CAROLYN Xmas 2023

GET

Lv.

Maggie

X

Ballet in Leicester Square

Also by Ivor Guest

Napoleon III in England
The Ballet of the Second Empire
The Romantic Ballet in England
Fanny Cerrito
Victorian Ballet Girl
Adeline Genée
The Alhambra Ballet
La Fille mal gardée (editor)
The Dancer's Heritage
The Empire Ballet
A Gallery of Romantic Ballet
The Romantic Ballet in Paris
Dandies and Dancers
Carlotta Zambelli
Two Coppélias
Fanny Elssler
The Pas de Quatre
Le Ballet de l'Opéra de Paris
The Divine Virginia
Letters from a Ballet-master
Adeline Genée: a pictorial record
Adventures of a Ballet Historian
Designing for the Dancer (contributor)
Jules Perrot
Gautier on Dance (ed. and trans.)
Gautier on Spanish Dance (ed. and trans.)
Dr John Radcliffe and his Trust

1 A group from Hansen's *Cupid* (Alhambra Theatre, 1886), with Emma Bessone as Cupid, and Lillie Lee as Hebe squeezing grapes into the hands of Mlle Marie as the Prince.

Ballet in Leicester Square

The Alhambra and the Empire 1860–1915

Ivor Guest

DANCE BOOKS
Cecil Court London

First published 1992 by Dance Books Ltd,
9 Cecil Court, London WC2N 4EZ.

A CIP catalogue record for this book is available from the British Library.

ISBN 1 85273 034 X

Distributed in the USA by Princeton Book Co.,
PO Box 57, Princeton, NJ 08534-0057.

Printed and bound in Great Britain by The Bath Press, Avon.
Design: Sanjoy Roy.

Contents

Illustrations

In the text

Provenance of illustrations

Bibliothèque de l'Opéra, Paris: 12, 14.
Mander and Mitchenson Theatre Collection: 9, 17, 55, 56, 60–62.
New York Public Library (Billy Rose Collection): 2.
Royal Academy of Dancing: 34, 45, 47–54, 57.
Theatre Museum, London: 18–20, 24, 30, 31.
Victor Glasstone Theatre Architecture Collection: 3.
Other illustrations from the author's collection.

Preface

This book is based on two monographs which I wrote many years ago – *The Alhambra Ballet*, published as the fourth issue of that excellent American journal, now alas defunct, *Dance Perspectives* (New York, 1959), and *The Empire Ballet*, published by the Society for Theatre Research in 1962. I am grateful to Dance Perspectives Foundation and to the Society for Theatre Research for allowing me to make use of those earlier works for this book. Both have been revised: that on the Empire Ballet to a small extent, but that on the Alhambra Ballet very extensively to give the work as a whole a proper balance. An introductory chapter has also been added, concerned with the conditions under which ballet moved from the opera house into the music hall, the merits and failings of the music-hall ballet, and why it vanished when it did.

This book concerns itself with a period in the history of ballet in London which happened to be associated with the two great music halls in Leicester Square, hence the book's title, and it should be borne in mind that it is not a history of those two houses as music halls. Those who wish to know more about the variety acts which accompanied the ballet performances are referred to histories of the music hall. However, to give a flavour of what was offered to patrons of the Alhambra and the Empire, I have included among the illustrations a selected number of playbills.

When I was preparing the two monographs, there were still a few people alive who were able to help me by recalling their memories of the ballet at the Alhambra and the Empire. Foremost of these were Dame Adeline Genée, whose biography I had just completed in a happy association with her, and Phyllis Bedells, who succeeded her as the prime ballerina of the Empire. Another former dancer, who had appeared at the Alhambra, was Theresa Heyman, with whom I spent a most entertaining afternoon listening to her memories. Also in the land of the living at that time was Philip Richardson, then a sprightly young man of some eighty-five summers, who sometimes spoke glowingly of the two music halls when we lunched together at the Moulin d'Or in Soho. For me, these were precious links, for there is nothing like a personal reminiscence to stir the historian's imagination. Nor must I omit to record my thanks to three of my colleagues who responded to requests for information contained in foreign archives – Knud Arne Jürgensen, Janina Pudelek, and Gunhilde Schüller.

I was also indebted to two private collectors, both now dead, alas, who generously gave me access to their treasures, William Beaumont Morris, an elderly balletomane whose eyes never lost their youthful brilliance, and that loveable figure of Edwin ('Puff') Kersley, who dug up many treasures from his Aladdin's cave in Maida Vale. Many of Monty Morris's cuttings are now in my own possession; Puff Kersley's collection is happily still intact in the care of his son Leo.

I must also record my indebtedness to the following libraries and public and private collections for providing facilities for research, answering enquiries and granting permission for reproducing material as illustrations: the British Library, the Victoria and Albert Museum, the Theatre Museum (which now holds the London Archives of the Dance), the Mander and Mitchenson Theatre Collection, the Victor Glasstone Architecture Collection, the Westminster Reference Library, the London Library, the Library of the Garrick Club, the Bodleian Library, Oxford, the Bibliothèque de l'Opéra, Paris, and the New York Public Library.

For permission to quote from the following books, I am indebted to the late Sir Compton Mackenzie (*Figure of Eight*), the late Miss Phyllis Bedells (*My Dancing Days*), the late Mme Lydia Ragosin (*Romantic Recollections* by Lydia Kyasht), and the Society of Authors on behalf of the Bernard Shaw Estate (*Music in London* and *Immaturity*).

Ivor Guest
Holland Park
London

INTRODUCTION

English ballet at the crossroads

'After a long and distinguished life, the ballet has died among us and gone to its grave, unhonoured even by a slight obituary notice,' began an article in Charles Dickens's popular weekly paper, *All the Year Round* in 1864. 'Once as much sought for in London as even that illustrious Italian guest, the opera itself, ballet is dead and gone. Her revengeful ghost usually haunts some scene of every grand opera, or revisits the glimpses of the footlights where burlesque or pantomime usurps her inheritance. But though her ghost walks, she is dead; dead past all galvanising into life again by the enterprise of opera directors. This was evident during the last opera season . . . '[1]

London's vogue for ballet seemed to have passed with dramatic suddenness, for not twenty years before those words were written, ballet had been sharing the honours with opera at Her Majesty's Theatre in the Haymarket on almost equal terms. Audiences had then been swept off their feet by an unprecedented clutch of ballerinas - Taglioni, Elssler, Cerrito, Grisi, Grahn, Rosati - who vied for acclaim with the divas of the opera, their artistry and skill displayed to well-nigh perfection by the creative genius of Jules Perrot, the most innovative choreographer of the age. For London Perrot had created the cream of his output: *ballets d'action* such as the poetic *Ondine* and the dramatic *Esmeralda* and *Catarina*, not to mention *Giselle* which Paris had already seen, and that unique series of multi-stellar *divertissements*, beginning with the *Pas de Quatre*, in which four of the greatest stars of the ballet put aside personal rivalries and joined forces in the most magical distillation of classical dance ever to have been seen. When later generations looked back upon this brilliant flowering, they would speak of it with almost sanctified respect as the Romantic ballet, recognising it as a major expression of the Romantic movement which had so profoundly affected art in every form.

Twenty years later, when Dickens's paper published the obituary of ballet quoted above, the *Pas de Quatre* was no more than a memory nostalgically cherished by the few who had witnessed it, and the triumphs, difficulties and disappointments of the director of Her Majesty's, Benjamin Lumley, whose managerial and diplomatic skills had made it possible, could be read in his recently published memoirs.[2] Lumley's management, which had begun so

1 *All the Year Round*, Sep. 3, 1864.

2 *Reminiscences of the Opera* (London, 1864)

propitiously in 1842, had closed unhappily in financial wrangles in 1858, but he could look back on it with a sense of achievement and a clear conscience. He had done his utmost to present the best of opera and ballet; a golden age it had been for both arts, but so far as the ballet was concerned, the shifting sands of fashionable taste had in the end been too much for him. Looking back to his first season he reminded his readers that 'those were the days when the *ballet d'action* still maintained a high *prestige* with the opera subscribers, though it was never so popular in England as in the gesticulating South, or even in France. It was not till years afterwards that the Lord Dundrearys of the opera came to regard the ballet as "something that no fellow could understand"; and to set their faces entirely against all pantomimic action, which, in order to follow "the story", required a slight effort of observation and memory. In fact, these critical gentlemen have now declared all ballet performances, beyond the mere *divertissement*, or string of consecutive dances, "a bore".'[3]

The success of Her Majesty's Theatre relied so heavily on foreign stars that both the opera and the ballet were offered as exotic importations, ballet being regarded as fundamentally French just as opera was Italian. In no way could the offerings at Her Majesty's — or, for that matter, Covent Garden, which had become a rival opera house in 1847 - be seen as part of the national theatrical tradition. There was no government subsidy such as supported opera houses on the Continent, and the viability of the enterprise depended largely on advance subscriptions exacted on the strength of a prospectus. For a high proportion of the subscribers attendance was as much a social obligation as an artistic experience. The opera season, which lasted for only a few months in the year, from March until August, when it was *de rigueur* to leave town for the country, was an essential feature of the social calendar. It added greatly to a person's social status to be seen there, for lists of those attending were published regularly in the newspapers and were eagerly scrutinised the next day. Under these conditions Lumley was, to a large extent, able to follow his artistic judgement, but his public was fickle and it was partly a shift of fashion - sparked by the enchantment of Jenny Lind, the 'Swedish nightingale' - that sounded the knell of the ballet. There were, of course, other factors: the departure of Perrot, the passing of an exceptionally brilliant generation of dancers leaving successors of lesser stature, and - a fundamental weakness - the lack of such solid foundations as supported the well subsidised Paris Opéra, which was open all the year round, had a permanent ballet company, continually refreshed by its large ballet school, and presented a ballet repertory that was recognised as an established expression of the national culture, even in times of decadence.

Yet, in the exotic but unstable flowering of ballet at Her Majesty's, there had long existed, virtually unnoticed, a substantial element that was entirely English. Although the heads of the ballet department - the *maître de ballet*, the

3 Lumley, 38.

régisseur de la danse and the teachers – together with the upper echelons of the company were almost without exception French or Italian, the *corps de ballet* was recruited from native talent. In time some of these dancers would be trained in the short-lived ballet school which Lumley established some years after taking over the direction. This was placed under Emile Petit, who was listed in the press announcement of the 1848 season as 'Master of the English School of Choreography', this last term being then used in a wider sense than it is today.[4] In 1851 it was recorded that the school comprised between thirty and forty pupils – apparently all girls – who were admitted at a minimum age of seven, formally apprenticed to the theatre for three, five or seven years, and taught there free of charge. A studio was set aside for their classes, its floor being raked at the same angle as that of the stage. After a year's initial training the pupils began to take part in performances, for which they received 4s. 6d. a week during the first year with the prospect of increases up to a maximum of 5s. a night (usually equivalent to 15s. a week). At the expiration of a pupil's period of articles, she might hope to be engaged in the *corps de ballet*, but she was free to leave if she chose.[5]

Apparently the school did not survive the closure of Her Majesty's Theatre in 1852. Although Lumley was able to reopen in 1856 and to direct three more seasons there, economies were imposed on him and the posts listed in the announcements no longer included the principal teachers. In the few years of its existence, however, the school produced a number of well-trained English dancers who found it helpful to announce that they had formerly danced, in however humble a capacity, at Her Majesty's. One who gained a measure of fame was Lydia Thompson, who as Mlle Lydia was appearing there in minor soloist rôles in 1852.

Away from the social spotlight that shone on Her Majesty's there were many stages in London where from time to time the dance flourished. It was there – at Drury Lane, the Lyceum, the Princess's, the Olympic, the Strand, the Surrey on the south side of Blackfriars Bridge, and the Grecian in the City Road – that English dancers might occasionally come into their own to entertain a public more numerous, if less select, than the frequenters of the opera. Their careers did not go unremarked, although it now requires diligence and patience to reconstruct them from surviving playbills and short notices scattered in the columns of the newspapers and periodicals of the time. Some became popular favourites, such as George Gilbert and his wife, Eliza Ann Ballin, and a brother-and-sister couple, the Marshalls; the promising but ill-fated Clara Webster who died of burns received during a performance at Drury Lane; Caroline Parkes, who played Giselle at the Grecian in 1852, and Rosina Wright, who four years later assumed another of Carlotta Grisi's rôles, the Peri, at Drury Lane, and was regarded by some as 'the first of our

4 Louis Gosselin was at the same time appointed Master of the French School of Choreography, presumably being responsible for company classes.

5 *Morning Chronicle*, Mar. 20, 1851.

English *ballerine*'.[6] The Christmas pantomimes were the exclusive preserve of English dancers, a number of whom specialised in the characters of the traditional Harlequinade, which in those days was an obligatory and central feature. Deriving from the Italian *commedia dell'arte*, it had evolved into a very distinctive English form in which knock-about comedy went hand in hand with acrobatic agility. To be acceptable as a Harlequin a man had to have panache as well as a crisp and strong dance technique, and his partner, Columbine, was usually a dancer too. One of the notable Harlequins of the eighteen-fifties, John Milano, was to play an important part in establishing ballet at the Alhambra Theatre. Pantomime Clowns were dancers as well, and two of these, Harry Boleno and John Cormack, would also be engaged at the Alhambra. The Bolenos, it should be added, were only one of a number of families who specialised in the Harlequinade, others being the Bolognas, Leclercqs, Lauris, Paynes and Lupinos. Their particular brand of comic pantomime and dancing influenced the style of English stage dancing for many generations, and many of the character dancers who appeared at the Alhambra and Empire theatres down to the First World War were brought up in this tradition.

The great majority of English dancers, of course, toiled in the anonymous ranks of the *corps de ballet*. For them employment was seasonal, but opportunities were seldom lacking. In the spring and summer the opera houses, even after ballet had been reduced in importance, always needed a *corps de ballet* for dance scenes in operas; pantomime provided many jobs at Christmastime (Drury Lane alone might engage up to a hundred girls for the ballets), and ballet was frequently being presented at one or other of the London theatres. Wages were not high, and were often not paid at all during a period devoted only to rehearsals. Also, hours were at times long, with rehearsals occupying the afternoons and only an hour or two's break before a performance, which might last until midnight. And during the pantomime season and at other heavy times rehearsals might even be called after the conclusion of the night's performance. In the eighteen-fifties a few *coryphées* earned 24s. or 21s. a week, out of which they had to provide part of their costume, but the average wage was around 15s. for a 'front line' girl or 12s. for those in the 'back line'; there were many others whose weekly pay was only 9s. a week, or even, as at the Strand Theatre, 6s., before any deduction for wreaths and flowers.[7]

A dancer was expected to equip herself with the basic necessities of petticoats, tights, fleshing and shoes, an outlay which entailed a considerable sacrifice. The cheapest petticoat, and a girl needed at least four, was made out of two and half yards of book-muslin, costing 2s. 8d. Many could not afford to buy the best tights, which cost more than £2, and made do instead by sewing pure silk stockings on to light brown cotton tops. To keep the

6 *Era*, Apr. 26, 1851.

7 'A Word for Ballet-Girls' (*Era*, Jan. 25, 1852); 'The Ballet' (*Era*, Feb. 7, 1858); 'Our Defence of the Ballet-Girl' (*Era*, Jan. 30, 1859).

colour, these had to be treated during the weekly wash with an application known as 'pink saucer', six-pennyworth being enough for three pairs. Then a fleshing for the body had to be bought at an outlay of 2s. Shoes had to be looked after particularly carefully, for they were expensive – 5s. 6d. for a pink satin pair and 4s. 6d. for one of lesser quality . . . and they quickly wore out. Dancers spent much time re-covering their worn shoes with satin or crape, and darning and mending them. All in all, it was estimated that the cost of setting oneself up as a dancer was about £1 13s. 2d., quite apart from the running expense of looking after one's effects and renewing them whenever necessary.[8]

Ballet in England was labouring under two irremovable disadvantages in the mid-nineteenth century: there was no native ballet troupe capable of becoming the nucleus of a national company, nor were there any established ballet schools. The school which Lumley had set up at Her Majesty's was never intended for anything else than to provide competent dancers for a *corps de ballet* supporting foreign principals; there was no thought of improving the quality of ballet presented on other London stages. The training of English dancers in those days was haphazard. A child employed in a theatre might hope to be regularly apprenticed to the ballet-master, but otherwise had to apply to some professional dancer who taught on the side.[9] Theatrical families in which dancing was a tradition not only provided training for their own kin, but took outside pupils as well. Clarissa Bennett, for example, who married Benjamin Conquest of the Grecian, had trained under Pierre Leclercq, father of the dancer and actress, Carlotta Leclercq. Mrs Conquest became a much sought-after teacher, training between forty or fifty pupils at a time at her school in the City Road, which was advertised from time to time in the theatrical weekly, the *Era*:

> MRS CONQUEST'S DANCING SCHOOL. Young ladies between the ages of 12 and 15 wishing to make stage dancing their profession can be taught the art without premium. Application to be made by the parents personally at the Eagle Tavern, City Road, before 12 o'clock daily, to Mr C. Montgomery, Acting Manager. Only a limited number required.[10]

For those lucky to be accepted by Mrs Conquest there was the chance of stage experience in the ballets she produced at the Grecian, which enjoyed a well earned reputation as 'a nursery for talent'. Augustus Harris, manager of

8 'Spoken by a Dancer' (*Punch*, Feb. 27, 1864). By the end of the century the dancer's lot had slightly improved. Front-row dancers then received 30s. to 35s. a week (40s. in pantomime) and second-row dancers, 12s. 6d. to 18s. They were still responsible for buying their own shoes and tights, shoes then costing 2s. 6d. to 5s. a pair, and lisle-thread or spun-silk tights, 15s. 6d. to 21s. Professional classes, another unavoidable item for the conscientious dancer, cost from 1s. to 5s. At a higher level, a principal might earn between 5 gns. and £20 a week. (Booth, *Life and Labour*, 2nd series, 4, 129–33.) An established star commanded more: in 1885 Kate Vaughan was paid £72 a week for dancing a solo in *Excelsior* at Her Majesty's.

9 Smith, 18, 91.

10 Fleetwood, 75.

Covent Garden, recruited most of his *corps de ballet* from Mrs Conquest's pupils who, as a contemporary observed, 'generally turn out the very best ladies of the ballet to be found in Europe.'[11] Similar opportunities were available to the pupils of another respected teacher, Mme Luiza, who was the wife of the Harlequin, Joseph Whitfield Collier, and made a speciality of adapting well-known ballets for smaller stages. It paid a teacher to be able to provide jobs, and a number of them doubled as employment agents by placing pupils in theatres, taking an agreed proportion of their meagre earnings, often as much as one third, as their commission.

Theatrical dancing was a humble profession in Victorian times, but in spite of the modest rewards and the taint of social prejudice, many of its practitioners were proud to belong to it. And no doubt dancers were united by a common bond just as they are today. For the majority of English dancers, however, the decline of ballet at the opera house had little material effect; prospects of employment were hardly affected, for almost simultaneously a new field opened up in the music hall.

For some decades music halls had been evolving from taverns which presented a variety of acts for the entertainment of their patrons. At first most of these halls were too small to offer much opportunity to dancers, but in 1860 the position was transformed by the opening of a music hall of unparalleled magnificence in Leicester Square. Accommodating an audience in excess of 3000, the Alhambra could not rely on the intimate contact between performer and public, and although for a few years it preserved the appearance of a tavern by serving refreshments during the performance to its clientele in the pit, a different form of programme emerged which depended to a large extent on spectacle and the dance. So successful was this formula that it was soon emulated by other music halls which were sprouting up all over the town: the Oxford, near Tottenham Court Road, where the troupe was headed by the Gunniss sisters and where the Kiralfys were engaged in the eighteen-sixties; the South London Palace, near the Elephant and Castle, where Luiza Collier produced the ballets in which her daughters Carrie and Lizzie were featured; the Canterbury, where in 1866–67 Henri Dewinne was ballet-master with a *corps* of a hundred and Pitteri as ballerina, and which was honoured by no less than three visits by the Prince of Wales; and finally the Empire Theatre which opened in Leicester Square in 1884 as a rival to the Alhambra. Thus ballet in England proved not to be dead after all, although it was assuming a different character through being unabashedly directed, with an eye on profit, to giving the public what it wanted.

By its very nature the form of ballet which flourished in Leicester Square for more than fifty years was non-élitist, a quality which distinguished it very significantly from the state-subsidised ballet presented elsewhere in Europe. Spectacle and entertainment value were the main considerations, and any attempt to present over-refined works which might appeal to only a small

11 'The Ladies of the Ballet.' *The Mask*, I (1868), 374.

section of what was a very large and broadly based public had to be resisted. The emphasis on pageantry and spectacle relegated the *corps de ballet* to the level of a chorus, employed more often than not as a background rather than as an integral part of the choreography. Although they performed with impressive precision, their evolutions were usually comparatively simple, and the technical skill required of them was limited. This deficiency was compounded by the general ignorance of the technique of ballet and its potential as an art. In London at this time there were few critics qualified to instruct the public. The specialised dance critic had not then made his appearance, even on the Continent, but there at least ballet was performed alongside opera and critics were generally musically cultured, whereas in London the ballets came within the province of journalists reporting on a music-hall programme. Their reviews might give a good description of the action, but comments on the choreography and the styles of the dancers were superficial in the extreme.

Among the more informed writers on ballet to emerge around the turn of the century was S. L. Bensusan, a writer of short stories much admired in his day. Being befriended by Adeline Genée, he acquired a sound basic knowledge which added authority to his pieces on ballet. He was himself able to recognise the lack of standards of judgement in the reviewing of ballet such as were to be found in France and Italy, and he drew attention to the effect this had not only on visiting ballerinas, who were aware that their art was not properly understood, but also on English dancers who 'as a class [did] not take the trouble to work hard enough to acquire the perfect control over limbs and movement that [was] the reward of their Continental sisters.'[12]

Another writer who was fascinated by the ballet at the music halls was the poet, Arthur Symons, who became music-hall critic of the *Star* in 1891. He gathered his knowledge at a lowlier level than Bensusan, becoming a habitué of the Crown public house in Charing Cross Road, a favourite haunt of dancers and their escorts. He was soon being admitted back-stage at the Alhambra, whose stage manager, John Hollingshead, called him '*l'enfant de la maison*'. He was well-known at the Empire too, and it was a humble dancer of that theatre's *corps de ballet*, Lydia (her surname is unrecorded), who inspired the great passion of his life which brought him not only physical pleasure and guilt, but great despair when the liaison ended.[13] His involvement with the ballet had a profound effect on his poetry, through which he attempted, perhaps not entirely successfully, to elevate the dancer into a symbol of her art. Much more evocative, though, was a prose piece, 'At the Alhambra – Impressions and Sensations', which he wrote for the literary magazine, the *Savoy*. There exists no more illuminating account of the bustling world of sweat and tinsel to be found back-stage at the Alhambra, with its rehearsals, its complement of 'girls travestied as boys, so boyish sometimes, in their slim youth, the feminine contours now escaping, now

12 Quoted in Flitch, 66–7.

13 A photograph of her is reproduced in Beckson, 101.

accentuated', the brilliance of the performances, and above all, the vision of the ballerina, 'the incomparable Legnani'.[14]

This description related to the year 1892, but more than ten years earlier a much greater literary figure, George Bernard Shaw, had penned from his personal experience what must be an accurate description of a typical Alhambra ballet of the late eighteen-seventies in his early novel, *Immaturity*. *The Golden Harvest*, as he called the ballet, is fictional, but it evokes the atmosphere of a performance more vividly than any other account that has come down to us.[15]

Whatever may have been their artistic shortcomings, it would be a mistake to dismiss the ballets produced in London's music halls between 1860 and 1914 as entirely lacking in artistic content. Many of them were carefully thought-out productions of not inconsiderable merit, and artistic standards certainly rose as the audiences acquired a taste for ballet. Indeed many of these ballets could compare not unfavourably with those staged at the Paris Opéra or any other European opera house outside Russia.

They were also an expression of the English theatre in a sense that the productions of the Romantic period and the creations of the Diaghilev Ballet were not. Ballet in the eighteen-forties had been 'the exclusive spectacle of the aristocracy, and only flourished in all its glory in such places as the Italian Opera House', while at the music halls it was, as a writer put it in 1869, 'the ballet of the million'.[16] At the opera house few ballets achieved a total of 20 performances in a season, but at the Alhambra and the Empire, where performances were given nightly all the year round, ballets usually ran for six months or more, and one was given for more than 400 consecutive performances. In the 'nineties the up-to-date ballet was born, based on a topical theme and with an English setting - an early expression of contemporary life in the dance theatre, but fated to be a short-lived phenomenon. For, as events turned out, the music-hall ballet died a sudden death, killed off by a combination of circumstances, of which the most potent in the longer term was the revelation of the Diaghilev Ballet. Such was the impact of the Russian dancers that ballet could no longer be dismissed as a mere diverting entertainment; it was to stake its claim, incontrovertibly, to be regarded as a major theatre art in which leading painters and composers were ready and willing to collaborate. But, more immediately, a new form of popular entertainment, the revue, was elbowing out the long-tried formula of interspersing ballet and variety at the Alhambra and the Empire. And finally, like a *coup de grâce*, came the First World War to shatter the old order beyond retrieval. Among many familiar features which had vanished beyond recall when the guns fell silent in 1918 was the music-hall ballet.

There can be no cause for regret that ballet in England took a different turn. But credit must be given where credit is due, and it has to be said that, even if none of its productions has survived, the era of the music-hall ballet

14 Symons, 77, 81.

15 Shaw, *Immaturity*, 72–5.

16 Anon., 'Stage Morality', 356.

was not devoid of achievements that would endure to the benefit of later generations. First, it had preserved a dance profession, which without the employment opportunities offered by the music halls would have been so emasculated that the modest but significant contribution of English dancers to Diaghilev and Pavlova might never have been made. And perhaps the move towards creating an association of teachers of ballet which resulted in the formation of what became the Royal Academy of Dancing might never have been made; it is significant that four of the five founders of the Academy - Genée, Cormani, Espinosa and Bedells - had been prominent at the Alhambra or the Empire.

Secondly, those two music halls created a public for the ballet, of which a nucleus certainly progressed to supporting the Diaghilev Ballet and later those modest English companies from which a national ballet would in time emerge.

And thirdly, the Victorian stigma was fading, and dancing was beginning to be accepted as a respectable calling by society at large - a development due in no small measure to the example of Adeline Genée, who performed a similar service for dancers to that by which Henry Irving had raised the status of the acting profession. But there had been other champions of the dancer's cause, notably a remarkable priest, the Revd. Stewart Headlam, who braved the disapproval of the Church of England establishment to give spiritual comfort to many dancers of the Alhambra and the Empire and vigorously pressed the claim of ballet to be considered as a fine art. To encourage greater understanding of the finer details of ballet, he published a new edition of Blasis's *Code of Terpsichore*; this and his library of books on dancing, today housed at the Royal Academy of Dancing, are further testimony to his lifelong fight to win respect for the dancer's profession.

For these reasons, as well as its purely historical interest, the rise and fall of the music-hall ballet - established in those two large theatres situated only a stone's throw from one another in the pleasure centre of Leicester Square - are part of the fabric of tradition that underlies English ballet as we know and love it today.

The Alhambra Ballet

I

Ballet comes to Leicester Square (1860–72)

When the imposing edifice destined to become the Alhambra Theatre, and for long one of London's main centres of ballet, began rising from its foundations in the Great Exhibition year, 1851, its promotors had more elevated plans for its future function. The site had been vacant ever since a row of tumble-down seventeenth-century houses had been belatedly demolished in 1840, but for one reason and another various plans for its redevelopment had come to naught until a group of high-principled gentlemen conceived the idea of erecting a museum devoted to 'discoveries in arts and manufactures'. With the Great Exhibition drawing unprecedented crowds of visitors from home and abroad to the vast Crystal Palace in Hyde Park only a short journey away by cab or omnibus, the moment seemed propitious for a venture designed to instruct the populace in the industrial progress of the Victorian age. And to see it on its way, a royal charter had been obtained for this worthy enterprise, which was inaugurated under the pretentious title of the Royal Panopticon of Science and Art.

As the building took shape its unusual design became apparent. The architect, T. Hayter Lewis, had sought his inspiration from the Saracenic forms which artists were then rediscovering. With its massive Moorish façade flanked by two lofty minarets, and a bulbous metal dome rising into the London sky behind, it dominated Leicester Square, then the centre of a district of foreign restaurants and cheap lodging houses. Within were to be found lecture rooms and laboratories, a massive organ, and a vast circular hall, surrounded by three tiers of galleries, from which visitors could gaze at an illuminated fountain shooting a jet of water nearly a hundred feet into the air.

That Queen Victoria did not grace the opening in 1854 with her presence spoke well for the royal judgement, for its attractions failed to come up to the expectations aroused by puffs in the press; all too few visitors turned up, and the ambitious and praiseworthy venture collapsed in financial disaster.

In 1856 the property was put up for auction, and was purchased as a speculation for a fraction of its cost by E. T. Smith, the lessee of Drury Lane Theatre, who appropriately renamed it the Alhambra Palace. Smith stripped it of its contents, disposing of the organ to St Paul's Cathedral. The great hall was found to be large enough to accommodate a circus ring, and the building was first let to Howes and Cushing's American Circus, which succeeded where the Panopticon had failed in tempting the Queen, who brought her children to see its special attraction, the wonder horse, Black Eagle. Smith's hopes of obtaining a theatrical licence were dashed, but in 1858, armed with a magistrate's licence for music and dancing, he set about converting the building at great expense into a music hall. Where the organ had been, a stage and proscenium were constructed, the circus ring being floored over and furnished with rows of tables at which customers were served with beverages of their choice - a brandy and soda perhaps, or a seltzer and sherry, or for simpler tastes, beer - while watching the acts. Capable of accommodating an audience of 3500, the Alhambra was by a long way the largest music hall in the metropolis. Among the offerings in the opening programme on December 10, 1860 was the Lauri family, who presented a 'musical, terpsichorean and dioramic illustration' called *The Fairy Ambuscade, or the Alhambra Rifle Corps*, featuring Louisa Lauri as the Sergeant. Ballet was not then an integral part of the theatre's programming in the sense that it later became; there was no permanent company, dancers being engaged *ad hoc* in the same manner as comedians, jugglers, singers and other acts. In 1863, to add tone and distinction to the bill, Smith engaged a company of Italian dancers, led by 'Signora Marianna and Signor Giuseppe, principal dancers from La Scala, Milan, and La Pergola, Florence.'[1]

The Alhambra's chapter in the history of ballet opened in earnest in 1864, when Frederick Strange became sole proprietor and adopted a policy in which ballet was to become a permanent feature. 'Just as the condition of Terpsichore appears to be most desperate,' noted *The Times* when the theatre reopened on Boxing Day, 'she starts up with fresh vigour in a new and unexpected place.'[2] Having engaged a 'large corps of admirably trained dancers', Strange was able to offer ballet as the corner-stone of his programmes, but since he possessed only the music and dancing licence that his predecessor had obtained, he had to take care not to contravene the Theatres Act of 1843 which placed London's theatres under the control of the Lord Chamberlain. The ballets he presented were therefore strictly *divertissements* as opposed to *ballets d'action* so as not to fall within the statutory definition of 'stage plays', for which a Lord Chamberlain's licence was required.

However, the threat which the Alhambra's energetic new manager posed to other theatres in town was not confined to the ballets. The historian of London, Sir Walter Besant, saw to the heart of the matter when he wrote:

> Mr F. Strange . . . was not a dabbler in half measures. He believed in the policy of giving the public the best of everything at the lowest possible price. He engaged a big band, a big chorus, and a big ballet, and covered the vast bare area of the ground floor, or pit, with an acre of valuable carpet. The carpet was important. It

1 These may be identified with Ermillina Mariana, one of the *prime ballerine italiane* of the Scala, Milan, in 1859–60, and Giuseppe Dan, a principal dancer at La Pergola in the eighteen-sixties and 'seventies. The Signora Rachele who supported them may have been either Rachele Conti (pupil *emerita* of the Scala School, 1859–62) or her contemporary, Rachele Fumigalli.

2 *The Times*, Mar. 16, 1865.

> not only helped to decorate and give an air of distinction to the first Variety Theatre or 'Palace' opened in London or in England, but it sealed the doom of dirt and discomfort in the leading London theatres. This was in 1864, and from that moment the immediate reform of badly-built, badly-kept, badly-ventilated, badly-lighted, and badly-furnished playhouses was inevitable. The managers knew it, and instead of imitating the example of the Alhambra Palace, and setting their houses in order, they resolved to prosecute their formidable rival for a breach of the law.[3]

It was a concerted offensive, in which no fewer than seven lessees - those of Covent Garden, Drury Lane, the Lyceum, the Adelphi, the Haymarket, Astley's and the Olympic - issued summonses against Strange, alleging that one of his ballets was a stage play and that he was guilty of an offence. Although wider issues were at stake, the case before the magistrate at the Marlborough Street police court concentrated on an analysis of a single item - the 'dagger dance', which had been added to a revival of a ballet originally produced for the Drury Lane pantomime of the previous winter.

In the pantomime, *Sindbad the Sailor*, this ballet had commemorated the recent discovery of the source of the Nile, and the stage designer William Beverley had devised a spectacular cascade of real water tumbling down a rocky mountainside. This had caught Strange's fancy and a similar construction had been erected at the back of the stage of the Alhambra, where the ballet was revived by its original choreographer, John Cormack, one of Drury Lane's two pantomime Clowns, supplemented for the occasion by the offending dagger dance. The *divertissement* opened with the entry of the *corps de ballet* down a path that wound its way down alongside the stream of water. Some of the dancers stopped to form groups on the rocks, while others, no doubt more competent, made their way down to the stage to perform a series of dances. No one could take exception to the charmingly devised dance which suggested the unfolding of petals and culminated in a singularly beautiful group when the *corps de ballet* came together to simulate one enormous bloom. The dagger dance which followed involved another group of dancers, who with much flourishing of daggers alternately retreated and advanced as if engaged in battle, and finally enacted the killing of an imaginary foe who had fallen to the ground.

Strange could congratulate himself on receiving some welcome publicity from the court hearing, which was fully reported together with evidence from witnesses describing the dance. After pondering for a week, the magistrate reluctantly felt obliged to find him technically guilty and imposed a mitigated fine of £3 1s., comforting himself with the thought that Strange would have an opportunity of reversing his decision on appeal to the Quarter Sessions.[4]

Strange's appeal was heard in May, when the Examiner of Plays in the Lord Chamberlain's office gave evidence favourable to his case. At the time of his appointment, this official testified, it was not the custom for the office to examine ballets. Occasionally complaints had been made after a ballet had

3 Besant, 195.

4 *The Times*, Jan. 5 and 12, 1865.

been performed, but these had been dealt with by remonstrating with the manager, in every case with the desired result that the offending matter was taken out. The Judge took the view that the question was to be decided on the facts, and on that footing he and the thirteen Middlesex magistrates who sat with him were unanimous that no offence had been committed, and so the conviction was quashed.[5]

Ballet proved to be a great attraction, and the public was soon regarding the Alhambra as an ideal place 'for a lounge or to pass a short evening, far the larger proportion dropping in late rather than sitting out the whole programme, and by no means caring whether there [was] a story in the ballet they [witnessed] or not.'[6] To cater to this shifting audience, the management advertised the times of the various items in the evening's programme, which might include three ballets: a comic ballet at 8.45, for instance, a light ballet at 9.45, and at 10.45 the grand spectacular ballet with its culminating transformation scene, none of them lasting for more than half an hour. It was all excellent value for money. Admission to the pit, where patrons could sit at tables with their drinks before them, cost two shillings, while half that sum entitled one to stroll in the wide promenade, with its bars, that encircled the central area. There was nothing like this in any other London theatre at the time, and for a significant proportion of the Alhambra's predominantly male clientèle the promenade had a special appeal, quickly becoming notorious for the beauty of the ladies of the town who were admitted unescorted. Moralists might thunder their disapproval of the 'Alcedama of licenced vice, the festering spot of all London',[7] but whatever might be said, the promenade filled a need and had come to stay.

A much less salubrious haunt was the canteen beneath the stage. Here many of the ballet-girls would make their way from their dressing rooms, easily recognisable by their make-up and the tights and slippers which could be seen beneath the travelling cloaks they wore for warmth. They would sit down on the wooden benches, waiting hopefully to be offered a drink by some swell with a roving eye, or a handsome soldier, or maybe one of the stray Americans who were already acquiring 'a reputation for reckless liberality'. It was a raffish place which the more senior dancers would seldom deign to enter, and something of its atmosphere comes across in a description by an American observer at the end of the eighteen-sixties, quoting the words of his cockney guide:

> You see, sir, these gals as is down here in the Canteen only gets ten to sixteen shillin' a week for the night's work, and that isn't much. They is only the figurantys, and can't dance a bit; but they gets a bad fashion from the swells who go behind the scenes a drinkin' champagne and sich like, and that fashion leads them to wuss nor hannything that you'll see 'ere. They comes down here and drinks between the balley, and then they goes hup on to the stage and dances again, and commes down hagain after the next balley, and by the time the Alhambra closes they are so blessed

5 *The Times*, May 9, 1865.
6 *The Mask*, 1 (1868), 81.
7 Kirwan, 463.

tight that they are ready for hanythink. I means, of course, the gals as is innocent yet; but the old hands are werry known' cards, so they is, bless you![8]

In Strange's time the Alhambra theatre acquired the reputation of being one of the foremost music halls in Europe, both for the excellence of its programmes and for the comfort it offered its patrons, and in no time even Parisians were speaking with envy of 'l'Alhambr-r-ra de Londres'. Strange, who had begun life as a waiter and made his money as refreshment caterer to the Crystal Palace, was essentially a showman with a flair for perceiving what the public wanted. Lacking any refined taste and culture, he saw ballet not as an art, but as a commercial product, a spectacle which would draw the public to his theatre in large numbers. His philistinism became a by-word in theatrical circles. One story told of his being approached by a writer whose ideas about ballet had no doubt been formed in its heyday at Her Majesty's, and who proposed a complex scenario set during the Danish invasions of King Alfred's reign. No doubt Strange paid little attention to the plot, which he could not have used anyway without a theatre licence, and after listening to an account of the effects which could be introduced, he enquired casually: 'Do you think you could get in a Chinese ballet?'

Taken aback, the author recovered his composure to suggest that he might arrange for some Norsemen to bring back some Chinese captives.

'Excellent!' replied Strange. 'I really believe I see my way. There is one other thing, but that won't be difficult if you can manage it properly. We must have a Minuet danced by shepherds and shepherdesses dressed *à la Watteau* in silk stockings, patches and powder.'[9]

Strange's first ballerina was Ernestina Bioletti, a dancer of somewhat obscure origins whose claim to have come from the Paris Opéra seems to have been highly doubtful. At the opening performance on Boxing Day 1864 she was featured in a *Grand Oriental Divertissement*, supported by a *corps de ballet* of nearly a hundred dancers. In February the programme was embellished with a *Royal Alhambra Bouquet Divertissement*, concluding with a stunning effect announced as the 'Golden Shower', which 'by some ingenious contrivance covers the front of the stage with scintillating splendour.'[10] May was celebrated with another novelty, an animated *Divertissement Espagnol*, arranged by Harry Boleno and Luiza Collier, in which Emma Boleno and Annie Cushnie, the latter in travesty, were nightly applauded. For this production the recent quashing of his conviction had emboldened Strange to countenance a fight scene in which a group of Spaniards brandishing knives become involved in a brawl before being brought to their senses by the angelus bell. Inevitably another summons followed, and then a third, but on each occasion Strange was acquitted.

For the next new *divertissement*, produced in August, a Russian background was chosen. *The Skaters*, as it was called, introduced a comic John Bull of an

8 Kirwan, 463.
9 Sherson, 186.
10 *The Times*, Mar. 16, 1865.

Englishman, some Russian dances and military marches, and culminated with the 'Golden Shower', which was too good to drop. By the end of the year it was estimated that more than a million people had paid to see the ballets at the Alhambra.

It was not without some pride and justification that Strange claimed the Alhambra to be 'The Greatest Spectacular Ballet Theatre in Europe - The Opera Eclipsed'. Each new ballet seemed to outshine its predecessors, not so much by the brilliance of its choreography as by the splendour of its scenery and the ingenuity of its effects. For the water effects a hundred and fifty tons of it were stored in tanks above the stage, and during a summer heat-wave the management was quick to exploit its added attraction as a cooling agent. What could be more inviting on a sweltering day in London than the Alhambra's inviting description of *The Titanic Cascades*, which was announced for July 2, 1866? 'The picturesque Ravine down which the Real Torrents pour,' ran the advertisement, 'has been solidly built upon the Stage, and THE SPORTS OF DIANA in this cool and glittering retreat are represented by more than a Hundred Graceful Dancers.' Not only was Strange particularly fortunate in his scene designer, William Callcott, who worked at the Alhambra until 1869, but he was continually on the look-out for ingenious new effects. One of the most striking of these was the 'Prismatic Torrent', invented and patented by G. Tanner and G. Parkes, which was the highlight of *The Watteau Fête*, presented on June 4, 1866. This consisted of a crystal curtain made up of thousands of pieces of glass which threw kaleidoscopic reflections of every colour on the forest scene beyond. After serving its purpose at the Alhambra, it was too good to be wasted, and Strange sold it to Marc Fournier of the Théâtre de la Porte-Saint-Martin in Paris.[11]

Appealing to another sense was the novel effect first introduced in the 'Magic Dance' at the first performance of *The Fairy Acorn Tree* on Boxing Day 1868, when the audience was sprayed with scent by Rimmel's Vaporisers.[12] Rimmel also provided some Bouquet Fans for *Pepita* (1869), and other trick effects were concocted by J. Bland of the Magical Repository in New Oxford Street: the Dryads' Flambeaux and scarves that turned into little baskets of flowers in *The Fairy Acorn Tree*, some Magic Branches in *Pepita*, and Bland's Magic Bottles, which at a touch of a spring released coloured streamers, in *The Spirit of the Deep* (1869).

The music for these ballets was generally supplied by the orchestral director and conductor - J. W. Hird until 1866, and from then Jules Rivière - but probably mainly amounted to selecting and arranging existing melodies. This was the weakest element in the early Alhambra ballets, although the standard of the orchestral playing was recognised as being unusually high for a music hall.

At first most of the spectacular ballets were produced by Luiza Collier, who

11 It was accidentally damaged in Paris and was resold to Jarrett & Palmer of New York for £15 000, being used for the transformation scene, 'The Palace of Dew Drops', in the New York production of *The Black Crook* in 1866.

12 A similar sensation was caused when rose perfume was sprayed through the old gas-pipes at the Paris Opéra in the 1952 revival of *Les Indes galantes*.

was succeeded in 1867 by John Milano.[13] In the eyes of the public and the critics, few of whom knew much about the technique of dancing, let alone being qualified to appreciate the finer points of choreography, the most immediate impression conveyed by the early Alhambra ballets was the brilliance of the spectacle and the special effects. The law's prohibition of staging ballets with plots remained a problem, but Strange's hopes for a resolution were encouraged by the formation of a Select Committee of the House of Commons to examine the state of the law on theatrical licences. In 1866 he was called to give evidence before this Committee, and was able to make some telling points: that the Alhambra employed 320 people at a total wage bill of £450 a week, that the wages of the ballet girls had only recently been increased by at least 20%, and that a large number of working-class people occupied the thousand seats in the upper gallery. However, the presence of prostitutes was too conspicuous to be passed over in silence, and Strange explained that what he euphemistically called the 'known evil' amounted to only 3% of the total house. Since the Alhambra could contain an audience of 3500, this element comprised, on his estimate, which was no doubt conservative, about a hundred women. When the Committee recommended in its reportthat music halls should no longer be restricted from giving theatrical entertainments, Strange must have thought he had triumphed, but Parliament had more pressing business to attend to than easing the life of music-hall managers. In 1867, when Strange was summonsed for presenting a comic sketch without dialogue challengingly entitled *Where's the Police?* he was not so lucky: the magistrate found the offence proved and fined him £240.

In the eyes of those who had the interests of ballet at heart, Strange was deserving of support, but at the same time in great need of guidance if ballet was to be restored to anything like the position it had held in the not so distant past. Advice of this nature was offered in an article in the magazine, *The Mask*, probably written by Alfred Thompson:

> We certainly cannot see any reason for refusing to this theatre the right of pantomime. There are many beautiful ballets which, with the addition of a *prima ballerina*, would prove an immense attraction. This is just the stage for the compositions of St Léon . . . and Espinosa, who was at the Lyceum, would have been just the man to appear in them, but pantomime story is tabooed, and seems likely to remain so, unless by some superlative attempt on the part of the management to bring out a ballet which would attract the upper ten thousand; such a success would be achieved as might overrule the Lord Chamberlain's injunction. But there is a tendency in all London caterers for amusement . . . to play down to the public instead of attempting to elevate taste and discrimination.[14]

13 Milano began his career at the Grecian Saloon and in the eighteen-fifties achieved distinction at Drury Lane as a Harlequin of remarkable agility and grace. He headed an English company which appeared at the Tivoli, Copenhagen, in 1858. Three years later he produced two *divertissements* at the Théâtre Déjazet, Paris. In 1870 he was working at the Circo, Madrid. He died in London in 1874 at the age of 49.

14 'The Almées of the Alhambra', *The Mask*, I (1868) 82–3.

For the time being, however, Strange had to tailor his policy to the situation as he found it, and it was now more important than ever to keep on the right side of the law if he was to continue to present ballet. His dilemma was that he could hardly avoid sailing close to the wind if he was to spice the ballets with variety, and for a time he introduced character dances and a discreet comic element to give flavour with impunity. *The Sprig of Shillelagh* (1868), for example, with its Barndoor Jig and Irish Lilt, the Spanish ballet *Pepita* (1869), and *Mabille in London* (1868), which featured the cancan, were all examples of ballets that kept within the law without being colourless *divertissements*.

Mabille in London, which was first given on March 16, 1868, introduced an original artist to the Alhambra. The year before, accompanied by the musical director, Rivière, John Hollingshead, the theatre's stage director, had gone to Paris in search of talent, and one evening they took out to supper, at the Café du Helder on the Boulevard des Italiens, 'a very handsome gypsy-like woman' who proved to be 'the somewhat uproarious belle of the evening'. Finette was a rising celebrity in the half-world of cancan dancers who exhibited their antics at the Bal Mabille and the Carnival balls of the Opéra. Unusually for a popular dancer, she had studied for a short while under the celebrated children's teacher, Mme Dominique, and even claimed to have appeared – perhaps 'walked on' would be more accurate – at the Opéra. But she soon forsook the ballet for a field that offered quicker rewards. Here her extraordinary elasticity stood her in good stead, and she was soon performing daring solos at the *bals publics*. She had then been spotted by the impresario, Raphaël Félix, and under his management had toured Germany in a musical extravaganza, giving a startlingly eccentric interpretation of the cancan. Hollingshead at once recognised her potential and brought her to London in 1867 to appear in the pantomime at the Lyceum. Wearing the short breeches and open-necked shirt of a Neapolitan fisherman she aroused no shocked protestations, and the following summer she was featured at the Alhambra in *Mabille in London*, coming, as one writer put it, like 'the champagne after the *vin ordinaire*'. In Hollingshead's own words, 'she was dressed as effectively as, and a little more decently than, a 'burlesque prince', and her dance had none of the offensive features of the cancan in petticoats. The most that could be said against it was that it was not a hornpipe.'[15] Having started a vogue for 'Parisian Quadrilles', Finette left London, her hour of glory over. In the summer of 1870 she was dancing in Edinburgh, but her career was destined to be short and not long afterwards Hollingshead heard from a friend who was a Foreign Office messenger that she had died in pain and poverty in Constantinople.

Ever on the look-out for new dancers, Hollingshead also kept in touch with Marie Taglioni, who was then principal teacher at the Paris Opéra school, to see if she had any promising pupils. For while the Alhambra *corps de ballet* was made up of English girls, a foreign background was considered essential in a principal dancer. So three remarkable Hungarian dancers, Imre, Bolossy

15 Hollingshead, i, 224–5.

and Aniola Kiralfy had been engaged in 1866, and the Parisian Anaïs Tourneur in 1867. In 1868 Mlle Sismondi,[16] whose origin remains something of a mystery, began her long association with the Alhambra, and Julie Feder made a brief appearance. And also in that year, on September 28, the first of the great Alhambra stars made her début.

Giovannina Pitteri,[17] a Venetian, became not only the prima ballerina but the favourite of Strange and the virtual queen of the Alhambra, where she was announced, a little excessively, as 'the acknowledged successor to Madame Taglioni'. In her heyday, around 1870, she and Strange were often to be seen driving about London in a splendid phaeton and pair. The well-known light opera singer Emily Soldene remembered her as

> a magnificent creature and great artiste . . . Her hair, naturally dark, was dyed a beautiful gold, quite an up-to-date proceeding then. She had a deliciously white, soft, satiny-looking skin. She told me she bathed in warm milk every day. Her dressing room was gorgeous, decorated with bric-à-brac and silken hangings. She had a French maid, and an Englishwoman to wait on the maid, also a toilette set of solid silver, and magnificent presents from many persons, some of them princes.[18]

Kind and generous to a fault, she was always very popular in the theatre. To express her appreciation of the scores which Rivière had composed for her ballets, she formally presented him with a silver baton in the presence of the audience. Emily Soldene was always grateful to her for interceding with Strange when the singer wished to be released from her contract. 'Years afterwards,' she wrote,

> asking an agent who had made much money out of the *danseuse* (and who licked the dust from her feet in the days of her prosperity) for news of her, he told me indifferently 'she was dead'. Dead in poverty and distress; died while filling an engagement in a low dance house among the sailors of Marseilles. She had spent all her money: the presents were gone, so were the princes.[19]

To display Pitteri in a ballet worthy of her position, Strange engaged Henri Justament, who had just completed a year's contract as *premier maître de ballet* at the Paris Opéra. His choice was quickly justified, for Justament's first ballet, *Flamma* (December 28, 1869),[20] surpassed anything produced before at

16 According to Edouard Espinosa, she was a pupil of his father, Léon Espinosa, and her real name was Betsy Simmons. After retiring as a dancer she became a teacher, and was placed in charge of the London school of John Tiller (founder of the Tiller Girls) at 143 Charing Cross Road. She is mentioned in an article in the *Dancing Times* (Apr. 1911, 170) by Helen Anstey, who wrote: 'In spite of a most attractive foreign accent and manner, [she] declares that she is quite English except for foreign extraction.'

17 Archibald Haddon asserted that Pitteri was a 'Miss Pitt, London East-ender', but there seems to be no truth in this, since her contract for her appearance at the Paris Opéra in 1859, long before she appeared in England, gives her name as Giovannina Pitteri (Archives Nationales, Paris, AJ[13] 486). She spent most of her career in London, but in 1864 she danced at the Scala, Milan, and in 1872–73 visited New York with Katti Lanner's company.

18 Soldene, 50–51.

19 Soldene, 55.

20 Justament's notebooks containing the choreography of *Flamma* and *The Fairies' Home*, described in words and stage plans, are preserved at the Bibliothèque de l'Opéra, Paris (B 217, 34 and 35).

the Alhambra; Pitteri had never been shown to greater advantage, and the transformation scene was so magnificent as to beggar description.

At about the same time Henri Dewinne, a Belgian ballet-master, produced the first of his ballets for the Alhambra. One of these, *Les Nations* (June 23, 1870), seemed an innocuous *divertissement*, but after a few weeks it was expanded to feature the Parisian Troupe of Mlle Colonna, who in private life was a Miss Newham. Across the Channel war had broken out between France and Prussia, and Paris was on the point of being besieged by the advancing German armies. 'Paris in sackcloth and ashes, and her national dance more vigorous than ever in Leicester Square,' was the dry comment of *Day's Doings*. 'The cancan . . . is simply a quadrille, with the most eccentric and extravagant figures which are devised by the fertile imaginations of the dancers themselves.'[21] One of the paper's artists drew a sensational picture of these dancers in action with results for which Strange had not bargained, for by a stroke of unfortunate timing the Alhambra's licence for music and dancing just then came up for renewal, and the police intervened to oppose it, attaching by way of evidence to their report a copy of the print. As a result the licence was refused, notwithstanding Strange's protests that some two hundred of his employees would be thrown out of work. In a letter to *The Times* he averred that he had not the slightest control over the 'sensational illustrated journal' which had published 'a highly overdrawn and exaggerated representation' of the dance, but a few days later *Day's Doings* revealed that the Alhambra management had in fact given facilities to the artist and purchased more than eighty copies of the print.[22] However, it certainly seemed unfair that the cancan should be permitted in *Orphée aux enfers* then playing at the St James's Theatre, and yet be prohibited in Leicester Square.

The police report described a visit to the theatre during a performance of *Les Nations*, 'in which Mlle Colonna and troupe (four in all) appeared and danced the Parisienne Quadrille, or ordinary cancan. Two of them personated men dressed in bodices and trunks to match, or flesh-coloured hoses; the others, as females, dressed as ordinary ballet girls, except that more of the thigh was visible in consequence of wearing very scanty drawers. The dance, on the whole, is indecent especially on the part of one dressed as a female, who raised her foot higher than her head several times towards the public, and who was much applauded. There was a loud influx of visitors shortly before the ballet commenced, but which decreased immediately after.'[23]

The cause of the trouble was a 'wispy slip of a girl' called Sara Wright, the daughter of a waiter at the Oxford Music Hall, where she had begun her career in Mme Louise's children's ballet. Her legs were unusually long, as everyone could see, since she wore her skirts very short. She was also astonishingly loose-jointed, throwing out her legs and dusting the floor with

21 *Day's Doings*, Oct. 8, 1870.

22 *The Times*, Oct. 15, 1870; *Day's Doings*, Oct. 8 and 22, 1870. When the Alhambra had to close, the ballet company, led by Pitteri, were engaged at the National Standard Theatre and performed *Estella*, which had been in rehearsal at the Alhambra.

23 *The Times*, Oct. 14, 1870.

PROGRAMME

For the WEEK ENDING SATURDAY, July 22nd.

Programme ONE PENNY

8. OVERTURE - - "Haydée." (Auber.) - - BAND.

8.10. FOURTH WEEK of a New Comic Ballet entitled

FIGNOLET ET ENTRECHAT.

In which M. BEKEFY and Mons. and Madame VARRAKE
Of the Theatre Imperial, Moscow, and Theatre Bordeaux, will appear in their eccentric National Dances,
(For the First Time in London.)
Assisted by Miss LIZZIE GROSVENOR and Mr. J. MARSHALL.

8.30. FOURTH WEEK OF DIBDIN'S Musical Farce of The

WATERMAN

Tom Tug ... ... Mr. W. PARKINSON
With the Songs of
"The Jolly Young Waterman," "Farewell, my trim-built Wherry," and "The Bay of Biscay."
Bundle ... ... Mr. G. YARNOLD, of the Theatre Royal St. James's.
Robin ... (with the Song of "Cherries and Plums) ... Mr. E J. ODELL
Mrs. Bundle ... Mrs. POYNTER, of the Theatre Royal, Haymarket.
Wilhelmina ... (With the Song of "Maggie's Secret) ... Miss MINNIE SIDNEY
Watermen ... ... Messrs. EVERARD and J. MARSHALL.

QUADRILLE - - "La Camargo." (O. Metra.) - - BAND.

SECOND WEEK of A NEW GRAND FAIRY BALLET D'ACTION, entitled The

SYLPH of the GLEN

Adapted from the Opera of
"THE MOUNTAIN SYLPH."
Arranged and Produced by - - Mr. J. MILANO.
The Music Arranged and Selected by M. J. RIVIERE.
The Costumes by Miss YATES. The Machinery by Mr. RAVEN. The Properties by Mr. DAVIDGE.
The New and Beautiful Scenery by Messrs. T. GRIEVE and SON.

Donald - (betrothed to Jessie) - Mr. J. RAYMOND
Jamie - (his Rival) - Mr. J. KELLINO
McCullom - - Mr. A. KELLINO
Saunders - (a Piper) - Mr. J. MARSHALL
Hag of the Glen - - Mr. EVERARD
Mrs. McCullom - Mr. W. KELLINO
Jessie - (betrothed to Donald - Miss LIZZIE GROSVENOR
The Sylph of the Glen - - Madlle. RITA SANGALLI.
Peasants, Bridesmaids, Sylphs, &c.,

By the Celebrated ALHAMBRA CORPS DE BALLET.
SYNOPSIS OF BALLET.

Scene 1.—HOME in the HIGHLANDS.
The Wedding Morn—The Presents to the Bride—The Rival Lovers—The Sword Dance, by Mr. J. RAYMOND, Misses F. PALMER, FREDERICKS, LEE, K. GRAHAM, MARS, FROST, BEYERS, HAZELWOOD, General Dance by the Ladies of the Ballet.

Alhambra Theatre programme, week ending July 22, 1871.

The Marriage Bells—**THE SYLPH of the GLEN.**—The Disappearance, Mystery—Come, come away

Scene II.—THE MOONLIGHT HOME.

Descent of the Mountain—Gathering of the Sylphs.

GRAND BALLET, BY MDLLE. RITA SANGALLI,

Assisted by Mr. J. RAYMOND, and the Ladies o the Ballet.—Dance of the Little Men of the Mountain.

Scene III—**THE STORM.**

In search of the Runaway Bridegroom—The Hag of the Glen, an unexpected Meeting and its results!

Scene IV **THE SYLPH'S HOME IN THE GLEN OF WILLOWS**

Union of the Lovers.—GRAND TABLEAU.

AN INTERVAL OF TEN MINUTES.

10.15

THE VOKES FAMILY,

In their Popular Sketch, entitled The

BELLES OF THE KITCHEN

Timotheus Gibbs - - (a Doctor's Assistant) - - Mr. FRED VOKES.
Wiggins - - - - (a Hair Diesser) - - - - Mr. FAWDON VOKES.
Lucinda Scrubb - - (Lady's Maid) - - Miss JESSIE VOKES.
Mary - - - - - (Housemaid) - - - - - Miss VICTORIA VOKES.
Barbara - - - - (Scullery Maid) - - - - Miss ROSINA VOKES.

1.-The DUET. 2.-The TRAGEDY. 3.-The OPERA. 4.-The BALLET.

POLKA - - - "Postilion d' amour." (Kunemann.) - - - BAND.

11. A NEW BALLET DIVERTISSEMENT, **THE**

BEAUTIES of the HAREM

Introducing

Mademoiselle SISMONDI,

The Music Composed and Arranged by M. J. RIVIERE.

The Costumes by Miss YATES. The Machinery by Mr. RAVEN. The Properties by Mr. DAVIDGE.

The Scenery by Messrs. T. GRIEVE and SON.

The Ballet Invented, Arranged, and Produced by Mr. J. MILANO.

Valse, by Mdlles. ELLIS, CLAYTON, CROME, and HOWE. Pas Generale, by the CORPS DE BALLET.

Grand Entree, by **Madlle. SISMONDI,**

Pas d'Ensemble - - **by Mdlle. SISMONDI,**

And LADIES OF THE BALLET. Mazurka, by LADIES OF THE BALLET.

Variation - - by **Mdlle. SISMONDI.**

GRAND GALOP FINALE—TABLEAU!

GOD SAVE THE QUEEN.

OPERA GLASSES Lent on Hire 1s. each, on application to Attendants.
LAVATORIES FOR GENTLEMEN under the Pit, entrances under Statues, at each end of Orchestra.
RETIRING ROOMS FOR LADIES, on Balcony Stairs, First Floor to the left of the Staircase
All the Pieces of Music, Published, Sung, or Performed at the Alhambra, can be had for Pianoforte, at the Musical Progress, HAWKES & Co., 33, Soho Square.
THE NEW ELECTRIC ORGAN, built by Messrs BRYCESON & Co. OPERA GLASSES by J. WHITEHOUSE, Optician 8, Coventry-street, Haymarket. The Wardrobe supplied by H. R. WILLSON, 10, Cranbourn-street.

J. W. ELLIOT, Theatrical and General Printer, 8, White Hart Street, Strand.

her back hair with such 'fiendish suppleness' as to earn her the sobriquet of 'Wiry Sal'.

Strange succeeded in extricating himself from his predicament by obtaining a regular theatre licence from the Lord Chamberlain, but it was to be several months before the Alhambra reopened - on April 24, 1871. The auditorium then presented a very different aspect. Gone were the tables in the pit, their place now taken by neat rows of brand-new stalls, and gone too was the smoke-laden atmosphere of old, smoking being permitted only in a specially designated 'smoke room'. In the temporary absence of Pitteri, Strange had engaged Rita Sangalli, a Milanese ballerina who, after graduating from the School of the Scala, had gathered laurels in America, first in New York and then touring her way across the States to San Francisco, where, in 1870, she had appeared with a small ballet company of her own. At the reopening of the Alhambra Sangalli danced in two ballets by John Milano - *The Beauties of the Harem* and *Puella* (for which the music was composed by Giovanni Bottesini, the double-bass virtuoso who was shortly to conduct the first performance of *Aida* in Cairo) - and three months later she was seen in another creation by Milano, *The Sylph of the Glen* (July 17, 1871).

This last ballet was especially interesting, for it was adapted from the ballad opera, *The Mountain Sylph*[24], which had itself been inspired by Filippo Taglioni's ballet of *La Sylphide*. In the process of adaptation, however, the simple, touching story of the original ballet had twice been subjected to 'improving' hands. The sad ending in which the Sylphide dies and the hero is left bereft, having lost both his mortal and his spiritual love, had been removed in the opera by the addition of a scene in which the hero rescues the sylph from the subterranean region in which she has been confined and, because she has conveniently been deprived of her immortality, is enabled to marry her. A sad ending was no less acceptable at the Alhambra, but this time the hero was to be united not with the sylph but with his forgiving fiancée. No one seemed troubled that the inherent poetry and romantic mystery of the original ballet had been drained away, not least the critic of the *Era*, who described the production as

> the most striking feature of the evening . . . produced with the utmost splendour and completeness. The ballet had been so well arranged that the dramatic incidents tell their own story as well without the aid of dialogue as if the story had been acted in the ordinary way. We are introduced to the Highland home upon the wedding morning of Donald and Jessie. Then we see Donald spirited away by the Sylph of the Glen, a magnificent ballet and sudden storm, then the search for the runaway bridegroom, and finally his restoration to the arms of Jessie. All this is displayed in a series of remarkably clever *tableaux* illustrated by 150 of the *corps de ballet* in the midst of beautiful scenery.

The direct link with Taglioni did not pass unnoticed. The *Era* described Sangalli as 'one of the most brilliant and fascinating heroines of the ballet we

24 *La Sylphide* was first produced at the Paris Opéra on Mar. 12, 1832. John Barnett's ballad opera, *The Mountain Sylph*, was first performed at the Lyceum Theatre, London, on Aug. 25, 1834.

have seen for many years. She recalls those palmy days at Her Majesty's Theatre when Taglioni danced in a ballet to the self-same subject. Some of Mlle Sangalli's solo performances were quite original, and the delight of the audience was shown by several hearty encores.'[25] It was nearly forty years since *La Sylphide* had been created, and twenty-four since Taglioni had retired. It is doubtful whether this critic had ever savoured the poetic quality of Taglioni's dancing, and he may be forgiven for failing to realise how different was Sangalli's style, although his reference to her originality suggests that he may at least have been conscious of the novelty of her *tours de force*. It was, of course, a very different ballet, and bearing in mind the ambience of the Alhambra, any comparison would have been pointless.

In any case its historical associations probably meant very little to Strange. More to his taste, one imagines, was the frenzy of the cancan, which he brought back to the Alhambra towards the end of the year in the interpretation of Esther Austin (sister of Emily Soldene), whose 'Quadrille du Grand Opéra de Paris' could not have been very different from the version which had caused such trouble twelve months before. This time it was to be received without objection, and fittingly marked the close of Strange's management, which came to an end in March 1872. Sadly, this man who had laid the foundations of the Alhambra ballet, then fell on hard times; he retired into obscurity, being once recognised as a steward on a Thames steamer, and his death in the summer of 1878 passed almost unnoticed.

25 *Era*, July 23, 1871.

II

Improving the image (1872–84)

With Strange's departure the Alhambra entered upon another phase in its history.[1] This coincided with the embellishment of Leicester Square in the 1870s, a process which was long overdue. Since 1861, when Wyld's Great Globe, which had occupied the central area, was demolished, the site had degenerated into an unkempt patch of sickly grass surrounding a statue of George I which was fast falling to pieces. Moves to tidy up the Square took some time to bear fruit, but eventually, in 1874, the ground was conveyed to the Metropolitan Board of Works and was pleasantly laid out around a marble fountain surmounted by a statue of Shakespeare. The tone of the neighbourhood also began to improve, and so too did that of the Alhambra, where, from 1872 until the music and dancing licence was recovered in 1884, variety was abandoned in favour of opéra-bouffe and extravaganza. While the programmes attained no lofty cultural level, the respectability of the house noticeably rose – without prejudice, it must be said, to the promenade, whose offerings were as eagerly sought after as ever and which had now, it seems, been accepted as a necessary evil. 'In days gone by,' commented an observer in 1880, 'one was supposed to visit the Alhambra disguised as a Californian gold-digger or an Australian stock-raiser or a Cape ostrich-farmer or with a false nose and blue spectacles, *mais nous avons changé tout cela* . . . The Alhambra, as a theatre licenced by the Lord Chamberlain, is now as decorously conducted as any other dramatic establishment in London.'[2] With spectacle remaining the key-note of every production and the tradition of ballet being assiduously maintained, the attractions of the theatre in the 1870s were concisely summed up as 'music to delight the ears, colour to please the eye, beauty to excite the imagination; nothing to make one think'.[3]

Much of the credit for raising the prestige of ballet at the Alhambra was due to its musical director, Georges Jacobi. Born in Berlin in 1840, Jacobi studied at the Conservatoires in Brussels and Paris before becoming first violin in the orchestra of the Paris Opéra. Doubtless it was there that the seeds were sown of an interest in ballet, an interest that extended to his private life

1 During this period the Alhambra passed through a succession of managements: John Baum (1872–75), J. A. Cave (1875–76), F. Leader (1876–77), Thomas Kittle (1877), Charles Morton (1877–80), J. Killingsworth (1880–81), Howard Paul (1881), Sydney Allport (1881–82), William Holland (1882–84). During Holland's management the theatre was licensed to James Howell.

2 *Illustrated Sporting and Dramatic News*, Sep. 11, 1880.

3 *Illustrated Sporting and Dramatic News*, Aug. 28, 1875.

when he married the dancer Marie Pilatte. In 1869 he was engaged by Offenbach to conduct the orchestra at the Théâtre des Bouffes-Parisiens, and early in 1872 he came to London to become musical director at the Alhambra, a post which, apart from a brief interruption from 1883 to 1884, he was to retain until 1898. Emily Soldene found him an ideal conductor, and her remarks, although made from a singer's point of view, were no doubt equally applicable to his handling of a ballet score:

> It does not matter whether you are full of sentiment or full of devilment, in good form or bad form, ill or well, he is always with you, waiting, coaxing, supporting, giving way to little unexpected fads of expression, phrasing or breathing. Attentive to every movement, to every sigh, he anticipated what you were going to do, and let you do it. The result was a delightful unanimity and perfect success.[4]

During the quarter of a century when he was musical director, Jacobi composed the music for nearly every ballet produced at the Alhambra, a total of forty-five competently written and eminently danceable scores.[5] In addition he produced music for *divertissements* in the Alhambra productions of *Die Fledermaus* (1876), *The Grand Duchess* (1878), *La Fille du Tambour Major* (1880), *The Bronze Horse* (1881) and other works that were lacking in ballet music, as well as composing several light operas of his own. *The Demon's Bride* (1874), *Lord Bateman* (1875) and *Babil and Bijou* (1882) were all his own compositions, while *The Black Crook* (1872) was a joint work by himself and Frederick Clay.

Without question he was the most important ballet composer working in London in his day, and when he retired from the Alhambra in 1898, the tribute that was paid him reflected the esteem in which he was held. The monster programme given in his honour lasted from noon until six o'clock in the evening. Taking part were three orchestras - those of the Alhambra, the Empire and the Palace theatres - and the audience was treated to no fewer than fifty-six acts. Henry Irving recited 'The Uncle', Dan Leno gave a comic song, Marie Tempest sang 'The Jewel of Asia', and in the *divertissement* of *The Roses and Butterflies*, from Carlo Coppi's ballet, *Beauty and the Beast*, Adeline Genée, the young ballerina from the Empire, came to dance on the rival stage of the Alhambra.

During the first twelve years of Jacobi's musical direction of the Alhambra, the more important ballets and *divertissements* were produced by D. Verli (1872), Hus (1872), Henri Dewinne (1873-75), John Lauri (1875), A. Bertrand (1877-82) and Joseph Hansen (who was engaged in 1884). The comic ballet, which had been such a feature of the Alhambra programmes during the eighteen-sixties, disappeared from the bills in 1873. Spectacle had become the essential ingredient, and scenic artists such as Albert Callcott, who carried on the tradition set by his brother William and designed most of the Alhambra

4 Soldene, 233.

5 Jacobi's manuscripts, consisting of full orchestral scores of nearly all his ballets, together with a number of *répétiteur* scores, a few orchestral parts, and some ancillary material such as printed synopses and press cuttings, were acquired by the London Archives of the Dance and are now in the possession of the Theatre Museum, London.

productions during the 'seventies, were given the widest scope for the exercise of their imaginations. The hundred and fifty tons of water were still stored over the stage, as audiences were reminded in *Cupid in Arcadia* (June 26, 1875) (which offered 'Real Water in Silver Streams, Gigantic Cascades, faithfully realising those fairy-like retreats, the O'Sullivan and Torc Waterfalls in Killarney') and again in *Yolande* (August 18, 1877). Similar attention was paid to the costumes: many were designed by Alfred Thompson, and in 1878 a young man who was to become renowned as the greatest ballet costume designer of his time was given his first commission. His name was Pitcher, but he was professionally known as C. Wilhelm. The Alhambra ballets, *The Golden Wreath* (May 20, 1878) and *Diona* (May 31, 1880), introduced his work to London theatre-goers, although it was at the rival house, the Empire, that he was to establish his reputation.

Although licencing difficulties were a thing of the past, the plot usually played a very minor part in the ballets at the Alhambra, while the *divertissements* in the operettas and extravaganzas of course had none at all. A rare exception - the first ballet to be produced after Strange's retirement - was a revival of a ballet which had been successfully created in Vienna four years earlier.[6] This was *Nana Sahib* (April 1, 1872), in which the principal character was based, with considerable balletic licence, on one of the ring-leaders of the Indian Mutiny, who became a fugitive after its suppression and mysteriously disappeared in Nepal. Announced as 'a New Grand Dramatic Spectacular Ballet' featuring '200 Coryphées in a style unequalled even at the Alhambra', it was attributed, not to the original choreographer, Henri Desplaces, but to one D. Verli, who, one may assume, followed the original choreography as faithfully as memory and notes would allow. For the original production in Vienna the music had been credited jointly to Giovanni Panizza and Matthias Strebinger, but they could not have collaborated in the strict sense since Panizza had died in 1860. Presumably, therefore, Strebinger had arranged the score from Panizza's music, making a number of additions of his own. The Alhambra programme in fact named Panizza as the sole composer.

The narrative of the ballet turned out to have nothing to do with the Mutiny, which was hardly surprising, since many of its incidents were still close enough to strike horror in English minds. *The Times* described the plot as being 'of the sketchiest character, and filled with violent but pleasing improbabilities'.[7] The curtain rose on a forest scene, where Nana Sahib (played by an actor, J. Bradshaw) is found casting jewels at the feet of a beautiful bayadère, Zita, with whom he is infatuated. The company was soon set dancing in a long *divertissement*, in which Rita Sangalli, who played Zita, performed a solo to an original accompaniment, her companions miming an accompaniment on musical glasses, the appropriate sound of course coming from the orchestra pit. There then arrives a hunting party of Europeans,

6 *Nana Sahib*, described as a choreographic drama in 2 acts and 5 scenes, was first performed at the Court Opera, Vienna, on Dec. 18, 1867. Apart from the Alhambra production, it was revived at the Teatro Regio, Turin, on Jan. 4, 1873.

7 *The Times*, Apr. 2, 1872.

including the Governor General, a young Englishwoman, Ophelia (Miss Rosine), and, to provide light relief, a dapper little servant, George, played in travesty by Elise Holt. The critic of the *Era* found the action confused at this point, but gathered that Nana took 'a violent fancy' to Ophelia and that Zita 'seemed to devote herself secretly to the service of the Europeans'.[8] The next scene took place in a street in Cawnpore (in the Mutiny the scene of a particularly nasty massacre), and introduced a bevy – the term is appropriate, for they were played by girls – of English sailors who danced a spirited hornpipe. The scene then moved to the Governor's Palace, where a 'Procession Dansante', remarkable for the splendour of the costumes, was followed by the intrusion of Nana and his men, who after a violent struggle seize Ophelia and carry her away to Nana's harem. Her captivity there is mercifully short, for Zita comes to rescue her, sacrificing her life in the attempt. The Goddess of Vengeance and Justice then appears to Nana, chastising him for the bayadère's murder, and the ballet concluded with a scene in the Temple of Brahma.

It was an ambitious production which probably left the largely unsophisticated Alhambra audience, who not only lacked the benefit of a detailed scenario but were unaccustomed to the art of mime, not a little puzzled by the events on the stage, although suitably impressed by the spectacle and the dancing. In its considered review, *The Times* passed a favourable judgement:

> The merit of the piece lies in its richness of setting, its continuous flow of incident, and its brilliancy of costume. For something between an hour and an hour and a half processions of rich dresses flit on and off the stage, each more glittering and many-coloured than its predecessor, yet with sufficient interval and accident between to prevent the display from sinking into a mere succession of transformation scenes.[9]

Processions were very popular at the Alhambra during this decade, and one of the more memorable among many was the State Procession in the Royal Gardens of Bambouli in Offenbach's operetta, *Whittington* (1874), which ended with an entrance of a troupe of dancers clad in black and gold armour that glittered in the gaslight with such barbaric splendour that the audience spontaneously burst into applause.

Typical of an Alhambra ballet of this period was *The Flower Queen* (November 8, 1875). The plot told of a youth who loses himself in a bleak region of snow, where the Ice King is holding court with his ice-fiends and ice-nymphs. He is rescued by the Snow Queen, with whom he falls in love. But the snow melts and the Snow Queen vanishes. The wintry scene was then transformed into a summer landscape and the lovers appear in different guises, the youth as Prince Butterfly and the Snow Queen now transformed into Queen Snowdrop, attended by bevies of bluebells, moss roses, fuschias, tiger lilies, tulips and dahlias. A grand *divertissement*, with different coloured lights playing on the dancers, brought the ballet to a close.

8 *Era*, Apr. 7, 1872.

9 *The Times*, Apr. 2, 1872.

Choice of subjects varied widely, from ballets about butterflies and birds and fish to Spanish, Barbaric, Turkish and Japanese ballets, Carnival ballets, Amazon ballets, Military ballets, and much else besides. The Fairy Musical Spectacle *Rothomago*, which filled the bill at Christmas 1879, included a Vintage *divertissement*, a ballet evoking the glories of ancient Egypt, and a Ceramic ballet. Only modern themes were, for the moment, eschewed.

The policy of staging 'nothing to make one think' presupposed the avoidance of drama in ballet. To this there was to be another exception, when A. Bertrand produced a four-scene ballet on the theme of *Carmen* (October 20, 1879), in which Erminia Pertoldi was a bewitching heroine and Theodora de Gillert, in travesty, an impassioned Don José. Gillert received special praise for her skilful acting. 'Every action of hers is full of meaning, and tells its own tale,' wrote the *Era*. 'Her hands and arms are as expressive as her face, every movement is full of signification, and if the ballet should prove slightly puzzling to those who have not made acquaintance with the opera and its story, the fault is most certainly none of hers.'[10] In the supporting rôles, Mlle Rosa, a pupil of the choreographer, played Michaella, and Elise Holt was the torero, Escamillo. The action followed that of the opera with a necessary degree of simplicifation to compress the ballet's length to about half an hour.

In the first scene, outside the tobacco factory, Carmen is arrested and then escapes from Don José. Next she is discovered in the smugglers' haunt, foretelling Don José's fate; here Escamillo makes his appearance, and he and Don José come to blows. The exterior of the bull-ring is the setting for a sung chorus, after which the bull-ring itself is revealed for the tragic dénouement when Don José kills Carmen. There being no question of using Bizet's music to accompany the ballet, Jacobi provided an entirely original score.

Whether matters might have taken a different course if an extraordinarily gifted dramatic ballerina - a Zucchi, for example - had appeared, there is no telling. But it must be remembered that the Alhambra catered for a much less sophisticated audience than those Continental opera houses which supported permanent ballet companies. Dancing and spectacle were elements which could be enjoyed by anyone, but the art of mime, or 'dumb show' as it was sometimes called, required a special understanding and a conscious effort. But some progress was being made, as was witnessed by the appreciation of de Gillert's miming even in the slightest of pieces. Her performance, for example, in *The Alpine Brigands*, a ballet scene inserted in Offenbach's *La Fille du Tambour Major* (1880), was specially remarked as 'almost worthy to rank with that of Mr Paul Martinetti [a celebrated pantomimist of the time] for its variety, its grace, and its intelligibility'.[11]

Although the age of the great Romantic ballerinas had passed, the ballets at the Alhambra did at times evoke nostalgic memories. In the ballroom scene in *La Fille du Tambour Major* there was 'a solemnly graceful minuet and gavotte danced by the *coryphées* in slow and stately measure to some quaintly

10 *The Times*, Oct. 26, 1879.

11 *Illustrated London News*, Aug. 28, 1880.

plaintive music by Lully . . . Do you remember,' asked a critic with a long memory, 'the "Menuet de la Cour" that Taglioni and Cerrito (or was it Carlotta Grisi?) used to dance in *Don Giovanni* at Her Majesty's Theatre, ever so many years ago? Ah, the sublimity of that dance! *Dis moi, soldat, t'en souviens-tu*? 'Tis fitting to ask the question, for only old soldiers can reply. And yet I had the honour to see Taglioni . . . the other night at Sadler's Wells, looking as fresh – well, a good deal fresher than the spectator who was respectfully gazing at her feet.'[12]

Giovannina Pitteri did not desert the Alhambra when Strange left. She returned in August 1873 to dance in Henri Dewinne's *The Enchanted Forest*, and remained as the theatre's brightest star until 1876. During these years she played the dual rôle of the Nereide and the Princess Topaze in Dewinne's version of Paul Taglioni's well-known ballet, *Flick and Flock*,[13] which had its first London performance on Boxing Day 1873 and had what was then a record run of 36 weeks. Two years later she was the Snow Queen in Lauri's *The Flower Queen* (November 8, 1875), and she was featured, too, in many of the operettas.

She soon had to contend with a rival. On October 9, 1874, a new name appeared in the programme, that of Erminia Pertoldi, 'a very handsome *danseuse* of statuesque proportions'. Pertoldi was to remain at the Alhambra until 1884; she married the ballad composer Tito Mattei and died in 1907. Her style of dancing contrasted strongly with Pitteri's. 'I should say,' wrote a critic after seeing them both dance in Jacobi's comic opera, *Lord Bateman* (1875), 'that Pitteri's style is pure motion, noiseless and perfectly symmetrical, while that of Pertoldi, though more vivacious and definitely fascinating, is suggestive of sound. Pertoldi touches the earth, Pitteri treads on the air.'[14]

Pertoldi was to be posthumously honoured by George Bernard Shaw, who introduced her into his novel, *Immaturity*, written shortly after his arrival in London in the late eighteen-seventies although not published until 1930. She inspired Shaw with what his latest biographer has called a romance of the mind.[15] There are cryptic references to her as 'Terpsichore' in his diary notebooks for 1876 and 1877. That they knew one another is beyond doubt, for in January 1888 he recorded having 'changed his coat and [gone] to Headlam's, where I had a conversation with Pertoldi whom I used to admire so much.'[16] With a novelist's concern for the authenticity of his background, Shaw must have called on her and enquired about her life, for in his novel

12 *Illustrated Sporting and Dramatic News*, Sep. 11, 1880. The writer's memory was a little at fault. Marie Taglioni had danced a Minuet and Gavotte called *La Romanesca* with Auguste Vestris at her benefit at the Paris Opéra in 1835, but the Menuet de la Reine and Gavotte which is referred to here was from Perrot's *Un Bal sous Louis XIV* and was danced by Fanny Elssler and Adèle Dumilâtre in 1843, and by Fanny Elssler and Fanny Cerrito in 1844. In 1880 Marie Taglioni was living in London and teaching dancing and deportment in Connaught Square. She was then seventy-six years of age.

13 *Flick und Flock's Abentheuer*, ballet in 3 acts and 6 scenes, choreography by Paul Taglioni, music by P. L. Hertel, first performed at the Royal Opera, Berlin, Sep. 20, 1858.

14 *Illustrated Sporting and Dramatic News*, Jan. 15, 1876.

15 Holroyd, 106.

16 Weintraub, II, 339.

he recorded that she was born in Trieste in 1850, that she had to struggle desperately at the Alhambra 'to uphold the tradition of the grand school of Italian dancing against the British ignorance of it which expects nothing from a stage dancer but loose morals and the power to kick off a man's hat in a cancan', and – an interesting detail – that 'her extraordinary grace and impetuosity of movement was very suitably accompanied by a beautiful singing voice which she could never be prevailed upon to use on the stage'.[17]

Other ballerinas, with shorter engagements, also enjoyed triumphs on the Alhambra stage. Betty Rigl, who appeared for a few weeks in the summer of 1875, had successes to her credit both in Paris and in New York, where she had danced in the first performance of the American version of *The Black Crook*. She was 'a most graceful and highly cultivated dancer, her style belonging to the poetic rather than the vigorous school. Statuesque and graceful in her poses and slow movements, she is equally brilliant and finished in the more rapid and elaborate *pas*, in all of which she called forth well-deserved applause, which culminated in her facile and expert execution of the rapid *tourbillons* round the stage on the tips of her toes.'[18]

Three years later, in 1878, the Alhambra audience had its first view of Judith David, a petite French-born ballerina, and in 1882 Consuelo de La Bruyère came to London, after a season at the Scala, Milan, to appear in the revival of *Babil and Bijou* – a very lovely woman whom one admirer compared to the bayadère of an Orientalist's dream, and who was renowned for her strong *pointe* work. In the days of Frederick Strange, the Alhambra had gained notoriety through the cancan, and the managements that followed were fully aware of the appeal of acrobatic dancing, particularly when it bordered on the lascivious. The most successful of the Alhambra's extravaganzas was *The Black Crook*, which ran for 204 performances in 1872 and 1873.[19] It included two ballets, in which Aladar Bekefy, Malvina Bartoletti and Signorina Baratti[20] were featured, and a cancan number which aroused stern condemnation from *The Times*; 'any merits the piece may have as spectacle,' wrote its critic, 'are neutralised so long as the manager retains the cancan in the

17 Shaw, *Immaturity*, 125–6.

18 *Illustrated Sporting and Dramatic News*, May 1, 1875.

19 This version of *The Black Crook* was very different from the spectacle of the same name that was so popular in America. Both versions, however, stemmed vaguely from *La Biche au bois*, a spectacle with music by Pilati, produced at the Théâtre de la Porte-Saint-Martin in 1845. The story of the American *Black Crook* has been told by George Freedley (in *Chronicles of the American Dance*, New York, 1948). A production of *La Biche au bois* was cancelled because the theatre where it was to have been given was burnt down. The proprietor of Niblo's Garden then bought the scenery and the contracts of the ballet company and, using a melodrama by Charles M. Barras as a scenario, presented *The Black Crook* in 1866. Unlike Barras's piece, J. and H. Paulton's book for the version given at the Alhambra in 1872 was recognisably based on the French original. The story was a variant of the Sleeping Beauty theme, Black Crook being the evil fairy who was not invited to the christening of Princess Désirée and who vents her spleen in diverse ways, including transforming the Princess into a fawn.

20 Probably Giovannina Baratti who danced at the Scala, Milan, 1859 and 1869–71, and the San Carlo, Naples, 1869–70.

performance'.[21] The Alhambra perhaps realised it was playing with fire, for the offending 'Folly Ballet' was quickly withdrawn. But in the next operetta production, Offenbach's *La Belle Hélène* (1873), the 'vivacious and preternaturally agile' Sara – the inimitable Wiry Sal – returned with her own troupe of English girls in a wildly abandoned 'Parisian Quadrille'. She became an established favourite, and her act was featured at the Alhambra for a year, being first interpolated in *Flick and Flock* and later in another Offenbach operetta, *Le Roi Carotte* (1874). Further successes may have awaited her at the Alhambra if she had not injured her leg on the stage that winter.

Now that the cancan could be given with impunity, eccentric dancers of all sorts followed one another on the Alhambra stage. There were the Majiltons, who performed an act called 'Les Trois Diables' to music by Victor Chéri in *Spectresheim* (1875). The following year a place was found in the operetta *Don Juan* for the Fiji Flutterers, a quartet of dancers dressed in extravagantly grotesque costumes – two of them as women with the most *outré* head-dresses – whose act was somewhat reminiscent of that of the Clodoches.[22] And two years later, in 1878, the Girards, a high-kicking trio of male dancers, were featured in the 'Bacchanalian Ballet' that ended *La Poule aux oeufs d'or*.

Eccentric dancing was only one aspect of the rich variety of dancing to be seen at the Alhambra. Spanish dancers were also popular there, the Casanobas from Madrid being engaged in 1876, and Maria Fuensanta and the Royal Spanish Ballet coming in 1879 to appear in *La Torera* and *The Costumes of Murcia*. And in 1880 a remarkable dancer with an original speciality made her appearance – Aenea, the Flying Fairy.[23]

Early in the morning of December 7, 1882, the Alhambra was completely destroyed by fire. For the first six months of 1883, while a new theatre was being designed and built on the gutted site, the company gave performances at Her Majesty's Theatre. The second Alhambra was ready well before the end of the year, and was opened on December 3, 1883, with Pertoldi, La Bruyère, Sismondi and Topsy Elliott heading the ballet company, the last being an English dancer who six years before had been the victim of the hazard that faced all dancers in the age of gaslight. Her costume had caught fire at the South London Palace, but she was fortunate and had survived to continue her career.

21 *The Times*, Dec. 27, 1872.

22 The Clodoches were a quartet of eccentric dancers who gained celebrity at the Opéra balls in Paris towards the end of the Second Empire. One was dressed as a Highlander, another as a fireman, and the remaining two in women's clothes.

23 Aenea, whose surname was Barry, began her career as an 'aerial dancer' with Mr Conquest's company at the Grecian, where she met her husband, W. P. Dando, who invented some of the mechanism she used. She first came into prominence in *Jack the Giant Killer* at the Gaiety Theatre in 1878. She was billed as 'a new ballet sensation, a flying dancer', and her act consisted of dancing interspersed with flying effects accomplished with the aid of a wire support virtually invisible to the audience. In 1880 she was featured at the Théâtre du Châtelet, Paris, in the ballet, *La Mouche d'or*, which was one of the principal features of the revival of the faery spectacle, *Les Pilules du Diable*.

Another major change in the theatre's policy was now imminent. It had been decided that the theatre would revert to being a music hall, and on October 9, 1884, a music and dancing licence was granted by the Middlesex magistrates, overriding objections that the re-establishment of a gigantic music hall in Leicester Square would place an increased burden on the police.

III

The return of the narrative ballet (1884–94)

In the decade when the Alhambra was given over to comic opera the ballet had firmly established its claim to a permanent place in the theatre's fare. As George Bernard Shaw perceived, 'people of taste went to the Alhambra in those days only to see Pertoldi and Gillert dance; and in the end it proved that even from a commercial point of view the ballet paid well enough to be worth retaining when the comic opera was dropped'.[1]

Over the next ten years[2] the standard of ballet would noticeably rise; although once again sharing the bill with variety acts, it increasingly became the main attraction. Vast expenditure was laid out on the scenery, costumes and effects for ballets which concluded each half of the programme. From a technical viewpoint, the dancers of the *corps de ballet* would remain considerably inferior to those of Paris, to take an example, but they performed the choreography given to them with impressive precision, which they were able to achieve by not having to keep a repertory in their memories and performing just two ballets nightly for runs of six months. They excelled in processions – military evolutions remained constantly popular – and within the limits of their capabilities formed a disciplined framework for the prima ballerina. Current taste required it to be an all-female *corps*, prepared to cope also with travesty rôles in which they could display their curvaceous figures and shapely legs without fear of protest.

Although a modest ballet element was retained in the opera seasons at Covent Garden,[3] it was only at the Alhambra – and from 1884, the Empire – that a choreographer could find sufficient opportunity to exercise his skill and that a ballerina could be presented with due regard to her importance. The music-hall ambience was no obstacle – ballet-masters and dancers had after all to earn their living, and the Alhambra could obviously pay them the going rate – and these ten years at the Alhambra were distinguished by a succession of four choreographers reared in the classical tradition, Joseph Hansen

1 Shaw, *Music in London*, I, 24.

2 Charles Morton was acting manager 1884–90, William Bailey in 1891, and A. A. Gilmer 1891–94.

3 Hansen was ballet-master at Covent Garden for the seasons of 1874 to 1876, and Katti Lanner from 1887 to 1892, but their tasks were mainly confined to arranging divertissements in opera productions. Several leading ballerinas were to be seen there: Virginia Zucchi (1878–79), Maria Giuri (1883, 1892), and Emma Palladino (1889–91).

(1884–87), Eugenio Casati (1887–90, 1893–94), Léon Espinosa (1890) and Carlo Coppi (1891–92, 1894–98, 1901–02), and by three of the most brilliant Italian ballerinas of the day, Emma Palladino, Emma Bessone, and the still more renowned Pierina Legnani.

In the days when the Alhambra was an operetta house, the dramatic interest of the evening's entertainment was concentrated in the operettas and the dance element was provided mainly in incidental *divertissements*; occasionally separate ballets were given, but with a few exceptions these contained little more than a shred of action. Now, under the new régime, the incidental parts of the programme were the variety acts and, with an organisation already in place, ballet became the dominant and permanent element around which everything else was fitted. Much more, therefore, was expected from the ballet-master than had been required of Milano and Bertrand, and very soon a trend could be observed of giving the ballets a stronger narrative.

The first choreographer to be engaged by the new management was already establishing an international reputation. A Belgian by birth, Joseph Hansen had served his apprenticeship at the Théâtre de la Monnaie, Brussels, first as a dancer, and later as *régisseur de ballet* and ballet master. He was then offered an engagement at the Bolshoi Theatre, Moscow, where on two occasions, in 1880 and 1882, he revived a ballet which had met with a certain amount of criticism at its first performance a few years before but was still considered worthy of preservation, no doubt on account of the eminence of its composer. This was *Swan Lake,*[4] which Hansen undoubtedly took as his inspiration for *The Swans* (December 1, 1884), his first work for the newly baptised Alhambra Theatre of Varieties. Tchaikovsky's music was not used, a score being provided, as usual, by the ever-obliging Jacobi.[5]

The plot, such as it was, can only be pieced together from contemporary descriptions, for no synopsis was published, but even so, the parallel with the second act of the Russian work is striking. The Alhambra curtain rose to reveal a lake shaded by overhanging trees, a line of painted wooden swans being drawn across while 'a score of scantily weed-draped maidens [danced] in the gauzy shadows'. The *répétiteur* score reveals these to be 'roussalkas', or water nymphs. The stage then filled with dancers representing the swans who have been briefly restored to human form. Soon they were joined by a party of young huntsmen (in travesty, of course) armed with spears, whose leader is smitten with the Swan Queen's charms. But a malign influence overpowers them; the huntsmen are 'ensnared by the wiles of the nereids [the *répétiteur* refers to them as sirens, but presumably they were the weed-draped

4 In its original version, *Swan Lake* was first performed at the Bolshoi Theatre, Moscow, on Feb. 20/Mar. 4, 1877, with choreography by Julius Reisinger. Hansen was responsible for revising the ballet in 1880 and 1882, and in 1883 the ballet, as then given, was dropped. The Petipa–Ivanov version, which forms the basis of most of today's revivals, was presented in St Petersburg in 1894 (Act II only) and 1895 (complete version).

5 Jacobi's *répétiteur* contains a note by the composer that this ballet was also produced at the Théâtre de la Bourse, Brussels, and at the Cercle Artistique and the Folies-Bergère. Paris.

roussalkas who appeared earlier] and are drawn into the lake'; and in the final apotheosis the lovers, united in death, are seen floating across the water in a swan-drawn car while 'the swans are left disconsolate'.[6] An engraving of this scene clearly shows the swans posing behind bands of transparent material stretched across the stage, an effect which had been used in Moscow.[7] The rôle of the Swan Queen was played by Emma Palladino, and the costumes were designed by Wilhelm. In contrast to the comparative failure of his *Swan Lake* in Moscow, *The Swans* retained its place in the Alhambra programme for an unprecedented run of 49 weeks in spite of having to compete with a spectacular production of *Excelsior* at Her Majesty's Theatre.[8]

Hansen's ballets contained little dramatic interest, but they were colourful, brilliant spectacles in which the setting or the theme suggested ideas both to the choreographer and to the costume designer. Although none was a work of major importance, they were competent, professional productions which without exception were well received. Some, though, had more than a thread of plot running through them. *Melusine* (December 22, 1884),[9] was based on the French legend of the fairy who cruelly imprisoned her father and was condemned to become, on one day in each week, a serpent from the waist down. After her marriage she attempts to conceal her secret, but her husband, overcome with curiosity, discovers it, and she is fated to walk the earth as a spectre until the end of time. It was not an unpromising theme, but in the absence of a printed scenario, the action mystified the greater part of the audience who were unfamiliar with the legend. *Nadia* (May 16, 1887), a ballet with a Russian setting, and *Algeria* (July 11, 1887) were each concerned with the rescue of the heroine, in the former from a demon who carries her off to his subterranean palace, and in the latter from a band of pirates. But plots were always of secondary importance at the Alhambra; it was the dances and the processions and the spectacle that counted. Speaking of the plot of *Melusine*, *The Times* wrote: 'As M. Hansen knows, this is a matter of supreme indifference to an audience who only requires that the stage shall be well filled with brightly dressed groups of pretty and graceful dancers'.[10] This was overstating the public attitude towards *ballets d'action*, for there was a proportion of the audience which did want to know what was going on. Writing of another of

6 *The Times*, Dec. 2, 1884.

7 The critic of *Moskovskie Vedomosti* (Jan. 15/27, 1880) noted that the stage was 'effectively wrapped in green tulle, which represented water', behind which danced the *corps de ballet* as the swans. (Quoted in Wiley, 61.)

8 *Excelsior*, ballet in 6 parts and 12 scenes, scenario and choreography by Luigi Manzotti, music by Romualdo Marenco, was first performed at the Scala, Milan, on Jan. 11, 1881. For London the ballet was reproduced by Carlo Coppi, later to become ballet-master at the Alhambra. It opened at Her Majesty's on May 22, 1885, and ran for 169 performances. The principal dancers were Adelina Rossi (later replaced by Giovanna Limido) and Enrico Cecchetti, and towards the end of the run a solo was added for Kate Vaughan. Malvina Cavallazzi, who was later to appear in mime rôles at the Empire, made her last appearance as a dancer in this production.

9 *Melusine* was revived by Hansen at the Théâtre de la Bourse, Brussels, on Apr. 16, 1886.

10 *The Times*, Dec. 23, 1884.

Hansen's ballets, *Cupid* (May 24, 1886), the *Era*, which published detailed reviews of ballets at the Alhambra, complained of the unavailability of a printed scenario – 'not,' it was pointed out, 'that the plot of a Terpsichorean *divertissement* is of much importance in itself, but some really clever pantomime is exhibited in the course of *Cupid* by several of the performers with the effect on the audience of interesting, but puzzling them.'[11]

Unfortunately there were no ballet critics in London with the knowledge and judgement of a Gautier, and a historian attempting to appraise Hansen's choreography must be content with the vague praise accorded, seemingly almost as an afterthought, to his skilful grouping of the *corps de ballet* in *Melusine* and his colourful dances of different nations – ranging from Albanians to Zulus, Nautch girls to Red Indians – in *Cupid*. Clearly, what most impressed the uninitiated were the processions. *Le Bivouac* (December 22, 1885), for example, the *bonne bouche* of that year's Christmas programme – was a classic example of the military ballet. 'No barrack yard drill could be more accurate,' wrote *The Times*, 'than the training which these stalwart female battalions have been put through under the direction of M. Hansen, with their brilliant evolutions and groupings. All branches of Her Majesty's services are represented, Irish jigs and Scottish reels alternating with English dances and hornpipes, the whole stirring up the house to a fever of patriotic enthusiasm.'[12]

But as often as not, what was most remembered in these ballets by Hansen were the costumes or some spectacular effect. For *Melusine*, the costumes were designed by Wilhelm and Bianchini, and the glitter of the armour in the limelight was a good match for the huge property dragons breathing fire from monstrous nostrils. *Dresdina* (November 15, 1886) was a particular triumph for another designer, Lucien Besche, who dressed the immense Alhambra *corps de ballet* in delicately colourful costumes representing various kinds of German porcelain, while a feature of *Nadia*, to which Besche also contributed, was the bevy of Stalactites scantily dressed in brilliantly colourful costumes.

Algeria, Hansen's last ballet for the Alhambra, was produced just six days before the death of Louis Mérante, the *premier maître de ballet* of the Paris Opéra. The vacancy was offered to Hansen, who left London to take up his new post no doubt well satisfied that his work had been appreciated there. For *The Times*, in praising the merits of *Algeria*, had written: 'Year by year under the present management of the theatre, the Alhambra ballets seem to improve in artistic merit, and there is probably no spectacle of the kind in Europe superior in point of taste, in musical design, or in richness and harmony of colour to the new ballet'.[13]

Hansen's successor, Eugenio Casati, came from Italy, where the tradition of mime had always been firmly established in ballet, and it was only to be

11 *Era*, May 29, 1886. In the Jacobi papers at the Theatre Museum, London, there are a number of printed ballet scenarios marked 'For Private Circulation', suggesting that they were printed not for the audience but for the cast and those concerned in the production.

12 *The Times*, May 29, 1886.

13 *The Times*, Dec. 25, 1885.

expected that greater emphasis would henceforth be paid to the narrative element. Account had to be taken of the attitudes of the public and the particular ambience of the theatre, but it had already become clear that audiences were not unresponsive to the introduction of mime. This development brought into prominence a new type of performer, a dancer skilled in the art of mime. Already, in Hansen's time, the Alhambra had been building up a group of dancers with sufficient acting abilities to mime rôles in plots of increasing complexity: Mlle Marie, who specialised in *jeune premier* parts, Lucia Cormani, who had excelled as the demon in *Nadia*, and Minnie Thurgate. In time, as stronger plots were introduced, these were to be joined by other actor-dancers. Casati was to be the first of a succession of Italian choreographers who would dominate the Alhambra ballet from 1887 to 1910 and consolidate the tradition in which they themselves had been nurtured.

He was undoubtedly still finding his feet in new surroundings when he produced his first ballet at the Alhambra, *Enchantment* (December 24, 1887). Its plot was dismissed by one critic as '[resembling] the stories of several other ballets at the Alhambra, and [being], indeed, of no particular consequence'. The ballet, however, did not lack novelty, although this was mainly provided by effects, such as the passage in which the dancers wore small bells on their wrists and ankles which they struck with little hammers 'in time and tune' with the orchestra. Another remarkable effect was an apparition of the heroine, 'managed [somewhat] on the principle of Pepper's ghost'[14], in which she appeared to grow in size as if approaching from afar until the moment when Bessone substituted herself for the vision and 'bounded on to the stage in person'. For the usual grand finale the *corps de ballet*, dressed in scarlet and wearing red wigs, went through a variety of evolutions, culminating in a whirling of 'gilded and fringed cones upon spindles' as Bessone was lifted aloft on a column radiating scarves of brilliant colours.[15]

Not for nothing was Casati an Italian. Reared in the tradition of dramatic ballets, he soon began to influence the general nature of the Alhambra productions. In *Antiope* (June 4, 1888), he chose a theme set in ancient Greece about the fury of a Queen of Ephesus when she discovers that the man she loves, an Athenian duke, prefers her sister Antiope. When he abducts Antiope, the Queen orders her warriors to invade, but is defeated and captured. The duke generously sets her free, and she finally gives her blessing to his marriage to Antiope. This happy ending provided an excuse to present the *corps de ballet* as 'vast battalions of glittering Amazons'[16] in the finale, parading in dazzling confections by Wilhelm, whose sure sense of colour never transcended the bounds of good taste. *Ideala* (September 3, 1888), a more muted work, was an Arcadian study. Casati's classical roots were also evident in *Irene* (December 17, 1888), which had a well defined plot about the

14 Pepper's Ghost, named after a certain 'Professor' J. H. Pepper who invented it, was an illusion by which a ghostlike apparition was made to appear to the audience by being reflected from below the stage on to a sheet of glass positioned at an angle on the stage.

15 *Era*, Dec. 31, 1887.

16 *The Times*, June 5, 1888.

ALHAMBRA THEATRE OF VARIETIES.

1. SELECTION BY THE BAND

"Iolanthe," *Sir A. Sullivan.*

Soloists.—*Flute*, M. B. Powell, *Piccolo*, M. Orchie, *Clarionet*, M. Hetherington, *Oboe*, M. Foreman, *Euphonium*, M. T. Busby, *Horn*, M. Cook, and *Cornet*, M. Lloyd Simon.

2. **THE BROS. PASSMORE.**

3. GEORGE BELVERE.

4. **THE BROS. GRIFFITHS AND THEIR BLONDIN DONKEY.**

5. **LYDIA YEAMANS.**

6. **ALGERIA**

Ballet Divertissement in Three Tableaux

MUSIC SPECIALLY COMPOSED BY C. JACOBI.

The Scenery by HENRY EMDEN. The Costumes from designs of L. BESCHE, by M. & Mdme. ALIAS. Properties by W. GARRETT. Stage Effects by F. FOX.

PREMIERE DANSEUSE—MDLLE. PALLADINO.

Supported by Mdlle CORMANI & Mdlle. MARIE

TABLEAU I. A Market-Place in Algeria.

1. Prelude, Introduction and Dance of Water-Carriers. 2. Entrance of Selim, Mdlle. MARIE, with Arabian soldiers. 3. Bamboula. 4. Almée's Dance. 5. Entrée Dansante, Mdlle. PALLADINO. 6. Scene & Pas de Deux., Mdlle. PALLADINO & Mdlle. MARIE. 7. Arabian Fantasia. 8. Algerian Dance and Rioting Scene.

TABLEAU II. African Interior.

9. Scene—Mdlle. PALLADINO and Mdlle. CORMANI. 10. Variation, Mdlle. PALLADINO. 11. Pas de Deux and Scene, Mdlle. PALLADINO and Mdlle. CORMANI.

TABLEAU III. Pirate's Encampment.

12. Dance of Pir[illegible] and Almée. 13. Moorish Dance. 14. Sword Dance. 15. The Arabian Tent. Andantino & Group. 16. Pirate's Drinking Valse. 17. Solo—Mdlle. PALLADINO. 18. Galop Finale. Departure and pursuit of the Pirates. Final Group.

Trade "SANITAS" Mark. THE BEST Fragrant, Colourless, Non-Poisonous, Does not Stain DISINFECTANT (Fluids, Powder & Soaps).

Alhambra Theatre programme, *c*. September 1887.

DAKIN & COMPY., TEA & COFFEE MERCHANTS, No. 1, St. Paul's Churchyard, E.C., and Oxford Circus, W., supply this Establishment.

7. **SISTERS BILTON.**

8. **BROS. BRAATZ.**

9. *First appearance in England of*
MDLLE. VANONI,
INTERNATIONAL SINGER AND DANCER

10. **SAM TORR, Comedian.**

CONCLUDING WITH

11. **NADIA.**

BALLET DIVERTISSEMENT IN TWO TABLEAUX.

The Music composed by G. JACOBI,

Costumes, designed by L. BESCHE, by M. & Mdme ALIAS.

The Scenery by C. BREW. Wigs by CLARKSON.

Premiere Danseuses—Mdlles. CORMANI and MARIE and Miss TOPSY ELLIOTT.

TABLEAU I. A Rustic Interior in Russia.

1. Prelude. 2. Scéne & Solo, Mdlle. CORMANI. 3. Pizzicato, Miss TOPSY ELLIOTT, Mdlle. CORMANI. Mdlle. MARIE. 4. Entrée Dansante of Wedding Guests. 5. Russian Dances: (a) Doumka; (b) Solo, Mdlle. MARIE; (c) Variation, Miss TOPSY ELLIOTT; (d) Trinka, Finale. 6. Scéne of Fascination.

TABLEAU II. A Stalactite Cave in the Silver Mines.

7. Andantino. 8. Dance of Stalactites and Solo, Miss TOPSY ELLIOTT. 9. Grand Ballabile—Groups of Stalactites. 10. Mazurka. 11. Variation Valse, Miss TOPSY ELLIOTT. 12. Grande Valse Finale. 13. Aurora Borealis.

12. **Finale by the Band.**

PURE WATER COMPANY'S AERATED DISTILLED WATER, Price per dozen—Syphons, 3s., Quart Bottles, 2s. 6d. *Lancet*—"*Perfection.*" *Food*—"*The Ideal Water.*" Works: QUEEN'S ROAD, BATTERSEA.

jealous rivalry of two goddesses for the favours of a young sculptor. It contained a colourful scene at a Neapolitan fair, peopled with masqueraders, and in the title-rôle it introduced to London a young Italian ballerina destined for future greatness but now venturing outside her native land for the first time – Pierina Legnani.

Casati was by no means his own master at the Alhambra, where he had to conform to the policy laid down by the management regarding not only the length of the ballets, but also on occasion the subject-matter. The decision to produce another patriotic ballet after the fashion of *Le Bivouac* certainly came from above. Musically, *Our Army and Navy* (April 1, 1889) was an augmented version of the earlier ballet, as Jacobi noted on the title-page of his score, but Coppi rearranged the dances which offered a panorama of high Victorian jingoism in the shapely forms of the superbly drilled Alhambra girls. There can have been no shortage of advice to get military details correct, and Casati accomplished his task with consummate skill, for the ballet ran for almost a year.

No doubt he saw this as no more than an interlude, for he was able to return to more familiar ground in his next ballet, *Astraea* (July 8, 1889). In classical mythology Astraea was said to be the daughter of Jupiter, and the ballet progressed from an Arcadian landscape where the gods of ancient Rome were introduced, first to a scene showing Jupiter in Vulcan's cave, and then to a colourful finale with the gods and goddesses paying homage to Jupiter on Olympus.

Dramatic interest and local colour were again the main features of *Asmodeus* (December 23, 1889), which was set in Spain and included a number of Spanish dances, which always found a warm response in London. The title was the name of the principal character in Le Sage's novel, *Le Diable boiteux*, but the limping devil had been transformed into a demon of remarkable agility to display the brilliant technique of a phenomenon most unusual for the time and the place – a male dancer, Vittorio De Vincenti. As in the novel, Asmodeus has been imprisoned in a bottle, from which he is accidentally freed by the student Cleofas, whom he rewards by assisting his wooing of the lovely Serafina, but the action had to be greatly simplified for a ballet lasting little more than half an hour – much more so indeed than in the celebrated ballet on the same theme in which Fanny Elssler had stirred the Parisians half a century before.[17]

This was followed by *Zanetta* (March 24, 1890), a short ballet in a single scene whose *divertissement* ensured its place on the bill, either complete or in truncated form, for sixty weeks, by the end of which it had attained a total of 419 performances, at the time the longest run achieved by a ballet at the Alhambra.[18] It was a 'melodrama in action' set in the Tyrol where a

17 *Le Diable boiteux*, ballet-pantomime in 3 acts and 10 scenes, choreography by Coralli, music by Gide, first performed at the Paris Opéra. June 1, 1836. Its choreographic highlight was the *Cachucha*, the stylised Spanish character dance forever after identified with its creator, Fanny Elssler.

18 *The Times*, Mar. 26, 1890.

diligence is waylaid by brigands, who are finally overpowered by a returning troop of soldiers. Commenting that 'in the hands of its expert manipulators at the Alhambra, the ballet [now] assumes as many forms as the drama proper . . . comic, passionate, tragic or romantic,' *The Times* noted with apparent approval that 'the fairy element, so common in this class of entertainment, has for once disappeared'.[19]

That there was a growing trend towards plots of increasing complexity dealing with real-life situations was further evidenced in *Salandra* (June 23, 1890), which evoked the following admiring comment from the critic of the *Era*: 'That actions speak louder than words is a generally accepted axiom, but it was hardly to be expected that by action could be set forth such an elaborate story as is told in [*Salandra*].'[20] As the heroine, Legnani played a gypsy queen who stirs the passions of a Bulgarian nobleman and is carried off to his private yacht where she dances for his pleasure, accompanied by the crew, which *The Times* picturesquely described as 'strangely hybrid . . . half sailor, half chambermaid'.[21] The wronged wife then appears and the husband meekly allows himself to be led back to the conjugal roof. The gypsies, who harbour grievances of their own, then burn down his castle and abduct his little son, whom they bring up as an acrobat. The child's parents search for him far and wide, and in the end he is restored to them through Salandra's selfless intervention. The action was considerably more complex than this brief summary conveys, and the dramatic action occupied a larger proportion of the performing time than was usual. The mimes were consequently given a new challenge, and acquitted themselves very honourably. The travesty tradition still held, and the rôle of the nobleman was very expressively played by Mlle Marie, who was ably supported by Mlle Zimmerman as the wife. De Vincenti was given the part of the gypsy chief, which enabled him to dazzle the audience with his high elevation and strong pirouettes, while a young acrobat, Master Etherdo, demonstrated globe walking and other feats in the small rôle of the son. Even so, there was a generous fill of dancing, including several variations for Legnani (including a *danse de fascination*), an umbrella dance for the nobleman's friends in the first scene, and a finale 'bewildering in its variety, exhilarating in its colour, and fascinating in its life and movement'[22] on which the curtain descended to a storm of applause on a stage crowded with dancers waving coloured streamers.

The introduction of themes more closely related to real life was to lead to the up-to-date ballet, but this development would never oust the more conventional type. In 1890, after Casati's engagement had come to an end, Léon Espinosa was engaged to produce *The Sleeping Beauty* for the Christmas attraction. Espinosa was a French-trained ballet master of Spanish-Jewish extraction who had appeared with success at the Théâtre de la Porte-Saint-Martin, Paris, during the Second Empire and whose travels had taken him as far afield

19 *Era*, Dec. 20, 1890.
20 *Era*, June 28, 1890.
21 *The Times*, June 27, 1890.
22 *Era*, June 28, 1890.

as Russia and the United States. He was a friend of Marius Petipa, first ballet-master of the Imperial Theatres in St Petersburg, who had stood as godfather to his son Edouard, and was no doubt aware of Petipa's splendid production of *The Sleeping Beauty*, to music by Tchaikovsky, at the Maryinsky Theatre. Espinosa's version, which was produced at the Alhambra on December 15, 1890, was in no sense a plagiarism, for it was presented with an original score by Jacobi, but the Russian production may have provided the initial impulse and a starting-point for the narrative which Espinosa devised.[23]

Espinosa's scenario told the well-known fairy story in five scenes beginning with the birthday celebrations of the Princess at which the Evil Geni, in his anger at not being invited, casts his spell. In the second scene, the Princess pricks her finger on the spinning wheel and is doomed to sleep, not for eternity but, thanks to the intervention of the good fairies, until reawakened by a kiss of love. Twenty years pass, and Prince Hubert learns the secret of the mysterious castle while travelling through a magic wood; he determines to rescue the princess, and overcomes the efforts of wood-nymphs who try to bar his way. When he arrives at her room in the castle, she rises from her bed and, without waking, dances a 'magnetic dance' before him, at the conclusion of which he brings her to life with a kiss. The final scene was devoted to the bridal festival, opening with a brilliant 'Grand Lace and Fans Valse' by the *corps de ballet*, divided into four groups, each representing a well-known lace – English Honiton, Irish Cut Cambric, Venetian Point and Black Spanish. In line with the tradition of the Alhambra, the rôle of the prince was played in travesty by Mlle Marie. De Vincenti appeared as the Evil Geni, here conceived as a male figure, not as a scorned fairy played by a man, as in Russia. His virtuosity seemed to draw down louder applause than the brilliance of Legnani. The ballet was an unreserved triumph, and at the close of one of the scenes, Espinosa, a modest man, had to be forcibly dragged before the footlights to receive the audience's applause.

The following spring the production was revised to introduce the pantomimist Charles Lauri as a sprite in the train of the Evil Geni. Two items in the opening scene and the woodcutters' scene in the third were omitted to add two dances for him in the scene in the magic wood – a 'shadow dance', which brought down the house, and a number entitled 'The Prince and the Spider'.

Espinosa was a demanding master, and he had been unafraid of imposing his will. As his son Edouard, who played the prince's equerry, remembered:

> At the very first call the fat was in the fire. Dad would not accept the girls to retain their various positions unless they had the ability to do so, and those who were in the front line from influence had to give way to the best dancers.
>
> Girls were brought from the back of the corps de ballet and put into the coryphées, girls from the extra ballet were brought into the front line of the corps de ballet.
>
> When matters were all fixed up, rehearsals began, with efficiency as the keynote.

23 See Appendix D for scenario. The Russian production had been first performed on Jan. 3/15, 1890.

Then there was a dispute with Jacobi:

> My dad's view was that a maître de ballet was like a captain aboard ship, not to be interfered with; on the other hand, the directors of the Alhambra had been accustomed to come on the stage and 'have a say' in the production, particularly dear old Jacobi, who was a director as well as the composer and chef d'orchestre. So at one of the rehearsals, up came various directors who made suggestions, in reply to which my dad requested them to mind their own business, and went off to his dressing room until they retired, which they did after a heated discussion.
>
> When my father returned, they had all left except Jacobi. Whilst he spoke of the music my dad accepted his views, but suddenly Jacobi made some suggestion about the miming, upon which my dad saw red and practically threw poor old Jacobi off the stage.
>
> The matter, of course, was patched up afterwards when their artistic temperaments had cooled down.[24]

So it may not have been surprising that, notwithstanding the success of *The Sleeping Beauty*, which ran for the customary six months, Espinosa was not offered the vacant post of ballet-master, which was filled by another Italian choreographer, Carlo Coppi. Coppi was a quiet, rather shy, benevolent-looking man with a beard, who wore a Holland suit and wielded a long stick at rehearsals. Like Casati, he was steeped in the Italian tradition, having been principal mime at the Scala, Milan, and staged *Excelsior* in both Paris and London. His association with the Alhambra was to last, with interruptions, for more than ten years, but his contribution to the English theatre was not confined to Leicester Square; he also arranged ballets for Drury Lane pantomimes and operas at Covent Garden, Irving engaged him for the productions of *Robespierre* and *Faust*, and he gave classes at Malvina Cavallazzi's school in Henrietta Street.

Coppi's first work for the Alhambra, *Oriella* (June 15, 1891), could hardly be called a dramatic ballet, although it could claim a plot of sorts. It had similarities with a ballet produced in London nearly fifty years before, *Alma*[25], but with a change of setting for the principal scene - Japan instead of Germany and Spain - and a marked dilution of action in favour of spectacle. Oriella - another rôle for Legnani - is a creature of the nether regions who, to relieve her boredom, is permitted to visit the Earth to taste the fruits of love. She and her accompanying demon - a part tailored to the nimble agility of Charles Lauri - emerge, presumably through a trap, in Japan, where during a festival of lanterns, complete with Japanese military band, she falls in love with a prince. The pageantry of this scene was a triumph for the designers, who made the most of the prevailing vogue for Japanese art; *The Times* described it as 'an enormously magnified view of the spectacular elements of *The Mikado*',[26] the most successful of the Gilbert and Sullivan operas which had been produced just six years before. The scene then changes

24 Espinosa, 28.

25 *Alma, ou la Fille du feu*, ballet in 4 scenes by Deshayes with *pas* by Perrot and Cerrito, music by Costa, first performed at Her Majesty's Theatre, London, June 23, 1842.

26 *The Times*, June 20, 1891.

to the Island of Love where Oriella's conquest is completed, and the lovers and the attendant demon finally make their way to the Infernal Regions, the prince having decided to become a demon himself. It was all very artificial and balletically conventional, with Mlle Marie playing the prince and Legnani dazzling the public with 'wonderful pirouetting and elastic agility' in her solos.[27]

Coppi's next production, *Temptation* (December 21, 1891), marked a return to the *ballet d'action*, although once again its plot was not remarkable for its originality. Set in mediaeval Italy, it told of a hunchback who is befriended by a country girl and on whom Hymen bestows the gifts of youth, beauty and wealth along with a series of temptations to test his fidelity. Two months later Coppi followed this with the skating *divertissement*, *On the Ice* (February 21, 1892), a slight piece which charmingly but conventionally culminated in a fall of paper snow, but his next two ballets, *Don Juan* (June 13, 1892) and *Aladdin* (December 19, 1892) were more ambitious productions.

Such was the taste of the time and the place that *Don Juan* was conceived in a modernised spirit, the title-rôle being played by Mlle Marie as 'an up-to-date Johnny' and the character of Zerlina, in which Legnani appeared most uncharacteristically as 'a giddy girl'. In short the ballet was devised with tongue in cheek, more as a light-hearted skit on the theme of Mozart's opera, the more tuneful melodies of which Jacobi had woven into his score. Modernisation, however, was not carried to its limits, for as Hollingshead explained in his programme note, it was 'dressed [only] in some parts *à la fin du siècle*'. Had the treatment been more serious, a travesty Don Juan might have appeared somewhat ridiculous, but as it was, Mlle Marie's 'abundant and ... eloquent pantomimic expression'[28] was received without disapproval. For the same reason no one objected to the action being transposed to Germany. The narrative was condensed into three scenes. Anna's repulse of the Don, the fascinating wiles of Zerlina, the fury of Elvira and the killing of the Commander were all rapidly sketched in the opening scene in a Bavarian beer-garden with its dancing highlight of a Hop-pole Waltz. In the second scene, revellers are seen returning from a masked ball, and Don Juan issues invitations to a banquet. Here much was made of Leporello's fright at being suddenly confronted with the Commandant's statue, which the Don cynically bids to his supper, a scene which George Lupino played for laughs, interspersing his comical antics with 'some astonishing *pirouettes en l'air*'.[29]

Aladdin, which was presented as the spectacular Christmas production for 1892, was not entirely an original work, although Coppi's choreography was new. Hollingshead, who was responsible for the scenario, had originally written it for a ballet produced by the d'Aubans and the Wardes at the Crystal Palace in 1871, and had based it on an earlier ballet in the repertory of the

27 *Era*, June 20, 1891.

28 *Era*, June 18, 1892.

29 *Dancing*, II, 14 (July 1892), 167. See Appendix D for scenario.

Berlin opera house.[30] Being the Alhambra's contribution to the Christmas season, a 'principal boy' was justified and Mlle Marie made an eloquent and dramatic Aladdin. Specially engaged to play the Magician was the seemingly jointless actor-dancer, Fred Storey, whose 'eccentric exploits in the way of somersault turning and strange steps, and the splendid looseness of his trips and flings, brought the house down in roars of applause'. For her part Legnani added the rôle of the Princess to her Alhambra triumphs, performing a skirt dance to an enchanting melody which Jacobi had entitled the 'Zerlina Gavotte' as a tribute to her success in *Don Juan*. Alongside her was a charming newcomer, Palmira Pollini, another Milanese ballerina, playing the part of the Spirit of the Lamp. The ballet concluded with an effect that stirred memories of the Alhambra's earlier glories – 'The Veil of Diamonds', a delicate curtain of 'crystal lacework' made out of 75 000 glass facets that were held together by twenty-four miles of wire and illuminated by lights of many different colours, the whole contraption weighing one and a half tons. 'The effect of the horizontal lines of liquid brilliancy' was dazzling; 'the prism-like hues produced by the facets, the streams of silver "rain" which fringed the curtain above, and the view through its network, of a beautiful central figure, with a branch of electric lights on each side of it' brought the ballet to a sensational close.[31]

After producing *Aladdin*, Coppi departed from the Alhambra for two years, his place being filled successively by Emile Grédelue and Eugenio Casati. Meanwhile a new development had been initiated with the production, on September 19, 1892, of the first truly up-to-date ballet, *Up the River*, which preceded the Empire's *Round the Town* by just a week. Devised by John Hollingshead and with the dances arranged by Dewinne, it was set on the banks of the Thames near Henley, where for the past half century the annual regatta had become a highlight of both the social and the sporting calendars. As the curtain rose a bevy of bathing belles emerge from the houseboats, running across the stage to take their morning dip. Tennis players and archers then appear, followed shortly by a boating party. Here a brief love interest was introduced, two of the men being in love with the same girl, and the issue being decided by a race between a couple of eights. It was all very topical, a reflection of the growing preoccupation with outdoor sports and activities: lawn tennis was still in its infancy, but archery was an established pastime for ladies. Then, after a spirited hornpipe by Minnie Thurgate, the sky darkened and a storm broke, a thin curtain of real water showering down from the flies into a trough running along the footlights. Blue skies at last return, and the black umbrellas turn into sunshades of many colours. Finally, when night has fallen, the curtain was lowered after a spirited galop.

The first of Grédelue's two ballets for the Alhambra was even more topical. *Chicago* (March 27, 1893) celebrated the great World Fair which had recently

30 *Aladdin, oder Dir Wunderlampe*, grand fairy ballet in 3 acts by Hoguet, music by Gührich, first performed at the Royal Opera, Berlin, on Jan. 19, 1834. It remained in the repertory there until 1884.

31 *Era*, Dec. 24, 1892.

opened in that city. It was also highly entertaining and extremely eclectic in the styles of dancing it contained, and it ran for more than a year. The critic of the *Sketch* described it in detail from the moment the curtain rose to reveal T. E. Ryan's set of the exhibition buildings, viewed across the artificial lake:

> The first people to present themselves are a mixed crew of Chinese, costermongers, comic tourists, and a man very much like Buffalo Bill. Some comic business is given, consisting of the wicked tricks played on the Buffalo Bill by two costers, who purloin his flask, and keep passing it so adroitly from one to the other that his efforts to recover it prove fruitless. Then the serious business begins with a dance of a bevy of Indian beauties. They are clothed in a vague diaphanous white with gold flowers printed on it, and bear huge cloaks of like material in dove colour. Gaily they dance what is called a Nautch dance - and it is not a bit like one - and wind up with a peg-top twirling to furious pseudo-Oriental music. After this nation after nation appears. First Spain, with Signorina Pollini, a study in black, red, and yellow, at the head of half-a-dozen girls, who dance a 'Jota Aragonesa', that delighted the audience and did not seem one bit Spanish. Then redskins, highly painted and be-feathered, dancing a war-dance, brandishing tomahawks, and uttering war-whoops not one whit more terrible than those one used to give forth in the streets when at the age of the Fenimore Cooper cult.
>
> Later on came three Russians to dance the Kimarinskaya, and one of them - Miss Seale, we believe - dressed as a moujik, danced with remarkable fire and life; indeed, hers was the success of the ballet. Of course, England was there, represented by Miss Seale again, and she performed a hornpipe delightfully. Twice over were we represented, for there was also a dance of mashers wearing big grey overcoats that suddenly changed to serpentine skirts, and very funny they were in their burlesque business. After many other individual dances came a procession of nations, and finally what is grandly called an 'Apotheosis of Universal Peace'. Perhaps a mere scholar would smile at the term 'apotheosis'; but, then, such people do not go to the Alhambra. Anyhow, it was a very pretty picture; at the back a huge statue of Liberty with a large electric light, in the centre of the stage a girl dressed all in white holding a large palm branch; she was mounted on a pedestal, from which were strands of laurel leaves like capstan bars, and seizing these the nations ran round in a sort of Maypole, and wound up in a picturesque attitude disclosing the monarchs of the earth in attitudes of friendship.
>
> On the whole, gorgeous dresses, pretty pictures, lively dances, exhilarating music, and a big success. Yankee-doodle-do![32]

The title of Grédelue's second Alhambra production, *Fidelia* (June 19, 1893), was an intentional pun, the ballet being about an infernally inspired violinist who teaches the troubadour hero some of his secrets so that he can win the girl he loves. The appearance of a holy friar spins out the story, and the lovers are only united at the end when the girl's father, who has been ruined at the tables in Monte-Carlo, relents to give them his blessing. Palmira Pollini was Fidelia; Mlle Marie having retired, the part of the troubadour was given to Lucia Cormani; while for the rôle of the demon violinist the Alhambra had engaged a speciality performer who styled himself Paganini Redivivus, 'Champion Violinist of the World and . . . Greatest Living Interpreter of Irish

32 *Sketch*, Apr. 5, 1893.

Melodies'. The ballet was memorable more for its dances and spectacle, however, than for its action: for a dance by the *corps de ballet*, clad only in their nightdresses and carrying electrically lit candlesticks; for the poultry *divertissement* with turkeys, geese, cocks and hens (complete with chicks breaking out of their eggs), and rabbits; for the long-suffering dancers who were suspended to represent stalactites, and an effective mirror scene in the nymphs' grotto; and for the finale in Monte-Carlo, with its swirling crowd of gaily dressed Pierrettes and Pulcinettes, Harlequins and Harlequinas, and Columbines – 'just the people one would want to see all the time,' exclaimed Arthur Symons, 'and their dancing is just what dancing should be.' Symons adored the ballet at the Alhambra, but disapproved of the recent trend of injecting comic pantomime, which he considered suitable for a Drury Lane pantomime, but for not for the 'Home of Ballet' which 'the Alhambra of a great tradition' prided itself to be. 'At its worst,' he pointed out with insular vision, 'it is, with the Empire, one of the two theatres in London where something more or less beautiful can always be seen; at its best it might easily become such a "Palace of Pleasure" as does not now exist in the world.'[33]

In 1893 Casati returned to produce two important works, beginning with an elaborate and picturesque *Don Quixote* (December 11, 1893), for which the costumes were based on the celebrated illustrations by Gustave Doré. The first-night audience's demonstrative enthusiasm was a sign of the growing appreciation of ballets based on an interesting narrative. As with all Alhambra ballets, the plot tended to peter out before the end, which by tradition was devoted to dancing and processions in which the whole of the *corps de ballet* participated. Athol Mayhew had based his scenario on Cervantes' novel, and had succeeded in selecting incidents that would capture something of the spirit of the original. The central rôle of Don Quixote was allotted, not to a travesty dancer, as might have been feared, but to Fred Storey, a tall, scraggy man who gave a convincing portrayal of the crazy 'knight of the doleful countenance' and danced with wonderful agility and suppleness. The first scene depicted Don Quixote's vision of Dulcinea and ended with him setting forth to seek knightly adventures with his servant, Sancho Panza. They come upon a group of millers and vintagers, and after 'a comic dance of a grotesque and eccentric sort', he attacks the windmill, being whirled skywards and flung to the ground (an effect achieved by the use of a realistic dummy). The scene ended with an intricate and exhilarating Jota and Sancho Panza being tossed into the air on a blanket. The action then moved to the Sable Mountains, where the Don slays a dragon, and the ballet closed with a brilliant display of dancing and pageantry in the courtyard of a Moorish palace.[34]

Sita (June 25, 1894), which succeeded *Don Quixote* in the summer, had an interesting and dramatic plot without any unbelievable twist or supernatural intervention. The action took place in New York, where the hero, Charles, is employed in a large workshop as an inventor. He is in love with his

33 *Sketch*, June 28, 1893.
34 *Era*, Dec. 16, 1893.

ALHAMBRA THEATRE,

LEICESTER SQUARE, LONDON. TELEPHONE No. 35,065.
Acting Manager—MR. ALBERT A. GILMER. *Secy. & Treas.*—MR. SYDNEY ALPORT. *Stage Manager*—MR. A. G. FORDE.
Maître de Ballet—SIGNOR CASATI. ORCHESTRA OF 50 PERFORMERS—*Conductor*, MONS. G. JACOBI.

Programme.

(1) "MARCHE LORRAINE" ... *L. Ganne.*

(2) THE SISTERS PARIS.

(3) THE PHANTOS, LES DIABLES ACROBATIQUES.

(4) FRANKIE MILTON, SERIO-COMIC.

SECOND EDITION OF

(5) **CHICAGO,**

NEW PANTOMIMIC BALLET. By M. AGOUST and M. GERDELUE. The Music from Popular and National Airs, selected and arranged by G. JACOBI. Scenery by T. E. RYAN. The Costumes by M. & Mme. ALIAS, from designs of HOWELL RUSSELL. Introduction. 1.—Comic Scenes. 2.—Opening of the Exhibition (Chicago, Miss HOOTON). 3.—National Dances:—*A.* Indian Nautch Dance. *B.* Spain (Jota Aragonesa), Solo, Signorina PORRO. *C.* Redskins (North America). *D.* Hungary. *E.* German Valse. *F.* French Fin de Siècle Dance (The AGOUSTS and G. ALMONTI). *G.* Russian Dance (Kimarinskaya), Misses SEALE, TULLY, and J. EMPSON). *H.* Dutch Clog Dance. *I.* Italy (Tarantella, Solo, Signorina PORRO & F. BRAITHWAITE. *J.* American Plantation Dance. *K.* Scotland (Sword Dance). *L.* England (Hornpipe, Miss SEALE). *M.* Ireland (Irish Jig). 4.—Comic Mashers' Dance (Mdlle. AGOUST, Mons. AGOUST, Messrs. M. E. & A. AGOUST, and Messrs. W. E. & G. ALMONTI). 5.—Grand March, entrance of all Nations—Turkey, Spain, Austria, Italy, Germany, Russia, France, America, England, Scotland, Ireland, Wales, and India. 6.—Grand Medley Galop. 7.—Apotheosis of Universal Peace, and Grand Final Tableau.

(6) ARTHUR REECE, VOCAL COMEDIAN.

(7) Mdlle. ARNIOTIS, IN HER UNIQUE FEATS OF STRENGTH. (First appearance in England).

(8) Selection "Reminiscences of Offenbach."

(9) HURLEY & WILTON, TRIPLE BAR ACT.

(10) KELSON TRUEMAN, TENOR—Specially Engaged will Sing
(*a*) Song .. .. "ONCE" ... ... *Hervey.*
(*b*) Song ... "WHEN OTHER LIPS" ... ... *Balfe.*

(13) **DON QUIXOTE,**

A New Grand Dramatic Ballet in Four Tableaux, adapted from Miguel Cervantes by A. MAYHEW and E. CASATI. The Music specially composed by M. GEORGES JACOBI. The Action and Dances invented by Signor E. CASATI. The Costumes by Mons. and Mme. Alias, from designs of Howell Russell. Wigs by W Clarkson. The Scenery by T. E. Ryan.

CHARACTERS:

Don Quixote .. .. Mr. FRED STOREY.
Sancho Panza .. .. Mr. F. YARNOLD.
Nicholas (a Barber, in love with Inez) .. .. Mdlle. COSSIO.
Professor Sampson Carrasco (of Salamanca) Mr. G. ALMONTI.
Dulcinea (Don Quixote's Visionary Love) .. Signorina PORRO.
The Duchess .. .. Miss HOOTON.
Tereza Panza (Wife of Sancho) .. .. .. Miss E. AUDUS.
Donna Rodriguez (a Duenna) .. .. .. Madame ROFFEY.
Cardenio (Son of the Duchess) .. .. Miss SEALE.
The Miller .. ..Mr. W. ALMONTI.
The Vintner / A Brigand Chief .. .. Mr. E. ALMONTI.
AND
Inez (Don Quixote's Niece) .. .. LA SALMOIRAGHI.
(Her first appearance in London).

TABLEAU I.—Study of Don Quixote.—Overture. 1. Dance of Servants. 2. Scene and Comic Dance (Mme. ROFFEY and G. ALMONTI). 3 Entrance of Nicholas and entree dansante of Inez (Sig. SALMOIRAGHI). 4. Don Quixote enters announced by Sancho; dispute, Scene and Dance. 5 Vision of Dulcinea and Solo (Sig. PORRO). 6. Finale **TABLEAU II.—Landscape in Spain.**—7. Scene. The Millers, and Procession of Vintners (Marche dansante). 8 Dispute and Galop (Sig. SALMOIRAGHI). 9 Scene. The Don's Battle with a Flock of Sheep. 10. Comic Dance (F. STOREY). 11 Scene and entrance of Duchess and Hunters and comic combat. 12. Windmill and Tossing Scene, and Dance finale (Jota.) **TABLEAU III.—The Sable Mountains.**—13. Scene. Don Quixote, Sancho and Brigands; wild dance and exit. 14 Scene (the Mad Boy) and solo (Miss SEALE). 15. Scene and eccentric dance (F. STOREY.) 16. The Wood Nymphs, slow valse solo (Sig. PORRO). 17. Scene with the Dragon and rescue. 18. Intermezzo Pizzicato (LA SALMOIRAGHI and Mdlle. COSSIO.) **TABLEAU IV.—Court of the Duchess, Moorish Palace.**—19. Dance of Pages. 20. Scene and grand Divertissement. 21. Grand Valse Ballabile. 22. Solo (F. STOREY and F. YARNOLD). 23 Variation (Sig. SALMOIRAGHI). 24. Galop finale and Apotheosis.

(12) RAYNOR & WOOD, MUSICAL GROTESQUES.

(13) THE AGOUSTS.

A SPECIAL MATINEE OF THE CHRISTMAS PROGRAMME ON BOXING DAY. OPEN 1 30.

Alhambra Theatre programme, *c.* December 1893.

employer's daughter, Alice, but the mulatto girl, Sita, one of the workers, is infatuated with him. On being spurned, she flies into a rage and after being restrained from striking an elderly servant who rebukes her, is dismissed. Seeking revenge, she returns to the workshop and, unseen by Charles, drugs a bouquet of flowers which has been left on his table. He falls into a deep sleep. She takes his keys and places in his pocket a bundle of banknotes, which she has extracted from the safe. Accused of theft, Charles is taken to prison, where he has an inspirational vision which enables him to perfect his invention, an 'aerial ship'. Sita, filled with remorse, then appears in his cell, confesses her love and begs his forgiveness. At that very moment Alice's father enters and overhears her confession. Charles is recognised as being innocent, and Sita herself is arrested. The ballet then moved into its finale, set in Central Park, where Charles is presented with a gold medal; Sita, repentant and now released, offers his bride a crown of orange blossom, and against a background of 'trophies formed of American flags on stands of electric lights', the Alhambra *corps de ballet* brought the work to its customary brilliant close. The rôles of the two women were played by Italian ballerinas: Legnani, as Alice, being given two *variations* which brought out the 'finished expertness and activity' of her *pointe* work, and C. Cossio as Sita making a sacrifice to verisimilitude by 'obscuring her charms of feature by an appropriately dusky make-up'. However, the decision to cast a man as the hero of the previous ballet did not appear to have set a firm precedent, for while Don Quixote had been an obvious character rôle for a man, the more conventional part of Charles was confided to Julia Seale, who played it, as the *Era* rather lukewarmly expressed it, in a 'quite acceptable' manner.[35]

The Alhambra ballets at this period were products of a close collaboration between choreographer and composer, for by this time Jacobi had gained an immense prestige and standing in the theatre, as Espinosa had discovered. A description of the creation of Coppi's *Don Juan*, was given by Athol Mayhew in an article he wrote for the *Idler*.[36] The work began to take shape in Jacobi's comfortable room just off the stage, with Coppi sitting by the upright piano and taking notes, while the musician's fingers strayed over the keyboard. Rehearsals then began for the *corps de ballet*, to whom Coppi conveyed his requirements wonderfully effectively for a man who still spoke little English. Most of the dancers were dressed alike, in coloured Garibaldis,[37] white cotton skirts and white linen 'tacks' or knickerbockers, with black or fancy stockings and practising shoes. Only when the *corps de ballet* had been thoroughly drilled did Coppi start working with the principal dancers. Meanwhile, the scene painter, T. E. Ryan, one of the leading figures in his profession, was preparing the sets, while the equally expert Alias was making the costumes in his Soho Square workshop. The contributions of these men were

35 *Era*, June 30, 1894.

36 'The Building of the Ballet', *Idler*, Aug. 1892, 61–69.

37 A form of blouse, based on the red shirt worn by Garibaldi and his thousand in their struggle for Italian independence.

fully acknowledged, particularly that of Alias, who usually came on with Jacobi, Coppi and Hollingshead to take a bow after a first night.

The Alhambra ballet of the eighteen-eighties was distinguished by several star dancers of great eminence. The first in order of time was Emma Palladino, who had been a favourite at the Alhambra for some years before the theatre became a music hall in 1884. She came from a dancing family, her father, Andrea Palladini – for some reason she slightly changed the spelling of her name – having been a distinguished dancer at the Scala. Emma was trained at the Scala school under Giovanni Casati, emerging as a ballerina of extraordinary promise and soon being launched on a brilliant career. After a triumphant visit to America, she made her London début at Her Majesty's in 1879, and two years later appeared at the Alhambra in a mythological ballet *Endymion*, inserted in an operetta, which *The Times* specifically advised Americans passing through London not on any account to miss. Palladino's technique was so faultless that she became known in the profession as 'the complete Palladino'.[38] She left the Alhambra in 1887, but continued to dance in London, at the Empire Theatre and the Royal Italian Opera, Covent Garden, before retiring shortly before the century's close.[39]

Emma Bessone, another Scala-trained ballerina, made her début at the Alhambra in 1885 and danced there until 1890. Born in Genoa in 1864, she was engaged at the Scala during the Carnival-Lent season of 1885, and in 1887 visited Russia, where Marius Petipa revised the production of *Giselle* for her début at the Maryinsky Theatre in St Petersburg. 'The opulent Bessone, "première danseuse assoluta" in *Asmodeus*,' wrote George Bernard Shaw, 'is complete from toe to top, a superb, passionate dancer, strong, skilful, and abounding in sensuous charm.'[40] As well as *Asmodeus*, she created rôles in *Enchantment*, *Astraea* and *Zanetta*, sharing the favours of the public with Pierina Legnani.

Legnani made her first appearance in London on December 17, 1888, and was to dance at the Alhambra with intervals until 1897. Shaw described her in 1890 as 'young, intelligent, and not yet in her prime', and '[holding] her own against the memory of the superb and magnetic Bessone, more by a certain freshness and naïveté than by her execution, which is nevertheless sufficiently brilliant.'[41] She is now celebrated for creating the rôle of Odette-Odile when *Swan Lake* was produced anew by Petipa and Ivanov in St Petersburg in 1895, and in particular for the series of thirty-two *fouettés* in the third act, a *tour de force* which she had already been performing in London before she ever set foot in Russia. In 1893 the *Sketch* published an interview in which she described one of her Italian-made shoes: 'a pretty little shoe, with a narrow sole that ended about the middle of the great toe, and had a stiffening in the part of the "upper" which covers the toes, giving it a rather Indian canoe shape in front.' 'With these,' she was reported as saying, 'I hardly ever

38 Espinosa, 'A Forgotten Dancer, Emma Palladino', *Ballet*, 3, 1 (Jan. 1947), 17.

39 She married an Englishman, Arthur Roger Carter, and died in 1922.

40 Shaw, *London Music in* 1888–89), 315.

41 Shaw, *Music in London*, I, 47.

get tired. In fact, in the last tableau of *Aladdin*, I turn thirty-two pirouettes on tiptoe without dropping my foot. Not many dancers can do that.'[42]

As well as disclosing this technical detail, the interviewer recorded that he found her 'a charming, honest, merry, pretty girl'. She received him in her dressing room, wearing a grey dressing gown and shawl, and looking very tired and hot. Fussing in the background was an aunt, grumbling that she was not eating enough and that the English climate did not suit her. Yet Legnani admitted that after injuring her knee, she had been cured by a week's recuperation in Brighton, where she sat watching the dancing of the waves and grew envious and sad. It was in Brighton, she added, that she realised for the first time how much she loved dancing.

Another notable addition to the Alhambra ballet during these years was Lucia Cormani, who joined the company in 1886. She was not a star of Legnani's or Palladino's magnitude, but she was greatly admired as a mime and was to stage a number of ballets herself between 1900 and 1905. Her greatest contribution to her profession, however, was as a teacher at the Alhambra's school, where many of the English members of the company graduated from her class. She taught according to the Italian method, and many years later she was to be one of the five distinguished founders of the Royal Academy of Dancing, remaining on its Grand Council until the Second World War.

Of the male dancers, only two can be said to have stirred the enthusiasm of Alhambra audiences during these years. One of these was that character dancer of extraordinary suppleness and strong interpretative gifts, Fred Storey; the other, Vittorio De Vincenti, a rather brainless virtuoso of the Italian school. De Vincenti relied for his success on his great strength and his ability to perform feats of extraordinary difficulty. He was the counterpart of the Italian virtuoso ballerinas who held a virtual monopoly of the star posts in the opera houses of Europe. After leaving the Alhambra in 1891, he was engaged at the Empire until 1895, and in 1905, at the end of his career, he returned to London to dance in a revival of *Excelsior* at the Lyceum. An interview he then gave threw a revealing light on his approach to his art. He seemed obsessed by the feats he had mastered, and lingered over a certain complex cart-wheel which was one of his specialities, but there was not a word about artistry or interpretation. 'With the [male dancer],' he declared, 'grace of action is out of the question. He must make great physical efforts and perform

42 *Sketch*, Apr. 26, 1893. Dancers had begun to exploit *pointe* work around 1820, but the blocked shoe did not make its appearance until the second half of the nineteenth century. Emma Livry's shoes in the Paris Opéra collection, dating from 1862, are darned at the toes but unblocked, and do not materially differ from those worn by Taglioni. Rosa Abrahams, who danced at the Alhambra between 1876 and 1884, later told an interviewer: 'In my day we really did dance on the *pointe*; nowadays, with the help of [the block] anyone could shuffle on the toes. But how big and ugly it makes your feet.' (*Dancing Times*, VI, 66 (Mar. 1916), 168.) The blocked shoe was fully developed by 1893, though then the block itself was much lighter than it has since become. The modern *pointe* shoe probably originated in Italy, where it no doubt played an important part in making possible the technical advances achieved by the Italian ballerinas of Legnani's generation.

moves (*sic*) which people think the human anatomy incapable of.'[43] No wonder male dancing was at such a nadir.

43 *Era*, Oct. 21, 1905. 'Chat with Signor Vincenti'. By contrast, in a 'chat' with Maria Bordin, published in the same issue, the ballerina revealed a clear understanding of the intellectual aspect of her art.

2 Leicester Square and the Alhambra Theatre around 1900.

3 The interior of the Alhambra Theatre on the occasion of the special performance of the ballet, *L'Entente Cordiale*, in 1905 in celebration of the new alliance between England and France.

4 Above: Milano's *The Caverns of Ice* (1867). (*Illustrated London News*, August 3, 1867)

5 Left: Rita Sangalli. Photo: Charlet & Jacotin.

6 Above right: Mlle Colonna and her Parisian Quadrille in *Les Nations* (1870). (*Day's Doings*, October 29, 1870)

7 Right: Reading the magistrates' decision not to renew the Alhambra's licence during a ballet rehearsal. (*Day's Doings*, November 11, 1870)

8 Giovannina Pitteri in Justament's *Flamma* (1869). From a drawing by Ch. Hamerton.

9 Erminia Pertoldi.

10 Emma Bessone.

11 Georges Jacobi.

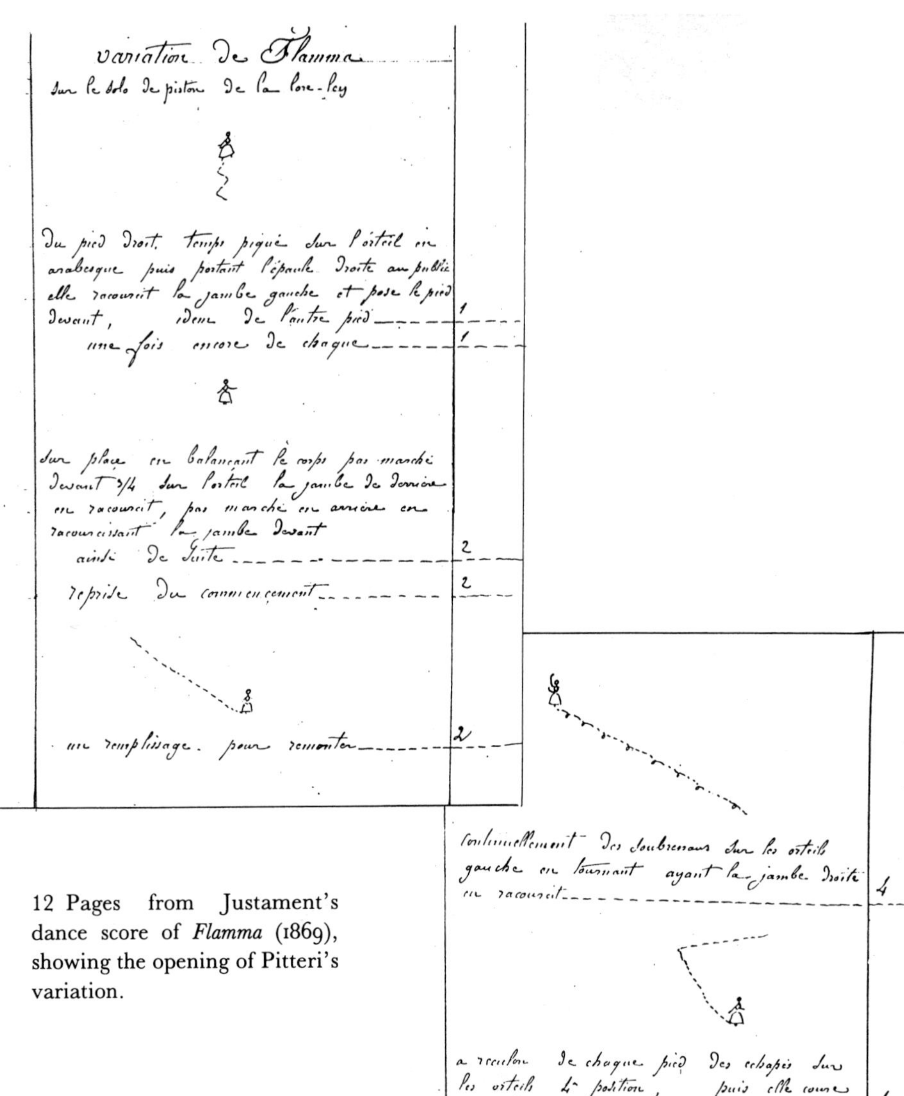

12 Pages from Justament's dance score of *Flamma* (1869), showing the opening of Pitteri's variation.

13 Hansen's *The Swans* (1884). (*Pictorial World*, December 11, 1884)

14 Emma Palladino. PHOTO: William Spalding.

15 Carlo Coppi conducting a rehearsal at the Alhambra. (*Sketch*, May 17, 1893)

16 Dewinne's *Up the River* (1892), the storm scene. (*Illustrated Sporting and Dramatic News*, October 1, 1892)

17 Cormani's *Carmen* (1903), with Edith Slack, Rosario Guerrero and M. Volbert.

18 Cormani's *My Lady Nicotine* (1905), with Edith Slack and Giovanni Rosi.

19 Curti's *Parisiana* (1905).

20 Curti's *L'Amour* (1906), with Maria Bordin (centre).

21 Curti's *Queen of Spades* (1907), with Julia Seale.

22 Curti's *Les Cloches de Corneville* (1907), with Julia Seale and Giovanni Rosi.

23 Britta and Leonora in Curti's *Femina* (1910).

24 Maria Bordin as Mylitta in *L'Amour*. PHOTO: Campbell & Gray.

25 Leonora and Britta in scenes from Curti's *Psyche* (1909). PHOTOS: Bassano. (*Sketch*, April 28, 1909)

26 Above: Gorsky's *The Dance Dream* (1910), Scene I (The Temple), with Vasili Tikhomirov, Marjorie Skelley, Agnes Healey and Gina Cormani. Photo: Foulsham & Banfield.

27 Left: Ekaterina Geltser and Vasili Tikhomirov in *The Dance Dream* (1910). Photo: Foulsham & Banfield. (*Play Pictorial*, 1910, No. 109)

28 Gorsky's *The Dance Dream* (1910), Scene III (The Rajah's Palace). Photo: Foulsham & Banfield. (*Play Pictorial*, 1910, No. 109)

29 Gorsky's *The Dance Dream* (1910), Scene VI (Old Russia, The Feast of Spring). Photo: Foulsham & Banfield. (*Play Pictorial*, 1910, No. 109)

30 Agoust and Clerc's *1830* (1911), with Poldi Müller, Emile Agoust and Greville Moore.

31 Berger's *Carmen* (1912), with María la Bella and M. Volbert.

IV

Changing fortunes (1894–1901)

The Alhambra ballets around the turn of the century, when Alfred Moul was General Manager,[1] enjoyed a justly earned reputation both for their spectacular staging and for the precision of the *corps de ballet*, which continued to play a prominent part, particularly in the spectacular finales, which were frequently quite complex. It being customary for the stage rehearsals of a new ballet to be spread over a period of some six weeks before the first performance, the company was most thoroughly prepared by the time the public saw it. The Alhambra *corps de ballet* prided itself on being the most competent in London. As a former Alhambra dancer recalled, 'they were expected to dance, unlike the *corps de ballet* of the Empire, who merely "held up the scenery" and were in attendance on the prima ballerina'.[2] Nevertheless, although many had been trained in the Italian method by Mme Cormani, company discipline was undoubtedly lax by present-day standards, and the routine of giving nightly performances of the same ballet, while it kept the performance level high, must have been psychologically deadening for the dancers. This was hardly noticeable when there was nothing better to compare it with, but some years later, under the impact of the Diaghilev Ballet, the deficiencies of the once-vaunted Alhambra *corps de ballet* could no longer be concealed. J. Crawford Flitch, one of the most knowledgeable of witnesses, undoubtedly struck a vein of truth when he described them in 1912 as 'rank after rank and file after file of honest bread-winners from Camberwell and Peckham Rye, performing mechanical manoeuvres with the dogged perseverance of a company of Boy Scouts'.[3]

While the old order was continuing, however, it needed the perception of a critic such as George Bernard Shaw to see that ballet was approaching a crisis. 'The veteran Jacobi,' he wrote in 1893,

> was still there, monarchical as *chef d'orchestre*, bold, ingenious, and amazingly copious as a composer of dance music, The danseuses were still trying to give some freshness to the half-dozen *pas* of which every possible combination and permutation has been worn to death any time these hundred years, still calling each hopeless

1 Alfred Moul was General Manager from 1894 to 1898, when he resigned. C. Dundas Slater was General Manager between 1898 and 1903. In 1902 Moul rejoined the Board. Douglas Cox was manager in 1903, and George Scott, 1904–06. Moul became General Manager again in 1908 and resigned in 1912.

2 Interview with Miss Theresa Heyman, Oct. 11, 1958.

3 Flitch, 65.

> attempt a 'variation', and still finishing up with the teetotum spin which is to the dancer what the high note at the end of a dull song is to a second-rate singer . . . [Ballet] is by no means unpopular . . . Unfortunately, it is so remote from life that it is absolutely unmoral, and therefore incapable of sentiment or hypocrisy. I therefore suggest that by getting rid of the dreary academic dancing, the 'variations', and the stereotyped *divertissement* at the end, and making the ballet sufficiently dramatic throughout to add the fascination of moral unreality to that of physical impossibility, it might attain a new lease of life.[4]

Jacobi, however, took a more optimistic view. 'The position of the *première*,' he said in an interview in 1895,

> is by no means at stake, as people affect to imagine. She is as important to ballet as the *prima donna* to grand opera. If their work has appeared a trifle monotonous of late, it is because they are nearly all pupils of the same mistress in Milan, and may have adopted certain mannerisms. Male dancers are not very interesting, but they are often required to support the *première* or for groups, while a good comic male dancer helps a piece along considerably. I find the public interest on the increase, and the musical taste considerably improved. Years ago, the demand for light simple measures and commonplace themes made it difficult for me to elaborate my scores, but today the public takes an intelligent interest in orchestration. I have added the harp to the orchestra, and the better the score, the greater its [i.e., the ballet's] success.[5]

The popularity of ballet, though perhaps a little precarious, was, as Jacobi observed, undoubtedly growing, for the Alhambra now had a serious rival in the Empire Theatre on the north side of Leicester Square, which in 1887 had been transformed into a music hall with a similar policy without seeming to affect the receipts at the box-office. In its publicity the Empire was boldly calling itself 'the Home of Ballet', and the Alhambra, unable to let such a claim pass, countered by announcing itself as 'the Original Home of Ballet'. With its smaller stage the Empire could not compete with the Alhambra in the lavishness of its productions nor in the excellence of its *corps de ballet*, but from 1897 it possessed a trump card in the person of Adeline Genée, a ballerina of the rarest calibre whom the Alhambra would never be able to match. Taking everything into account there was probably little to choose between the two houses.

There was no break with tradition during Carlo Coppi's association with the Alhambra, which lasted intermittently from 1894 until 1902. The policy of presenting a major production at Christmastime was continued with three ballets on themes frequently associated with the traditional English pantomimes: *Ali Baba* (December 13, 1894), *Blue Beard* (December 16, 1895) and *Beauty and the Beast* (January 4, 1898).

4 Shaw, *Music in London*, III, 38–39.

5 *Sketch*, Aug. 7, 1895.

'Perhaps some of us old fogies,' wrote one critic of *Ali Baba*, 'will declare that [it] is rather pantomime than ballet, and has an excess of comic business.' There had been some talk of late that the Alhambra seemed to have lost some of its former glory, but for this ballet the management had opened wide its purse and presented a spectacle of exceptional magnificence. If Howell Russell's costume designs did not match the artistic blending of colours which Wilhelm was achieving at the Empire, there were electrical effects to marvel at. The incandescent electric light bulb was still something of a novelty, and the use of wreaths containing bulbs that changed colour during the course of one of the dances created a great stir. Jacobi, as usual, provided the music, and for once a gentle note of criticism was sounded in the surmise that it was perhaps too much to expect 'much novelty of treatment or originality of melody and rhythm', considering the burden of writing two ballet scores a year. 'One is inclined to think,' added this critic, 'that it would be as well to give some of our younger composers a chance.'[6]

The story of *Ali Baba* was of course well known, and if the dramatic element in the ballet had been somewhat sacrificed to the spectacle, the engagement of the Agousts, a family of pantomimists who were to enjoy an association with the Alhambra, introduced the element of broad comedy which had shocked the 'old fogeys'. One of them played Ali Baba himself, another had a hilarious scene as a comic donkey, a third played the rôle of a sergeant, and a fourth, Louise, gave an expressive performance in the important mime part of Morgiana. Their antics must have diverted attention from the new ballerina, Cecilia Cerri, who was no doubt anticipating a triumphant London début. Cerri was an accomplished technician produced by the school of the Scala, Milan; in later years she was to be the resident star of the ballet in Vienna, but in *Ali Baba* her part seemed very incidental and was overshadowed by the novelty act of Preciosa Grigolatis and her aerial ballet. Using equipment invented by her husband, Grigolatis's act was much more elaborate than Aenea's, involving a supporting company of six flying *coryphées*, not to mention a small flock of pigeons trained to alight on her arms. But her most striking effect, and one of real beauty, was her slow descent to pose her toe on the centres of six pink scarfs wafted in the air by her flying companions.

A year later, in *Blue Beard*, Cerri did not have to contend with such formidable competition, and made a much stronger impression, particularly in an automaton dance. The Agousts were again very much to the fore, with Henry in the title-rôle and Louise as Fatima; another member of the family, A. Agoust, played one of a couple of comic servants (his partner being George Almonti, a member of another family of pantomimists) who enter Blue Beard's secret chamber, making fun with the severed heads of the murdered wives, one of which appeared to move across the floor of its volition, and being scared out of their wits by a dancing skeleton which fell to pieces and reassembled itself in an effective but not entirely unfamiliar trick. The

6 *Sketch*, Dec. 26, 1896. Review signed 'Monocle'.

spectacle was as lavish as ever, culminating in some brilliant dancing, including a delightful number performed to xylophone accompaniment, and a dazzling effect when the curtain fell on a web of golden ribbons glowing with hundreds of electric light bulbs which had floated down behind the massed *corps de ballet*.

Beauty and the Beast was a more cohesive and artistic production than had been seen for a very long time. Its action was presented without that surfeit of comic business which many had thought marred its predecessors. The leading rôles were presented in straight-forward fashion by Josephine Casaboni,[7] a newly engaged dancer of French extraction, as the Beauty, and Julia Seale, once again the 'principal boy', as the Beast. The opening scene in the Beast's Palace contained some original character dancing by a group of dwarfs, the Kromo family, as the guardian gnomes, and unusually the highlight came, not in the finale, impressive though that was, but in the second scene, the 'Garden of Roses', in which the *corps de ballet* represented a luxurious mass of roses of seemingly every type and hue, 'weaving . . . into ever fresh and endless harmonies of colour and enchantment'.[8] This also provided the setting for an effective variation by Cerri, who, to quote a typically vague effusion by a critic of the time, displayed 'her surpassing skill, and won enthusiastic appreciation by her active and elastic efforts'.[9]

Interspersed with these Christmas offerings were other ballets by Coppi of varying character. *Titania* (July 30, 1895) was of course based on Shakespeare's *Midsummer Night's Dream*, and was conceived primarily as a vehicle for Mlle Grigolatis, who was inevitably cast as Titania, with one of her flying ladies, Emma Haupt, as Puck. Julia Seale not unexpectedly played Oberon, the male element of the company being mainly employed in the parts of the 'mechanicals'. The long-suffering Cerri once again had to compete with the formidable aerial ladies, but managed to achieve a decided success as Hermia. *The Gathering of the Clans* (October 7, 1895) was an exhilarating little piece featuring Scottish dancing, with a plot based on Scott's poem, 'Young Lochinvar', and *Donnybrook* (June 4, 1896) was an Irish *divertissement*.

A more substantial offering was *Rip Van Winkle* (July 29, 1896), a literary ballet based on Washington Irving's story of the Dutch colonist in New York who drinks a magic potion that sends him to sleep for twenty years and who wakes to find himself an old man and America an independent nation. For once the music was not provided by Jacobi, being written by the French light opera composer, Richard Planquette. The production succeeded 'more as a ballet of action and interest than as a banquet for the eye', its success resting largely on the masterly performance of the dancer who played Rip. Loud shouts of 'Storey' at the close brought Fred Storey before the curtain to receive a personal tribute for another remarkable interpretation:

7 She may have been the daughter of M. Cazaubon, who was named in the 1890 Alhambra programmes as leader of the orchestra.

8 Perugini, 265.

9 *Era*, Jan. 8, 1898.

> The character lends itself easily to interpretation in dumb show, that it needs a master of the art like Mr Storey to fully develop the pantomimic possibilities of the part. In his indication of Rip's weakness in the first act, in his expressions of surprise, amusement, and terror when confronted with the strange beings on the Kaatskills, and of bewilderment and puzzled distress, Mr Storey was superb. A more artistic, impressive, and picturesque performance has seldom been seen on the Alhambra boards.[10]

Somewhat more lavish, being a winter offering, was *The Tzigane* (December 15, 1896), a tale of a villainous gypsy and a girl who becomes infatuated with him and is sorely ill-treated before being rescued by her steadfastly faithful sweetheart. The heroine, eloquently portrayed by Josephine Casaboni, had to repeat her solo to xylophone accompaniment, and enthusiasm was stirred again by the Kermess scene at the end which was performed with the closest approximation to Magyar vigour that an all-female English *corps de ballet* at that time could manage.

Evidence of the improving standard of ballet music at the Alhambra to which Jacobi had drawn attention was provided by the commissioning of a ballet score from Sir Arthur Sullivan, the most celebrated living English composer. Terms were agreed for a fee of £2000 and a share of the takings, Sullivan retaining the copyright in the music. The first subject to be suggested - Byron's tragedy, *Sardanapalus* - was quickly rejected, no doubt as being too lurid, and with the approach of Queen Victoria's Diamond Jubilee, it was decided instead to honour the occasion with a patriotic ballet. So it was that Sullivan directed his mind to a scenario entitled *Victoria and Merrie England*. Early in January he set to work seriously in a villa he had taken on the Riviera, where he was visited by Moul and Coppi for a consultation; by the end of March the score was in its final form, apart from a third solo for Legnani, who was returning to London specially to dance in this ballet. Coppi must have begun rehearsing as soon as the music was delivered, and such was the efficiency of the Alhambra's organisation that the ballet was ready for performance on May 25, 1897, ten days before the Jubilee itself.

Although Sullivan was in poor health, there was nothing dispirited in his music. If it suffered from a certain monotony of rhythm, it was ingeniously orchestrated and full of charming melodies, and possessed a polish and a refinement rarely found in ballet music of that period. Most of it was newly written, but Sullivan had incorporated two numbers - a mazurka and another piece to accompany a flirtation scene between Robin Hood and Maid Marion - from an earlier ballet, *L'Ile enchantée*.[11] Musically, one of the most interesting numbers was a fugue in waltz-time for a comic dance by four servants. Sullivan realised it was 'a little daring', but why, he asked himself, 'shouldn't you have a minute or two of severe counterpoint in a ballet?'[12]

10 *Era*, Aug. 1, 1896.

11 *L'Ile enchantée*, a *divertissement* with choreography by Henri Desplaces and music by Sullivan, was first performed at the Royal Italian Opera, Covent Garden on May 16, 1864, with Guglielmina Salvioni as prima ballerina.

12 Williamson, 400.

He seems to have enjoyed a very private joke, for none of the critics noticed that its theme was a 'naughtily elaborated side-sweep at the National Anthem.'[13]

Sullivan's prestige and the brilliance of the spectacle attracted nearly a score of royal visitors to the Alhambra during the ballet's six-month run. Described as a 'grand national ballet', it had no consecutive theme, but was a series of characteristic English scenes evoked by the Genius of Britain in the person of Pierina Legnani.[14] There was a coming-of-age party set in Elizabethan times; a May Day scene in which Legnani returned in a new guise as the May Queen and which included a passage evoking Robin Hood; the legend of Herne the Hunter; a Restoration Christmas revel with another solo for Legnani as the Snow Fairy; a *tableau vivant* of the Queen's Coronation to Sullivan's stirring Imperial March; and finally a lavish pageant, in which the *corps de ballet* had been specially augmented, to represent the armed services of the Empire from the elite regiments of the British Isles to troops from the Cape, Canada, India and Australia, all portrayed in the shapely forms of the Alhambra dancers. The ballet was brought to an appropriate close with the National Anthem, accompanying the final grouping of the enormous cast around four statuesque women who reproduced the figures of the Continents which occupied the four corners of the base of the Albert Memorial. Carried away by a spontaneous burst of national pride, the first-night audience responded with unusual enthusiasm. Encores were very rarely allowed at the Alhambra, but an exception was made on this occasion when Julia Seale was made to repeat her dance as a tipsy jester, for which Sullivan had inserted a witty cadenza for the bassoon. And such was the fervour evoked by the coronation scene, with one of the loveliest women in the company portraying the girl Queen in her robes, that three curtain calls were demanded before the final scene could be got under way.

* * *

The year 1898 was one of radical change for the Alhambra ballet, marked by the departure of virtually the entire team which directed this side of the enterprise. At the beginning of the year the two men who were responsible for decisions of policy, Alfred Moul, the respected general manager, and his stage manager, A. G. Forde, both retired. Their successors were also to exercise a close control over the ballets. Charles Wilson, the new stage manager, was to be credited with the scenarios of most of the new ballets during the next eight years, as well as being responsible for their production, the choreographer being subordinated to his authority to a greater extent than before. Moul's successor as manager was C. Dundas Slater who, as the man in over-all charge, was probably primarily responsible for the retrogressive trend of introducing song and dialogue; during the five years of his management the ballets were always announced as being produced under his direction, and significantly, the vocal element disappeared when he left the

13 Tillett, 21.

14 See Appendix D for scenario.

Alhambra in 1903. Another familiar figure who retired in 1898 was Jacobi, whose vast experience of ballet had given him an influence that extended beyond purely musical matters. The new musical director, George W. Byng, was also to prove adept at producing ballet music to order, but he would never be used so exclusively as a composer, nor did his voice carry the same weight as his predecessor's. Another vacancy that fell to be filled was that of *maître de ballet*, for Carlo Coppi also departed. It is possible that Byng played a part in the choice of his successor. The year before he had been involved in the production of the pantomime, *A Pierrot's Life*, at the Prince of Wales Theatre, and it may have been at his suggestion that one of the Italian mimes taking part, Giovanni Pratesi, was engaged to fill Coppi's place at the Alhambra.

Coppi was to produce a somewhat mixed bag of ballets over the next two and a half years. Three of these, *Jack Ashore*, *The Red Shoes* and *Napoli*, were traditional *ballets d'action*; *A Day Off* was in the up-to-date vein; and *Soldiers of the Queen* was another patriotic military pageant.

On seeing Pratesi's first effort, *Jack Ashore* (August 8, 1898), *The Times* expressed regret that 'the glories of the ballet, strictly so-called, seem to have been banished - it is hoped only for a time'.[15] Gone was the splendour and the pageantry, and to the horror of purists, dialogue had been introduced to help along the story, which told of a young man in eighteenth-century England who narrowly escapes being caught by a press gang. Unremarkable though it was, it was nevertheless performed with great spirit and remained in the programme for a full eight months.

Happily, *The Red Shoes* (January 30, 1899) marked a return to traditional ways, being, exceptionally for the Alhambra, a version of a ballet successfully produced elsewhere. In August 1898 Josef Hassreiter had presented *The Red Shoes*[16] at the Vienna Opera, and the Alhambra had negotiated an arrangement to use Hassreiter's scenario and the score by Raoul Mader for a new version by Pratesi. Based on Hans Christian Andersen's well-known fairy tale, the ballet was a skilfully devised work with 'sufficient dramatic interest, and varied and beautiful without being over elaborated or surfeiting'.[17] Set in a Russian village, it contained some picturesque local colour, closing with an Eastertide scene outside a village church with all the villagers dressed in rich and vivid costumes. The vivacious Josephine Casaboni was the heroine, Darinka, who is tempted to try on the red shoes which are revered for their healing powers, and finding that she cannot remove them, is condemned to dance until she is finally granted forgiveness. The travesty tradition was breached by casting a handsome male actor who had joined the company, Lytton Grey, as her sweetheart, Gregor. Julia Seale, who in former times might have expected it for herself, was given the part of the Spirit of Temptation, while the double rôle of the Avenging Angel and the Angel of Mercy

15 *The Times*, Nov. 1, 1898.

16 *Die Roten Schuhe*, as it was called, had been created at the Vienna Court Opera on Aug. 18, 1898. It remained in the repertory until 1922, achieving a total of 80 performances. It was also successfully produced at the Scala, Milan, by A. Coppini in 1900.

17 *Era*, Feb. 4, 1899.

was entrusted to a glamorous visitor – Emilienne d'Alençon, celebrated on the other side of the Channel as one of the reigning beauties of the Parisian *demi-monde*.

Napoli (August 21, 1899),[18] for which George Byng wrote the music, was a short ballet, lasting only half an hour. The action was fast and furious; Naples was depicted in Carnival mood, with one lively dance following another, culminating in a rousing tarantella. A less than happy innovation was the introduction of the Alhambra choir which joined forces with a singer, Ian Colquhoun, who was cast as a captain of the Bersaglieri. On the other hand, Josephine Casaboni as the heroine was again spared the indignity of a travesty sweetheart, the rivals for her hand both being played by men, one by Lytton Grey, and the other by the choreographer himself, who was singled out for special praise by S. L. Bensusan as 'a pantomimist who has no equal on the London stage since Madame Cavallazzi retired from the Empire. It is no exaggeration to say that his work shows what London has lost through the growing neglect of pantomime.'[19] Comic characterisation, however, remained very much an English speciality, and a young man recently engaged, Fred Farren, aroused gales of laughter with his brilliant caricature of a valet.

Much of *A Day Off* (April 24, 1899) was a romp about a motley party (which included a couple of variety artistes to provide a part for the decorative Emilienne d'Alençon) setting out on a trip to Boulogne, but its *pièce de résistance*, indeed almost its *raison d'être*, was a 'Grand Valse Politique' inspired by the current international situation. Although Europe was still to enjoy many years of peace, the nations were beginning to align themselves into two opposing camps. The Triple Alliance of Germany, Austria and Italy was already being regarded as an unsettling factor in the balance of power, and after years of colonial rivalry in Africa, England and France were tentatively moving towards a *rapprochement*. Meanwhile, on the other side of the globe China was on the point of collapse, and the European powers were scrambling for rights to build railways and other concessions. This was the background to the dancing on the Alhambra stage, which the *Era* described in some detail:

> First, France receives her foreign visitors, including Russia and the members of the Triple Alliance. China, in her endeavours to please all nations, accidentally pushes against Germany. That power immediately demands reparation for the insult and tears off a sleeve from China's rich mantle. But appeals to Russia for sympathy only cause that nation to take the other sleeve, so that matters may be equalised. At this moment England enters, and protests strongly against the outrage, telling them that China is not for one nor the other, but is for the benefit of the world. To show them fully her meaning she takes off the greater portion of China's garment, the other nations dividing the rest of her once-gorgeous apparel, leaving China almost bare. To conciliate poor China, England offers her a railway. China is delighted with the toy until Russia presents her with one of greater value. India is announced, and while France coquets with England Russia seizes the opportunity of taking to himself

18 Pratesi revived the ballet, with Byng's music, at the Scala, Milan, on Feb. 4, 1906, but it was given only a single performance. Cecilia Cerri was the ballerina.

19 *Sketch*, Aug. 23, 1899.

> India. England's attention is called to these designs, and, taking India upon his arm, she warns Russia that India is for England alone. Turkey enters, bringing in Egypt and Greece. Russia and France pay their attentions to Egypt, but again England bars the way. Spain enters, trying to keep two unruly children in order, viz. Cuba and the Philippines. They break away from her jurisdiction, so Uncle Sam intervenes, and finds there are more than he can manage. The other nations offer to assist him, but are kept at a distance by England, the ballet winding up with a dashing galop full of fiery vigour and 'go'.[20]

At the end of the year, instead of the usual Christmas fare, Dundas Slater decided that a patriotic spectacle was called for to satisfy the chauvinism of the hour. The Boer War had broken out in October, and in the week before the ballet's first performance a series of Boer victories had left three British garrisons besieged. To a people whose pride had been fed for so long with a regular flow of glorious feats of arms in distant colonial fields, the events of 'Black Week' were especially shocking and served only to strengthen their resolve to fight to the finish. *Soldiers of the Queen* (December 11, 1899) was perfectly timed to respond to this mood, and the Alhambra found itself riding on the crest of the patriotic tide. Although performed by the principals and the *corps de ballet*, it was not so much a ballet as a military pageant, devised with careful attention to accuracy on the advice of a 'very popular officer known as much in Bohemia as in military circles', who concealed his identity under the pseudonym of 'A. Sol Dato'. After an opening scene depicting *reveillée*, the changing of the guard and stable drill at Aldershot, the audience was treated to a display of lance drill and a first-aid dance of Red Cross nurses, and finally a stirring climax introduced by Leslie Stuart's latest song, 'Soldiers of the Queen', sung by Ian Colquhoun and the Alhambra choir, and concluding with an imposing march-past of detachments from famous regiments. 'There was not a suspicion of confusion,' wrote the *Era* admiringly, 'and the intricate marching, counter-marching, wheeling, deploying, were carried out without a halting or faltering step. The fair Amazons looked as smart as possible in the uniforms so admirably designed by Mr Louis Edwards.'[21] It proved just the right tonic. Moved by the sight of the nation's fighting men portrayed by 'the most ravishing beauty and the most divine lower limbs', the critic of *Black and White* felt strangely reassured. 'Send these gay dogs to South Africa,' he urged, 'and the Boers would lay down their arms incontinent.'[22]

The vocal element provided by solo singers and the Alhambra choir, which was increasingly becoming a feature of the ballets, was a departure from the traditional roots of the *ballet d'action* towards a hybrid form more closely allied to musical comedy. Following Pratesi's departure, both of the ballets presented during 1900 were of this nature. Choreographed by Egidio Rossi, *The Handy Man* (September 24, 1900) was constructed around a romantic story about a girl, the sole survivor of a shipwreck, who is rescued by her sweetheart from a fate worse than death in a bey's harem, while *The Gay City* (December

20 *Era*, Apr. 29, 1899.

21 *Era*, Dec. 16, 1899.

22 *Black and White*, Dec. 23, 1899.

19, 1900) was a topical piece, celebrating that year's International Exhibition in Paris with a slight but amusing plot and several entertaining dances arranged by Lucia Cormani and (for one number) Fred Farren. In both works a young dancer with a famous name, Judith Espinosa, daughter of Léon, stood out from the rest of the cast: as a jealous slave girl in the first, and a vivacious Pierrette in the other. Neither ballet added much to the Alhambra's prestige as a ballet house, but the public did not complain, and both enjoyed long runs.

The experienced Coppi returned in 1901, but in his next work, *Inspiration* (June 10, 1901), he too found himself hamstrung by this new obsession with song and dialogue. It was an allegorical ballet, in which the Goddess of Inspiration, a speaking part like a number of others in the ballet, convinces a band of bacchanalians that her influence upon the world was infinitely more beneficial than that of their bibulous god. When the Genius of Inspiration – a dancing rôle this – is forced to drink with the revellers, the Goddess plunges the world into darkness. The leader of the bacchanalians remains defiant and demands proof of her powers, and in the finale she evokes the arts of drama, poetry, painting and music. As the Genius of Inspiration, Judith Espinosa added to her growing reputation as 'a dancer of the Milanese school, perfectly trained', her classical grace contrasting effectively with the style of Edith Slack who was featured in a scene based on Sir Edward Poynter's popular painting, 'A Greek Dance'. But to anyone who had the well-being of ballet at heart the work was fatally flawed. For all the excellence of the dancing, and the *corps de ballet* never had such complex work to perform, the human voice obtruded. The perceptive S. L. Bensusan was greatly put off by the dialogue and the singing of the Alhambra chorus. 'The human voice,' he wrote,

> is killing pantomime quite surely, though slowly, at the Alhambra, and while one must praise the excellent quality of the voices heard there, it is impossible to forget that with the end of pantomime comes the end of ballet's intellectual attraction. It becomes merely sensuous. A Cavallazzi or Jane May is a great artist though dumb, but when the spoken word avails (*sic*) stage deportment will be as dead as the other deportment cultivated by Mr Turveydrop in Georgian days.[23]

Ballet at the Alhambra certainly seemed to be approaching a crisis. 'The old order of entertainment changes,' wrote a critic in 1901, 'and nowhere more distinctly than at the Alhambra, which used to call itself the home of ballet. There is no ground for complaint; ballet has outlived its welcome, and in its place has come a spectacular display that is nearer to the theatre than any of its predecessors.' Certainly the two new ballets produced in the last months of 1901 gave no sign of any improvement. *Gretna Green* (October 10, 1901) was, as the same observer remarked, 'so very much like a comic opera that the official description "vocal divertissement" does nothing to hide the resemblance.'[24] Even the heroine burst into sung, with a rendering of 'The Honeysuckle and the Bee'. The next work, *Santa Claus* (December 23, 1901), a seasonal piece introducing popular nursery figures, passed unremarked.

23 *Sketch*, June 12, 1901. Mr Turveydrop, a character in Dickens's *Bleak House*, was a relic of the Regency, a teacher of deportment whose art had become irrelevant in the reign of Victoria.
24 *Illustrated London News*, Oct. 19, 1901.

V

The Edwardian years (1902–10)

The election of Alfred Moul at the beginning of 1902 as chairman of the company which owned and ran the Alhambra was a hopeful sign that the fortunes of the ballet were to be restored. Indeed it was not long before signs of improvement were evident. One can perhaps perceive the influence of his cultured background and musicianship in the first new ballet of the year, *In Japan* (April 21, 1902), which was entirely lacking any vocal element and had a charming score, specially composed by Louis Ganne, which *The Times* happily noted was 'free from Wardour Street Orientalisms'.[1] It was based on a story entitled *Dédé* by S. L. Bensusan, who was now rapidly developing an intelligent interest in the ballet. Its heroine was a country girl who is brought to Kyoto, where she arouses the interest of the City Governor. His intentions towards her are, however, thwarted by a geisha who, instead of doing his bidding and teaching the girl to dance, assists her to escape. Unluckily the girl and her sweetheart are caught and face the direst consequences. But a couple of English naval officers persuade the Governor to allow the geisha to dance before him one last time, which she does so enchantingly that all is forgiven. It was a light work, but full of charm and atmosphere, which for once was undisturbed by the intrusion of a star ballerina. Among the special effects which the Alhambra was specially well placed to supply was a troupe of jugglers spinning plates on tall rods in a street scene; Coppi skilfully devised a number of characteristic dances, including a dance for swordsmen who went through 'a showy drill' with their weapons drawn,[2] and a beautiful 'Ballet of Blossoms'; and in the pageantry at the end there was a prophetic hint of Japan's emergence as a modern military power in a march-past of Japanese soldiers.

At the dawn of the twentieth century, Britain was conscious of entering a new age. Queen Victoria had gently passed away at Osborne early in 1901, and the accession of her son, the genial Edward VII, was symbolic of the nation's renewed confidence as the South Africa war moved towards its victorious conclusion. Changing too was the attitude towards the Empire; its acquisition was now being justified by a sense of mission to lead the peoples over whom the British flag flew to share in the benefits of civilisation. At the Alhambra the moment seemed ripe for celebration, and Charles Wilson was

1 *The Times*, Apr. 24, 1902. Ganne also wrote scores for a number of ballets for the Folies-Bergère and the Casino de Paris.

2 *Era*, Apr. 26, 1902.

encouraged to produce a patriotic ballet, for which Landon Ronald, a rising young musician who was a *protégé* of Moul, was brought in to compose the score. *Britannia's Realm* (June 16, 1902) was presented only a few weeks after the signing of the peace treaty at Vereiniging, but it celebrated - naively to more cynical eyes of a later age, but at the time with conviction - not the military victory that lay in the past but the nation's destiny as it was then perceived. One scene depicted one of the evils which Britain had sought to eradicate, the slave trade in the Sudan. Another showed an Australian lad bidding farewell to his parents to answer the call of the mother country, his affection for which being seen as 'evidence of Britannia's wisdom in the work of colonisation'. All in all it was 'one of the best planned and most extraordinarily sumptuous productions ever seen at the Alhambra',[3] the *corps de ballet* being fully employed in three spectacular set-pieces - first as bejewelled dancers in an Indian scene of great magnificence, then as skaters whirling in carnival mood on a frozen Canadian lake to one of Ronald's most haunting melodies, and the grand finale in which a Union Jack took place in a dazzling display of electric light.

Britannia's Realm was Coppi's last work for the Alhambra. He left London to resume his career in Italy, where he was to revive *In Japan* with success at the Scala, Milan, the following spring.[4] Meanwhile the Alhambra sought a successor, turning first to its own company and trying out Lucia Cormani, who had already given proof of her choreographic skill in *The Gay City*. Of the four works in which she was to collaborate, the first two were distinguished by their dramatic content and continued the return to the more conventional type of *ballet d'action*. The hero of *The Devil's Forge* (January 12, 1903) was Karl, a sword-maker, who is on the point of being betrothed to the Burgomaster's daughter, Gretchen, when a rival challenges him to a test of weapons and with his sword cleaves through a steel helmet. Taking the sword he has just made to give to his future father-in-law, Karl fails in his attempt, and in consequence the Burgomaster calls off the betrothal. A fairy disguised as an old woman appears to Karl in his misery and tells him of a burning cavern where he can forge a sword of matchless strength and temper it in a magic stream. Karl makes his way to the mountain, and overcoming all manner of difficulties, forges a new sword, which restores his good fortune when he returns to claim his bride.

Perugini recalled the ballet as 'a charming and dramatic work, beautifully staged, and uncommonly well acted',[5] and seemed undisturbed by the return to the travesty tradition in casting Edith Slack, a pupil of Katti Lanner and formerly a member of the Empire company, as Karl. She was in fact widely praised for her performance, although criticised for taking her miming too fast - a shortcoming no doubt forced upon her by the music and the need to keep the ballet to an acceptable length. An attractive young ballerina of no

3 Perugini, 267.

4 First performed at the Scala on Mar. 1, 1903, it achieved a respectable number of 18 performances during the season.

5 Perugini, 267–8.

great renown, Alma Mari, took the leading dancing rôle as the Fairy of the Mountain, being succeeded in the course of the run by Marjorie Skelley.

Most of the dances occurred in the scene in the Devil's Forge, Edith Slack being brought in to support Alma Mari in her Grand Adagio. Cormani produced some 'quaint and grotesque' dances for the goblin-guardians of the great cauldron whose movements contrasted starkly with the graceful measures of the white-and-silver-clad nymphs of the torrent.[6] Her choreography was on the whole competent without being particularly outstanding, and could not, as one critic wrote, 'make us forget Sig. Carlo Coppi, who has more ingenuity and freshness in his treatment of masses'.[7]

Although it was 'an ordinary two-act spectacle of the usual Alhambra type',[8] it enjoyed a longer run than most ballets, remaining in the programme for ten months. The next ballet, *Carmen* (May 7, 1903), was to be even more successful, running for three weeks longer. It was conceived to take advantage of the exceptional expressive gifts of the Spanish dancer, Rosario Guerrero, and was described as 'a powerful play without words'. Guerrero's Carmen was 'a fine, resolute, instinctive animal - cunning, pitiless, amorous, and fearless',[9] much closer to Mérimée's original than any of the divas whom London had seen in Bizet's opera. Perugini, whose reminiscences of the music-hall ballets of the Edwardian era are a vivid and valuable first-hand source, described those highlights of her performance which remained etched in his memory:

> Apart from Guerrero's fine presence, her magnificent dancing, the breadth, realism and intensity of her acting throughout . . . there were two particularly memorable moments of that production; one was the fortune-telling scene, the other - the scene in which Carmen flirts with the Lieutenant of Gendarmes in order to lure him away from the gypsy camp, and is dividing her attention between her flirtation and the knowledge that Don José has only just been frustrated from stabbing her while so engaged . . . In the card scene, Guerrero gave in all its fullness the sense of a tragic, overhanging doom. In the other, all the combined cunning and fighting instinct of a savage animal at bay with circumstance, and trying by sheer cunning and audacity to master it, came out, and it was not acting but reality, the real Carmen of Mérimée extricating herself and her comrades from discovery and disaster by superb daring in the use of her dazzling, unconscionable charm.[10]

The travesty tradition of the house was happily relaxed to enable Don José to be played by a male dancer, M. Volbert, whose stage presence reminded some of the handsome allure of the actor-manager Johnston Forbes-Robertson, but it was still necessary to find a rôle for Edith Slack. Her appearance as a travesty 'toreador', stealing the heart of a passionate gypsy from a masculine Don José, was an obvious error, even at a time when travesty was still an accepted element, for as one critic pointed out, 'Escamillo should

6 *Era*, Jan. 13, 1903.
7 *Sketch*, Jan. 14, 1903.
8 *Era*, Jan. 13, 1903.
9 *Era*, May 9, 1903.
10 Perugini, 268.

be the essence of exuberant masculinity, the adored of the ladies – virile, imposing, and magnificent'.[11] In his score, Byng had incorporated many passages from Bizet's opera, but had added several numbers of his own: a Cigarette dance, a Hungarian dance for Carmen, and a Grand Valse for the splendid last scene outside the bull ring. During the ballet's long run Guerrero was to be followed by two other Carmens, first by Josephine Casaboni, who was 'more sparing of shrugs and tossings of the head',[12] and then by another Spaniard, María la Bella, whose Carmen was 'sensuous rather than passionate, a shallower-hearted young woman than was either of the other two.'[13]

The third work to which Cormani contributed, *All the Year Round* (January 21, 1904), came from a very different mould. It might best be described as a dance revue of the months of the year, introduced by a short prologue in which the Spirit of Happiness shows a blasé young Marquis how to keep himself amused and cheerful during the coming year. This provided a linking theme for a sequence of spectacular scenes containing a variety of dancing, mostly of the more popular kind such as step-dancing and cake walks. Fred Farren and Giovanni Rosi – a remarkable mime who had recently joined the company – were associated with Cormani in arranging this ballet, but by general consent the highlight of the production was Cormani's ballet of swallows and mayflowers in the May scene.

It had become clear, however, that Cormani was going to work no miracles at the Alhambra, and in 1904 an experienced choreographer was brought over from Italy. Alfredo Curti had been reared in the mainstream of the Italian tradition, learning his art at the Scala, Milan. Endowed with a highly developed sense of tradition, Curti regarded the works of Noverre and Blasis as sacred texts, and without being in any sense an innovator, had sufficient imagination to give his ballets the required touch of originality needed to retain the fancy of the music-hall public. The erudite Perugini had many an interesting discussion with him. 'Signor Curti,' he wrote,

> whose scholarship in the history of the dance was remarkable, was an enthusiastic follower of the traditional school, and as an accomplished dancer and mime, an artist, trained geometrician, and devotee of literature and music, he brought to bear on his work as composer of Ballet, a theatrical experience and artistic sympathy, somewhat akin to that of Blasis himself; and while the action of his ballet was always coherent and dramatic his appreciation of stage effect and handling of massed groups of dancers in motion, were uncommonly fine.[14]

In appearance and in temperament, Curti was a typical Latin. Sallow of complexion, with black hair and a magnificent black moustache, he was very fiery at rehearsal and if a dancer failed to do his bidding, he was prone to fly into a furious rage, directing a stream of Italian oaths at the unfortunate girl. His English remained very limited, and Cormani's niece, Gina, who was a dancer in the company, would frequently be called upon to interpret. A perfectionist

11 *Era*, May 9, 1903.

12 G. E. Morrison press-cutting albums (Theatre Museum, London), VII, 85.

13 Morrison, VIII, 19.

14 Perugini, 272.

at heart, he took infinite pains when preparing a ballet. The literary research required for his scenarios was carried out by an Italian crony, who kept a bookshop and who was occasionally rewarded for his trouble with a small rôle, and the choreography was then meticulously recorded in notebooks, beautifully written down in different colours with diagrams.[15]

It would take Curti some time to impose his artistic ideas on the Alhambra, where his first task was to arrange the *ballet d'occasion*, *The Entente Cordiale* (August 29, 1904), celebrating the new Franco-British alliance. For this Moul's friend, Landon Ronald, supplied a score full of 'tripping melodies'. After a reference to the Russo-Japanese War – a bevy of Russians brandishing knouts being put to flight by geisha girls with umbrellas was the Alhambra's comment on the siege of Port Arthur – the ballet moved on to its apotheosis showing the nations of the world uniting in a single grand alliance, a chimera that ten years later was to be shattered on the battlefields of Flanders.

Ballets were now being retained in the Alhambra's repertory longer than ever before, both *All the Year Round* and *L'Entente Cordiale* running for more than a year. Consequently, more than six months passed before the next new ballet entered the programme. As its title suggested, *My Lady Nicotine* (February 27, 1905) was a comment on the habit of smoking, which after being long regarded as an exclusively manly pleasure was now becoming a socially acceptable accomplishment among younger women. To capitalise on this, the Alhambra decorated its front entrance with coloured playbills showing a young woman provocatively smoking a cigarette. Apart from disapproval from the older generation, the habit was considered innocuous, for no one then suspected its danger to health, while by many women it was seen as a sign of liberation. This 'idealisation of Tobacco', as one critic called it, was devised and produced by Charles Wilson, the rôle of the choreographer, Mme Cormani, being restricted to arranging the dances. The staging came up to the Alhambra's generous standards, the action unfolding briskly in a variety of settings – a Virginian plantation, a Turkish harem and a Dutch scene (which offered an excuse for a sabot dance) – before being brought to an end with an allegorical finale of great splendour. The public greeted it with 'uproarious applause' and seemed never to tire of it, for, like its two predecessors, it was more than a year before it was taken off.

Parisiana (December 11, 1905) was another production by Charles Wilson, who devised a series of Parisian sketches from Revolutionary times to the twentieth century. Once again there was no continuity of narrative, but there was no shortage of opportunities for dancing, which enabled Curti to reveal his versatility in ranging from a minuet, a polka and the Carmagnole to the exhilarating 'maxixe'[16] that brought the ballet to a close. A feature of the

15 Interview with Miss Theresa Heyman, Oct. 11, 1958.

16 This dance had been introduced at the Alhambra in Sept. 1905 by Anne Dancrey and Egidio Rossi as a variety number. It is not to be confused with the Maxixe Brésilienne which became popular in 1914 as a ballroom dance. The earlier dance was described as 'essentially a voluptuous dance of the Cabaret or low music hall' and was danced to 'a most fascinating tune known either as "La Mattchiche" (*sic*) or "Sorella"'. (*Dancing Times*, IV, 43 (Apr. 1914), 427.)

ballet was the appearance in one of the sketches of Jane May, a mime artist whose performance in *L'Enfant prodigue* had been the talk of the town some fourteen years before[17] She was now seen in a moving vignette of a Parisian *gamin* who adroitly protects some young men from the unwelcome attentions of a couple of pickpockets, and later, entering a poor artist's garret with thieving intent, is moved to pity at the sight of a sick girl shivering on a bed and covers her with his coat.

The ballet had to be revised in a second edition when Jane May's engagement expired, and it closed its long run with another unusual star – the exceptionally supple and slender American eccentric dancer, La Sylphe.

Having dispensed with a prima ballerina assoluta for a number of years, the Alhambra reversed this policy in 1906 to engage Maria Bordin of the Scala, Milan. Curti may have been pressing for this, but he was aided by the increasing rivalry of other theatres: the success of Genée at the Empire had overshadowed the Alhambra ballets for some years, there had been another revival of *Excelsior* at the Lyceum in 1905, and in the summer of 1906 Covent Garden presented Messager's *Les Deux Pigeons* with Aida Boni as Gourouli. Bordin, who had been seen recently in *Excelsior* and was already known in London, was a dancer with a vivacious personality and a fine classical technique, being particularly noted for her *équilibre*. She had little gift for character work, and Curti fashioned her part accordingly in the new ballet he prepared for her Alhambra début. *L'Amour* (June 11, 1906) marked a return to the conventional spectacular grand ballet, with a fanciful and not undramatic narrative set in ancient Assyria, and an unusually fine score by Thomé. The scenario was the joint work of Charles Wilson and Mrs Thomas Hay Ritchie.[18] King Darius is seeking a worthy husband for his daughter, Mylitta, and the various suitors are put to a daunting test – they are required to pierce a golden apple with a javelin, a task made doubly arduous by the dazzling flame of purity that shines into their eyes. Prince Nashur alone succeeds, helped by Mylitta who shades his eyes with her long hair. But now there is another ordeal to be faced: he must pass a night in the temple, resisting the temptations of the sirens who haunt it. He remains unmoved until Mylitta arrives in disguise. Succumbing to her wiles, he is imprisoned by the priests, but all ends happily when the princess claims his release. In the rôle of Mylitta, Bordin's Italian style was found by one observer 'rather out of keeping with the Oriental surroundings, and her ballet dress . . . very strange amid costumes suggestive of Assyria', but there could be no two opinions of the 'wonderful grace, vigour and lithe subtlety' of her dancing.[19] Still a fine figure of a man, Curti cast himself as Nashur, and was outstandingly dramatic in the somewhat over-long temptation scene. Several other Italian mimes were included in the cast, notably Giovanni Rosi as the High Priest.

17 *L'Enfant prodigue*, a mime play by Michel Carré fils with music by Wormser, was first performed at the Prince of Wales Theatre on Mar. 31, 1891, with Jane May as Pierrot and Francesca Zanfretta as Phrynetta.

18 Mrs Ritchie was the daughter of Sir Arthur Sullivan's mistress, Fanny Ronalds.

19 *Morning Post*, June 12, 1906.

Visually, the ballet was exceptionally magnificent. A wonderful atmosphere of mystery was achieved in the temple, with its erotic overtones of dances of *aphrodysiaques*, *charmeuses*, and *cheveux*, the last a *pas de quatre* in which the dancers wore wigs of flowing hair of unbelievable length; and the ballet closed with a scene of such richness and spectacle as had never been seen before – 'even', added the critic of the *Era*, whose memory was long, 'if we go back to the palmy days of Pitteri and Charles Morton'.[20]

Curti produced his next ballet, *Queen of Spades* (February 25, 1907), not for Bordin but for the speciality acrobatic dancer, Mlle Alexia. He had based his theme on the dangers of gambling. To play the hero, Julia Seale returned to the Alhambra after an absence in France and Italy. She had clearly profited from her spell abroad, having presumably studied under some of the great mime teachers who practised in those two countries. The ballet's action relied heavily on her interpretation, in which she displayed 'considerable dramatic force and no little pathos'.[21] Her part was that of a young sculptor, who is taken up by the fashionable set at a German health resort. There he falls under the spell of a Parisian dancer, and in an attempt to find the wherewithal to secure her favours gambles disastrously at the tables. To drown his misery he drinks himself into a stupor, at which point the services of the cinematograph (which in its infant form had been a novelty feature of the Alhambra programmes for some years) were called upon, probably for the first time in a ballet. In flickering black and white, the moving picture depicted his dream of entering the dancer's boudoir and in a fit of jealousy shooting his rival. When the picture faded, the screen was raised to reveal the spectacular set for the Dream Visions, with its playing-card dances and *valse des liqueurs*, interspersed with some effective dancing for Alexia representing the unlucky card of the Queen of Spades. Later in the ballet's run, this section of his choreography had to be recast with more classical solos for Bordin, who took over the rôle in the summer. The Dream Visions scene was followed by a dramatic Temptation scene, preceding the spectacular apotheosis in the Nymphs' Grotto of 'La Source' that featured a shapely *figurante* in the pose of Ingres' celebrated painting.

Bordin's last creation at the Alhambra was the Spirit of the Bells in Curti's adaptation of *Les Cloches de Corneville* (October 7, 1907), one of his finest ballets. Praised as more dramatically constructed than the original opera, which was then well-known to London, it had a continuous run of over seven months and was to be revived in 1909 with the young Danish ballerina, Britta. Among its memorable moments were the entrance of the knights in glistening armour, played by tall show-girls, and the exquisitely rustic scene in the apple orchard with its kissing waltz. As the old miser Gaspard, Giovanni Rosi had a wonderful moment when he was seen gloating over his hoard of gold, to be suddenly struck with terror when the castle's bells peal out. Another fine character study was provided by Julia Seale as the timorous Grénicheux.

20 *Era*, June 16, 1906.
21 *Era*, Mar. 2, 1907.

Bordin's attempt at character work in a sabot dance in the apple orchard scene was not so successful, but Curti had thoughtfully arranged a variation more suited to her style in the final *divertissement*.

Maria Bordin could not stand the treacherous English climate with its winter fogs, and was glad to return to her native Italy. The Alhambra did not replace her immediately, and for a brief while Curti had to return to a lighter style. *Cupid Wins* (January 27, 1908) was an amusing trifle, an unpretentious piece with *commedia dell'arte* characters, while *The Two Flags* (May 25, 1908) was essentially a topical production, capitalising on the newly formed alliance between France and England and timed to coincide with the state visit of President Fallières. Predictably, it contained an effervescent scene of Parisian gaiety, in which a delightful French dancer called La Pomponnette performed a *danse excentrique*, and ended with a patriotic *défilé* in which, to drum accompaniment, troop after troop of girls descended a massive staircase at the back of the stage, fancifully dressed in uniforms of the country's crack regiments.

A new ballerina was not long in appearing, and this time the Alhambra looked to Denmark, spurred no doubt by the popularity of Adeline Genée. The choice rested on Britta Petersen,[22] a young dancer still in her teens who resembled Genée in size and colouring and bore a marked likeness to the actress, Nina Boucicault. She was also gifted with a strong personality and a certain ability as an actress. Appearing under her first name of Britta, she made her London début on October 12, 1908, in Curti's new ballet, *Paquita*. As the title suggested, the setting was Spain, Paquita being a young gypsy whose lover, the impecunious Don Gomez, is arrested for fighting a duel in her defence. The gypsies make their way into the castle, where the couple is married according to the gypsy rite, and Don Gomez makes his escape. Paquita, however, is arrested, but her flight arouses the pity of Prince Philip, who is also smitten with her charms, but is man enough to accept his rebuff with good grace, and Don Gomez is freed and reunited with Paquita. A sign that the travesty tradition was no longer so acceptable was given in the casting of Rosi as Gomez, Julia Seale being compensated with the lesser rôle of the disappointed prince. The *corps de ballet* was fully employed in the finale, set in the Ambassadors' Hall of the Alhambra, a 'sensuous and brilliant spectacle' of contrasting colours and movement. Towards the end of the ballet's run the local colour was enhanced by the participation, in the scene in the gypsy camp, of the acrobatic act of Bobker's Moorish Arabs.

Shortly before Britta's début there had appeared at the Alhambra a dancer of a very different type. La Belle Leonora came from Paris, and excelled in what might be called a pseudo-Greek style of dancing. Moul took a great fancy to her, and on March 30, 1908, presented her in a one-woman number called *Sal-Oh-My!* a satirical parody of the erotic 'Vision of Salome' with which Maud Allan was drawing the crowds at the Palace Theatre. Later in the year Leonora returned in two more short works designed specially for her, *Narcisse*

22 She entered the ballet school of the Royal Theatre in 1894, and left the Royal Danish Ballet in 1908. For some reason Hans Beck had not promoted her as principal dancer. She later married a businessman, and died in 1965.

Alhambra Theatre

CHARING CROSS ROAD AND LEICESTER SQUARE, LONDON.

Managing Director—ALFRED MOUL.

The National Variety Theatre.

Business Manager & Secretary. H. Woodford.
Treasurer. A. E. Corrick.
Stage Manager. Clarence Hunt.

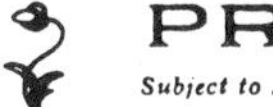

PROGRAMME.

Subject to Alteration at the Discretion of the Management.

Maitre de Ballet. Signor Alfredo Curti.
Musical Director. Geo. W. Byng.
Sub-Conductor and Leader Julian Jones.

Programme for Week commencing Monday, February 1st, 1909.

1. OVERTURE 8.0
MARCH "THE CATCH OF THE REGIMENT" *Fredericks*

2. FRANK LAWTON, 8.5
Siffleur

3. CHARLENE & CHARLÈNE 8.15
In their Drawing Room Entertainment.

4. VICTOR FERREROS 8.30
Musical Clown with his Dog "Virt."

5. 'PAQUITA' 8.45

A ROMANTIC BALLET

Arranged and Produced by Signor ALFREDO CURTI
Music Composed by GEORGE W. BYNG
Costumes by ALIAS from designs by COMELLI Scenery by E. H. RYAN
Master Machinist, A. WILLIAMS. Electric Effects by J. WEBBER.
Properties by A. WILLIAMS and ALIAS. Wigs by GUSTAVE.
Floral Decorations by BAUMLER

Presented under the Personal Direction of ALFRED MOUL.

Prince Philip ... ... Miss JULIA SEALE
Don Gomez de Sylva ... ... Sig. G. ROSI
Duke of Alcala ... ... Sig. SANTINI
Roderigo Perez (Captain of the Guard) ... Mr. TOM COVENTRY
Piquilo (Gaoler) ... ... Mr. G. ALMONTI
Pedro ... ... Sig. FRIELLI
Silvio (Page to Prince Philip) ... Mdlle. CARLOTTA MOSSETTI
Concita (Proprietress of the Posada) ... Mdlle. JACQUELINE BLANEY
Inez (the Favourite of Prince Philip)... Mdlle. JACQUELINE BLANEY
Manolita ... ... Miss L. BRYANT

AND

Paquita .... Mdlle. BRITTA

(First Appearance in England.)

SCENE I—A Gipsy Encampment in Old Spain—Daybreak
Cloak Dance. Serenade to Concita. Card Dance. Mdlle. BRITTA.
Mazurka. Pas Seul. Mdlle. Carlotta Mossetti
Pas de Deux. Mdlle. BRITTA and Miss G. CORMANI
The Farandole. The Challenge. The Duel, and The Arrest.

SCENE II. The Castle Terrace.
Don Gomez a Prisoner. Paquita's Interview. Pas de Fascination.
The Meeting. The Gipsy Wedding & the Escape. Arrest of Paquita.

SCENE III La Fete Galante in the Ambassadors' Hall at the Alhambra.
DANCES—Fan Dance. Danse Crotale.
Bacchanalian Dance. March. Pas Seul. Mdlle. Carlotta Mossetti
Pas Seul. Mdlle. BRITTA. Valse Oriental. Apotheosis.
FINALE.

6. "L'INCOGNITA" 9.35
WILL SING
"LO! HERE THE GENTLE LARK" *Bishop*
POLONAISE from "MIGNON"

7. SCHICHTL'S WONDERFUL MARIONETTES 9.45
(First appearance in England).

8. ORCHESTRAL SELECTION 10.0
"TAMBOUR MAJOR" *Offenbach*

9. LEONORA 10.10
IN
"LA PETITE BOHEMIENNE."
AN EPISODE.
Music by FRANCIS THOMÉ.

Characters

Carita } ... (Strolling Minstrels) { Mdlle. LEONORA
Manuel } ... (Strolling Minstrels) { Miss JULIA SEALE
Count Lagrange ... (An Artist) ... ... M. VOLBERT
The Countess ... (his Wife) ... Mdlle. SALANDRI

Scene I.—Christmastide. Scene II.—The Artist's Studio

Costumes by ALIAS from Designs by COMELLI.
Scenery by E. H. RYAN.

10. BOBKER'S ROYAL MOORISH ARABS 10.40
(First Appearance in England)

11. JURY'S IMPERIAL PICTURES. 10.55

In accordance with the requirements of the London County Council:
(*a*) The public may leave at the end of the performance by all exit and entrance doors, and such doors must at that time be open
(*b*) All gangways, passages, and staircases must be kept entirely free from chairs or any other obstructions.
(*c*) The Safety Curtain must be lowered about the middle of the performance so as to ensure its being in proper working order

The Management earnestly trust that Ladies will very kindly remove their Hats (if so desired) and thus add to the comfort of all
Gentlemen are respectfully notified that Pipes are not permitted in the Fauteuils or Box Stalls Circle

"Scott's" TOP OF THE HAYMARKET, W. Suppers *After the Theatre.*

"Scott's" TOP OF THE HAYMARKET, W. Suppers *After the Theatre*

Alhambra Theatre programme, February 1, 1909.

(December 14, 1908) and *La Petite Bohémienne* (January 4, 1909). It thus turned out that Curti found himself with two principal dancers for his next work, *Psyche*, which was presented on April 5, 1909, only a month before Diaghilev and his dancers arrived in Paris for their historic first season. *Psyche* was very much a ballet in the traditional mould, harking back to an age that the Russians would make old-fashioned at a stroke. Its plot was unashamedly anacreontic, treating lightly of the divinities of ancient Rome. Psyche, played by the statuesque Leonora, is being acclaimed as the queen of beauty when Venus rises, in jealous wrath, from the waves. For her sacrilegious impertinence Psyche is chained at the entrance of a sea-monster's cave. Venus entreats her son, Cupid, in the person of the sprightly, classically trained Britta, to assist in her vengeful designs, but he falls in love with the hapless captive and carries her off to his bower. Their idyll is interrupted by Venus, whose anger is finally appeased when Cupid begs her forgiveness. Psyche is not only pardoned, but is given the cup of immortality and herself becomes a deity. The contrast between the two principal dancers gave spice to the action, and a further point of interest was the score, composed by Alfred Moul himself, who in an interesting passage made effective use of the glockenspiel.

Britta was next featured on her own in another patriotic ballet, *Our Flag* (December 20, 1909), a celebration of the Empire in which Julia Seale was rather incongruously cast as John Bull, but some months later the talents of Britta and Leonora were again combined in Curti's last and most ambitious ballet for the Alhambra, *Femina* (May 30, 1910). Its underlying theme was the power of vanity over woman, which was illustrated in five episodes set in the First Garden, the Stone Age, Ancient Assyria, Spain, and – for the obligatory spectacle at the end – the allegorical Kingdom of Vanity. Described as a ballet with a moral, it was hardly flattering to the fair sex, whom Leonora personified, in various guises, as spurning true love for base reward. Leonora's beauty was displayed to such effect in the first scene, in which she appeared as Eve, that she insisted on a corridor of curtains being installed from her dressing room to the stage, and the stage-hands being instructed to turn their backs if they crossed her path. *Femina* was full of incident, the most striking scene of all showing an Assyrian high-priest struck dead for snatching a jewelled necklace from an idol to satisfy the desire of a lovely priestess. As lightning strikes the temple, the priestess turns to flee. But Vanity exerts its power even in her terror, and as she passes the body of the priest she snatches up the necklace and bears it off in triumph.

In his seven years at the Alhambra, Curti had done much to restore the prestige of its ballet, and his departure left a vacancy that would be difficult to fill. Instead of looking to Italy for his successor, Moul made an unexpected decision, calling on an Englishwoman from the company and testing her in light, vivacious works. Whether he hoped that in time she might progress to more substantial productions will never be known, for ballet was already entering a new phase and for the moment the Alhambra was offering its public a series of entertaining pieces of no great consequence. Elise Clerc had already revealed a talent for arranging striking dances in the up-to-date ballet, *On the Square* (February 22, 1909), a 'breathless, up-to-date, idealized motion-picture of New York gone dancing mad',[23] which had included a marionette dance for Britta and Carlotta Mossetti, a whistling solo for Frank Lawton, and an apache dance by Frank Lawton and Elise Clerc herself. This was followed, after Curti's departure, by *The Polar Star* (February 28, 1910), which in a fanciful way, by evoking a fairy realm among the snows and making fun with a penguin dance, echoed the public interest in the search for the poles: only a year had passed since the North Pole had been reached by Peary, and the South Pole still remained out of reach. Elise Clerc's next effort was a one-scene 'frolic', *On the Sands* (August 1, 1910), constructed around the predicament of some bathing belles whose clothes are stolen by some Eton boys, and containing a number that was to have a special significance in the light of future developments. This was a burlesque of two Russian dancers then appearing at the Palace, Anna Pavlova and Mikhail Mordkin – a good-humoured acknowledgment of the new force that was so shortly to ring the death knell of the Alhambra ballet.

23 *Sketch*, Mar. 31, 1909.

VI

The last years of the Alhambra ballet (1911–12)

In the summer of 1909 London's music-hall managers, always on the look-out for novelties to whet the appetite of their public, were alerted to a potent new source of talent. In Paris Diaghilev's Ballets Russes had opened their first season to an acclaim that left no doubt that a theatrical event of major importance had taken place. The illustrated magazines dwelt at length not only on the extraordinary artistry and technique of the dancers and a plastic quality hithero unseen in the choreography, whether in romantic mood or in displays of animal vigour, but on the visual splendour contributed not by commercial scene painters but by artists of first rank. Upon a world where male dancing had sunk into insignificance the young Nijinsky had burst with the force of a revelation, and accompanying this new god of the dance were two ballerinas, Karsavina and Pavlova, who themselves were to become legends in the years ahead. Two years were still to pass before London would have the chance of welcoming the Diaghilev Ballet, but in the meantime the music-hall managers had managed to tempt several of its dancers to cross the Channel and appear individually or in scratch groups on their stages. Thus Karsavina had appeared at the Coliseum in June 1909; Georgi Kyaksht, brother of Lydia Kyasht of the Empire Theatre, and Ludmila Schollar were billed at the Hippodrome in October; and the summer of 1910 saw a further spate of Russian visitors - Pavlova with Mordkin at the Palace, Karsavina at the Coliseum in the second act of *Giselle*, and a company from the Bolshoi, Moscow, headed by Preobrazhenskaya in *Swan Lake* at the Hippodrome.

There was fierce competition between London theatre managers to exploit the new-found revelation of Russian ballet in 1911, the coronation year of the new monarch, George V. Alfred Moul, the General Manager of the Alhambra, was not a man to drag his heels, and in the previous summer he had been in correspondence with the Paris theatre agent, C. Ercole, about the possibility of engaging a Russian company.[1] Ercole warned him that the terms would be high. '*Stupendous offers* are being made to these people in view of securing them for the Beecham season at Drury Lane,' he advised on June 23, 1910. 'They are therefore tempted by these different offers and their terms are naturally very much bigger than they would even have been a year

1 Moul's correspondence with Ercole and Braff is now in the Theatre Museum, London.

ago.' Two sets of proposals were put forward for consideration: one for a Moscow company headed by Yekaterina Geltser and Vasili Tikhomirov, with Kuznietsov as ballet-master,[2] and the other for a company under Mikhail Fokine. At first it was the second proposal that found most favour. Fokine was asking £5000 a month for a company of thirty-three, with his wife as ballerina, and was holding out as an additional bait the possibility that he might secure the services of Pavlova. 'I beg to *insist most particularly*,' advised Ercole, 'that if you wish to make a *great coup* you should accept this proposition which if the Alhambra wants to keep its foremost rank in the production of up-to-date ballets [by which he meant ballets in the new Russian manner] *would be the only way to achieve same*. Trading on the name of Foukine (*sic*) which none can approach at present would be an excellent way of getting ahead of *all the other* productions of Russian ballet.'

Ercole found the Russians both difficult to deal with, and exorbitant in their demands, and wrote to Moul on July 28:

> I am not very much astonished at what you say respecting the numerous interviews that Mr Wollheim has had with Foukine. This gentleman and Mr Stoll ought to be put for some time in straight jackets and have ice put on their heads – they are rendering the market impossible. It is very evident that as everything in life like the Stock Exchange is based on offer and demand these people who are kneeling down to the Russian dancers and offering them engagements on golden trays are causing them to ask unheard of salaries . . . Respecting your friend's criticism regarding the Russians contained in your letter of the 26th I agree: they are perfectly correct. They are the most unreliable scheming and thick-headed lot of idiots in the world and their brains are located in their feet.

In the end Thomas Beecham engaged the Diaghilev Ballet for Covent Garden, and the Alhambra had to be content with the Moscow company. Negotiations were conducted through Tikhomirov, who was able to persuade Alexander Gorsky, ballet-master of the Bolshoi Theatre, to come to London to produce a ballet for a fee of £300. Of the dancers engaged, the highest paid was the senior ballerina, Geltser, who would receive a weekly salary of £90; Alexandra Balashova, who was to replace Geltser after eight weeks, settled for £40 after asking for £60, and Vera Mosolova, who was to follow Balashova, would be paid £50. Tikhomirov's fee was £40 a week for a twelve-week engagement, at the end of which Alexis Koslov was to take over at £35 a week. Four second dancers were also engaged: two women, Ekaterina Adamovich and Elisaveta Anderson, each at £20 a week, and two men, Leonide Zhukov and Lavrenti Novikov, each at £15 a week.

As soon as contracts were signed, Gorsky began preparing the new ballet in Moscow, and sent a reassuring progress report through the London

2 There was no ballet-master by the name of Kuznietsov in Moscow at this time, but the company included a dancer of that name, Vladimir Nicolayevich Kuznietsov, who had been engaged in 1898 and appeared in secondary rôles such as the Chinaman in *Coppélia* and one of the Prince's friends in *Swan Lake*.

theatrical agent, A. Braff: 'Everything is going ahead all right. We are already rehearsing. The music will be light and very gay. I expect to find some music in London.' It seems that he had been warned that the Alhambra audiences might not be so musically discerning as the opera-goers of Moscow. Gorsky's plan was to come to London with his principal dancers already familiar with their parts, so that he could concentrate on the sections for the English dancers and the *corps de ballet*. Meanwhile Geltser and Tikhomirov were having their costumes made in Moscow, as Moul had agreed.

When Gorsky arrived in London, the Alhambra *corps de ballet* was immediately captivated by his gentle and courteous manner. But no one was allowed to forget that Geltser was the reigning diva, and when she arrived for rehearsal, Gorsky always made a great ceremony of kissing her hand. Everyone soon learnt not to offend her, for she seemed perpetually to be in a bad temper. And her insistence on wearing four different costumes during the rehearsal of the new ballet seemed to the English dancers a pointless display. They were much more sympathetic to Gorsky, appreciating his talent as a choreographer, particularly in the Hungarian scene, in which he gave them soft undulating arm movements, so different to the vigorous flailing they had been required to do by other choreographers.

Gorsky's *The Dance Dream*, the only ballet this celebrated choreographer produced outside Russia, was first performed on May 29, 1911, nearly a month before the Diaghilev Ballet was due to open at Covent Garden. In form it was little more than a glorified *divertissement*, filled with spectacular set-pieces and brilliant dances, linked by a slender thread of a story about an Indian warrior, who, transported by opium to the land of dreams, searches in vain for his ideal woman. She appears to him in various forms, in different surroundings and in different ages – in the cloud-covered Himalayas, in Bronze-age Scythia, in Hungary, and finally at a spring festival in old Moscow – but she always eludes him. The structure of the score, cobbled together by George Byng from a selection of pieces by Brahms, Glazunov, Luigini, Rubinstein, Tchaikovsky, Drigo, Minkus, Koreshchenko, and Bleichmann, to which Byng added several pieces of his own, suggests that most of the dances were extracted from works by Gorsky already in the Moscow repertory and therefore familiar to the principals. The ballerina's variation to music by Koreshchenko presumably came from *The Magic Mirror*, which Gorksy had created for Geltser and Tikhomirov in 1905; parts of the Hungarian scene were undoubtedly borrowed from his version of *Raymonda*, staged in 1908; and 'the wonderfully vivid war-dance' in the Scythian scene was reported to be stylistically similar to a passage in his more recent ballet, *Salammbô*, produced in January 1910. However, no one was in a position to object if any of the dances had been seen before in distant Moscow, and London was delighted with a splendid feast of dancing, with opportunities given to three girls of the permanent company, Marjorie Skelley, Gina Cormani and Agnes Healy, whose dances were praised as being 'out of the conventional rut'.[3] Even if

3 *Era*, June 3, 1911.

the ballet could not be counted among Gorsky's important creations, it was skilfully and artistically crafted. As J. E. Crawford Flitch pointed out, it 'had the crowning virtue of breadth and simplicity of treatment. A sense of space was created; the tumult of action was varied by passages of sobriety; an effect of beauty was produced, larger and serener than any that has been seen in the English ballet during recent years.'[4] Perhaps the only disappointment was that, at thirty-four, Geltser was a little too mature and heavily built for the taste of the Alhambra audience, who failed to appreciate the spectacular lifts in her *pas de deux* with Tikhomirov.

The Dance Dream was performed nightly until the last days of October. When Geltser had to return to Moscow for the rehearsals of Gorsky's new production of *Le Corsaire*, her replacement, Balashova, was so apprehensive that she came to London with sufficient cash to pay the penalty under her contract if she wished to return home. However, all was well, for Tikhomirov was there to partner her for the first half of her engagement and she saw the remaining four weeks out in the safe hands of Alexis Koslov. Before the end of the ballet's run all the Russians had departed, and for the last performances, the hero was played by a Signor Protti, and a young English dancer stepped confidently into the shoes of Geltser, Balashova and Morosova. This was Marjorie Skelley, who had previously been at the Empire Theatre, where she had understudied Genée; she had been in *The Dance Dream* from the beginning, having created the small but significant rôle of the Bayadere whose love for the hero is not returned, but her possession of the star rôle was sadly brief.

Moul had assessed the value of Gorsky and the Russian dancers as soon as *The Dance Dream* entered the programme, and within a few days he was exploring the possibility of a return visit in 1912. The Russians were no less astute in appreciating the realities of the theatrical marketplace. Geltser and Tikhomirov had made it known that they would require increased fees of £120 and £50 respectively, and Gorsky too had raised his sights. On June 8, 1911, only ten days after the first performance, the theatrical agent, Braff, wrote to inform Moul of Gorsky's proposals:

> He is willing to come over to London next summer for 8 or 10 weeks to put on a new Ballet for a sum of £400 . . . and he would work all the winter to prepare a ballet for you with a new subject, novel dances and *good music*!! Mr Gorsky is of the same opinion as yourself that there should be no lady dancers booked next year from Russia, and he thinks he could choose some very good dancers out of the Alhambra corps de ballet. I would suggest that Mr Gorsky should plan his future ballet with one or two eccentric numbers for male dancers, as was done last year at the Chatelet Theatre, Paris, a number of BOUFFONS with ROSAY[5] and others. This number was a terrific success in Paris and I feel sure that they would appreciate such a thing in London.

4 Flitch, 176.

5 Giorgi Rosay had been a member of the Diaghilev Ballet in its first season in 1909, arousing great enthusiasm on the opening night as the principal jester in the 'Danse des Bouffons' in Fokine's *Le Pavillon d'Armide*. Braff is presumably referring to this occasion. Rosay repeated this triumph in the 1911 season in London. His career was short: he was discharged from the Maryinsky Theatre in 1915, and died two years later at the age of thirty.

Moul's plans were to dispense only with the supporting female Russian soloists, for in his reply of June 13 he told Braff that the Alhambra management was prepared to re-engage Gorsky, Geltser and Tikhomirov, provided they could bind themselves to a twelve-week term. He also required that Gorsky should submit for his approval both the scenario and the music for the new ballet he was proposing to mount. Further, an ambitious suggestion had been floated for the designing of the ballet, and Moul expressed his hopes that 'if possible, the idea of securing the cooperation of Mr Bakst be carried out. As to that, I should be glad to know as soon as possible to what expense such collaboration would commit us.'

These seeds bore no fruit. Since the Alhambra was apparently ready to meet the financial terms, it seems likely that the Bolshoi Theatre would not release the choreographer or the dancers or all of them for the period the Alhambra required.

* * *

Meanwhile Diaghilev's Ballets Russes had at last given their first London season, at Covent Garden in June and July, and when *The Dance Dream* ended its run in October, were drawing full houses in a return visit with a company headed by Kshesinskaya, Pavlova and Nijinsky. In the space of these few months, the whole course of ballet in England had been radically changed. In the years ahead, until a truly British ballet was established through the efforts of Ninette de Valois, Marie Rambert and others, the main fare of the British ballet-going public would be the Diaghilev Ballet and other Russian-oriented groups. As for the ballet at the Alhambra, which had still seemed healthy under Curti, it had clearly lost its *raison d'être* and would survive for no more than a year after *The Dance Dream*, expiring when the theatre changed over from variety to revue under the new management of André Charlot.

For the moment, however, its fortunes were resting on the slender shoulders of Elise Clerc, who produced two new works in 1911. The first of these, *The Mad Pierrot* (March 13, 1911) was a vehicle for an unusual visitor, not a Russian but an extraordinarily loose-jointed acrobatic dancer from America, Bessie Clayton, whose speciality was an ability to dance on *pointe* in unblocked black shoes. The dramatic posssibilities of the Puckish rôle of the Pierrot might have been more fully developed, but she managed to convey a strange elfin quality in the character, and in the dances composed for her, 'pirouetted with quite remarkable velocity and astonished all by her backward-flings.'[6] Later that same year Clerc followed this ballet with *1830* (October 9, 1911), an 'enchanting and elegant' ballet about Bohemian life in Paris, which starred the charming Poldi Müller, a Viennese ballerina who had the additional and at that time rare distinction of being a cinema actress. Her acting talent enabled her to give a delightful portrayal of the heroine, a simple grisette, loved by a penniless artist, whose suit is threatened by a wealthy Baron. Thinking he has lost her, the young man consoles himself with a mysterious siren, 'a kind of vampire woman, raven-haired, ashy-pale-faced,

6 *Era*, Mar. 18, 1911.

scarlet-gloved and stockinged . . . who completely hypnotises [him] with her sinuous beauty and passionate caresses' in a striking scene acted by Emile Agoust and a glamorous newcomer, Xenia Greville Moore.[7]

The history of the Alhambra ballet concludes with the engagement of Augustin Berger, an experienced ballet-master who had worked for many years in Prague and Dresden and had more recently directed the ballet in Warsaw. Negotiations with him had opened in November 1911, when the last hopes of re-engaging Gorsky had faded. A star ballerina was needed as well, and it was hoped that Berger might bring with him one of the leading Polish ballerinas. The lady of his choice, Anna Gaszewska, turned out not to be free. Overtures were then made to another ballerina, who made impossible demands, refusing to dance more than three times a week and requiring two fares from Warsaw to London.[8] It then transpired that Gaszewska was available after all, and a contract with her was signed, only to be cancelled almost immediately on payment by the Alhambra of a week's salary and £100. The reason for this drastic step was almost certainly connected with the choice of subject for Berger's ballet. Presumably it was originally planned to leave this to him, but ultimately he was asked to mount a new version of *Carmen* – a project the Alhambra had had in contemplation for some time. When Berger agreed to stage this ballet, the opportunity arose of presenting it with María la Bella, one of the Carmens of the 1903 production, and clearly no Polish dancer could hope to be preferred to her.

Berger arrived in London in time to see some of the last performances of *The Dance Dream*, by which he was suitably impressed, although he saw at once that the company was not particularly well trained by his standards. When he started rehearsals, he found it hard work to achieve what he wanted, and his frustrations rubbed off on the unfortunate dancers. Nor was the situation helped by his parade-ground manner of barking out his orders in German. Although the Alhambra dancers had cheerfully endured Curti's rages to the point of making fun of him, Berger's bullying treatment was something they could not stand, and they came close to revolt.

His talent as a choreographer, however, was never in doubt, and his new version of *Carmen* (January 24, 1912) was no less successful than its predecessors. Like 'a bright wild bird', María la Bella returned to give a performance as Carmen that was tinged with 'passion and exquisite grace, allurement and the power of expression by look and movement of tragedy'.[9] Volbert was back again as Don José, and – a sign that the lessons of the Russian ballet were beginning to be learnt – the part of Escamillo was assigned not to a woman but to the strikingly handsome Emile Agoust. Berger's ballet contained more Spanish dancing than had Cormani's version of 1903, for

7 *Era*, Oct. 21, 1911.

8 The identity of this dancer is a mystery. She was named as 'Mlle Dombrowska' in the correspondence between Moul and Braff, who reported that Berger was very keen on presenting her to London in the ballet scene from Jose Manen's opera, *Acte* (Theatre Museum, London: Alhambra 3 folder). But there was no solo dancer of that name in the Warsaw company.

9 *Evening Standard,* Jan. 25, 1912.

Alfred Moul had brought over from Spain a number of Spanish dancers, led by La Malagueñita and Antonio de Bilbao, to appear in the final scene outside the bull ring. Dressed in male costume of dazzling white, La Malagueñita danced several flamenco numbers on a table; and Antonio de Bilbao displayed his legendary wizardry in *zapateado*. 'Never before,' declared a contemporary critic, 'had *Carmen* been so genuinely Spanish as in the ballet produced with exceptional *éclat* at the Alhambra.'[10]

By then the process of winding down the Alhambra's ballet establishment was well under way. The dancing school, if it could so be called, which had been started in Coppi's time during the eighteen-eighties and where Mme Cormani had been turning out pupils for almost quarter of a century, had long existed on sufferance. No space could be spared exclusively for these classes, which were held in far from satisfactory conditions on the stage itself. There they were continually disturbed by rehearsals and scene-shifting, and it was difficult to maintain order because of 'dark corners and overshadowing wings'. Both Cormani and Moul recognised a need for improvement. Curti had in fact submitted proposals for a more varied spread of training, to include such subjects as 'speciality dancing', which included national dances and acrobatic dancing, and 'modern dancing'. Cormani, however, was primarily interested in the strictly classical training which she had undergone in Milan. 'I make dancers and pantomimists,' she told Moul, 'I do not profess to teach acrobatism.'

Moul's concern was to service his theatre. It was not his intention, he made it clear, to produce dancers for other theatres. As he saw it, the school's function was to provide the Alhambra *corps de ballet* with 'all the material [it] may require (outside of Première Danseuses), as the English temperament is even more adapted to the requirements of Ballet dancing, than the foreign'. It was to be the means of assuring a supply of pretty girls to replace 'those whose contracts have expired and who, on account of their age, appearance, and lack of ability, are useless'. He therefore envisaged two series of classes, taking place on alternate days, one for girls newly apprenticed and the other for 'such of our girls who care to join', and comprising, in addition to ballet, 'the Swedish method, which is best adapted to the requirement of Modern Dancing'.

Nothing, it seems, came out of these discussions, and the classes were eventually discontinued altogether. It was not long afterwards that the *corps de ballet* itself was disbanded. The event, which must have taken place some time in 1912, went unrecorded, and the general public remained unaware that a tradition had been snapped in the unfolding history of the London stage. As for the dancers themselves, they were only dimly conscious of any tradition and moved on to take jobs elsewhere. It required a novelist's imagination to perceive that sense of the past which had bound dancers of one generation to another at the Alhambra. In Compton Mackenzie's novels *Carnival* and *Figure of Eight*, the Alhambra is thinly disguised as the Orient Palace of Varieties, where

10 *Globe*, Jan. 25, 1912.

> for nearly sixty years ballet had succeeded ballet without a break except when the theatre had been closed for cleaning and decorating, and even then the girls had been paid half salary. The place on the deal form at which Lucy Arnold sat to make herself up had been sat on before her by Jenny Pearl. The place of Jenny Pearl before she came to the Orient from Covent Garden had been the place of a girl called Maisie Rawlins, whom Rita Vitali could remember when she herself first came to the Orient in 1899. Before that there was no tradition in the dressing room of the occupant, but occupant there had been and before her another and another, back to the days when crinolines were hanging on the dressing-room hooks and ringing black and white stockings flung down upon the forms. Every one of them had learnt the same steps, practised in the same way, talked the same jargon of the dance, dreamed the same dreams of triumphant pas seuls, and pondered with the same anxiety such dancers' problems as if their walking when they were off the stage was getting pigeon-toed or if that bone in the instep was likely to develop a very ugly bump.[11]

Not by any means did the dance disappear from the Alhambra stage when the theatre became the home of revue. In 1913 the new management engaged Natalia Trukhanova, partnered by Quinault, to give selections from her repertory, and several of the revues produced both before and during the First World War included short ballets. A number of these were produced by Theodore Koslov: a Pastel Ballet, and a 'Flowers of Allah' ballet, costumed by the celebrated *couturier*, Poiret, in *8d. a Mile* (1913), and an Assyrian Ballet in *Keep Smiling* (1913). Serge Morosov was the choreographer of 'The Temple of the Sun' ballet in *5064 Gerrard* (1915) and 'The Spirit of Egypt' ballet in *Now's the Time* (1915), the latter being written and produced by the distinguished Egyptologist Arthur Weigall, who also designed the costumes and scenery and the property Sphinx. In 1916 Adeline Genée appeared at the Alhambra in a 'Spring' ballet arranged by her uncle, Alexander Genée, which was inserted in a revised edition of *Now's the Time*, and in the same year – the year of *The Bing Boys* – Morosov produced *Aleko*, a balletic adaptation of Serge Rachmaninov's opera. That the house still had a vestige of pride in its ballet tradition was shown in the sequel to *The Bing Boys*, *The Bing Boys are There* (1917), with its scene, 'The Alhambra – Formerly', nostalgically evoking the ballet as it was in 1887, even with some of Jacobi's tripping melodies.

The coming of peace brought the Diaghilev Ballet from its haven in neutral Spain back to London. English balletomanes, culturally starved for more than four long years, found a company which had changed in many ways since pre-war times, and now possessed a bewitching comedienne-ballerina in Lydia Lopokova and a young choreographer of modernistic leanings in Leonide Massine. After a season at the Coliseum the company moved, in April 1919, to the Alhambra (in Osbert Sitwell's opinion 'the best house in the capital in which to show ballet')[12] and there two ballets that have since become classics were created: *La Boutique fantasque* and *The Three-cornered Hat*. In 1921 the

11 Mackenzie, *Figure of Eight*, 142–3.
12 Sitwell, 14.

Diaghilev Ballet was back at the Alhambra again, with the fabulous but commercially ruinous, ballerina-studded revival of *The Sleeping Princess*.

Reverting to a variety theatre, the Alhambra never reconstituted its ballet department, although the dance, and occasionally ballet, continued to find a place on its boards. In 1923 Massine produced his *Zéphyre* there for Vera Savina, and in 1928 Anton Dolin staged a ballet to George Gershwin's *Rhapsody in Blue*, with himself and Vera Nemchinova. Occasionally English companies found a place on the bill: J. W. Jackson's English Dancers (1924, 1925, 1929), the Haines English Ballet (1926), and a company led by Molly Radcliffe and Stanley Judson, which appeared in Morosov's *The Rosebud and the Bee* and an aerial ballet, *The Garden of Happiness*, in 1926. Among individual acts were Maud Allan (1923, 1924), Errol Addison with Mitrenga (1924), Nicolas Legat and Nadezhda Nicolayeva (1925), Robert Sielle and Annette Mills (1925, 1929), and Carola Goya and Carlos de Vega in a recital of Spanish regional dances (1928).

After a brief spell as a cinema the Alhambra reopened as a theatre in 1931 and during the last few years of its existence was to present many distinguished dancers on its stage. In the Strauss operetta, *Waltzes from Vienna* (1931), Albertina Rasch arranged the dances for a company headed by Alexandra Danilova, while *A Kiss in Spring* (1932) was memorable only for an excellent ballet by Frederick Ashton featuring Alicia Markova and Harold Turner, which so excited the audience that they 'shouted themselves hoarse and nearly flayed their hands in enthusiasm'. Ashton also arranged the dances for *The Flying Trapeze* (1935), for which Pearl Argyle and Hugh Laing were engaged. In another musical comedy that same year, *Tulip Time*, Wendy Toye and Frederic Franklin were featured in dances by Buddy Bradley.

In the nineteen-thirties a native English ballet was establishing itself at Sadler's Wells and the Mercury Theatre, but notwithstanding the dispersal of the Diaghilev Ballet after the great impresario's death, Russian companies still commanded a wide and enthusiastic following whenever they appeared in London. The 1933 season of Col. de Basil's Ballets Russes de Monte Carlo at the Alhambra was extended from three weeks to four months, when London fell captive to the charms of the baby ballerinas - Tamara Toumanova, Tatiana Riabouchinska and Irina Baronova - and witnessed the creation of Massine's symphonic ballet, *Choreartium*. In 1935 Vera Nemchinova and Anatole Obukhov were the stars of the National Ballet of Lithuania for a brief and not particularly successful season at the Alhambra, and they returned in 1936 with René Blum's Ballets de Monte Carlo, in the company of Nathalie Leslie, Helene Kirsova, Leon Woizikowski, André Eglevsky and Igor Youskevitch, dancing in a repertory consisting mainly of works, old and new, by Fokine.

This was the Alhambra's swan-song, for after a short season by the magician, Dante, the theatre closed its doors to the public for the last time and the demolition contractors moved in. The face of Leicester Square was changing, and it was now the turn of the Alhambra - 'that strange temple', as H. M. Walbrook called it, 'with its vast distances, Moorish ornamentations, and starry dome, its promenades, and its buffets, its traditions, its echoes, and its ghosts. There, long ago, some of us saw *Don Giovanni* as a ballet with Mozart's music, and M. Jacobi conducting an orchestra as full and as superb as that of Covent Garden itself . . . There some of us first saw Pierina Legnani dance in her grand way . . . The great promenade at the back of the dress circle was for years one of the nightly sights of London. In it stood a crowd two or three deep watching the show on the stage, and between them and the buffet at the back strolled a throng of men and women chatting in all the tongues of London. I have seen J. McNeill Whistler there and Aubrey Beardsley; the fierce-looking Henri Rochefort, and the important looking little M. de Blowitz. Others also whose names are too august to be mentioned in so frivolous a connection.'[13]

13 *Observer*, Oct. 11, 1936.

The Empire Ballet

VII

The Empire Theatre's beginnings (1884–86)

From 1884 those in quest of an evening's pleasure had a double reason to make their way to Leicester Square, for in that year there arose on its northern side an elegant new theatre, the Empire, which soon bid fair to challenge the Alhambra's supremacy in the realm of ballet. The site on which it stood had some curious associations with the entertainments of the town. In Ailesbury House, built there in the seventeenth century, when it was on the very fringe of London, Peter the Great had been entertained during his visit to England in 1698. Passing into the possession of the Saville family, the mansion then became known as Saville House, and this name was retained after it was rebuilt early in the nineteenth century and became a 'sort of "Noah's Ark" for exhibition purposes'.[1] For many years its eastern wing housed Miss Linwood's exhibition of needlework, which long rivalled Madame Tussaud's waxworks in popularity. On Miss Linwood's death in 1845, her needlework copies of famous paintings were dispersed and Saville House was given over to a succession of bizarre entertainments, from a panorama of the Mississippi to giants and dwarfs, monstrosities and strong men, and finally the *tableaux vivants* and *poses plastiques* of Madame Wharton.

Madame Wharton and her troupe of shapely women in their pink fleshings were to be seen over a number of years exhibiting themselves in a room of Saville House, variously known as the Walhalla and the London Eldorado. A surviving playbill of the London Eldorado[2] gave a hint of the Empire's future status as a centre of the dance when it announced the double attraction of 'Madame Warton's (*sic*) grand new tableau of Giselle & the Night Dancers'[3] and 'the celebrated Spanish dancers – Señor, Señora y Señorita Escudero'.[4]

1 Walford, III, 165.

2 Broadley Collection, Victoria Library, Westminster.

3 *The Night Dancers* was an opera by Edward Loder, based on the ballet, *Giselle*. Presumably this playbill may be dated shorrtly after the revival of the opera at the Royal English Opera, Covent Garden, on Nov. 10, 1860. See 'Parodies of *Giselle* on the English Stage' by Ivor Guest, in *Theatre Notebook*, IX (1954–55), 38–46.

4 Escudero is a distinguished name in the annals of Spanish dance, but I have been unable to discover any connection between the Escuderos of the London Eldorado and the celebrated dancer, Vicente Escudero.

On a cold February evening in 1865 Saville House caught fire. Its gaunt ruins remained standing for many years, the long unfulfilled ambition of its owners being evidenced by a board announcing the imminent erection of the Denmark Theatre, in honour no doubt of the Prince of Wales's Danish bride, Alexandra. In the end it was a French company which rebuilt the ruin, to house the Royal London Panorama with a representation of the Battle of Balaclava. But this was only an intermediate stage in the history of the site, for not long afterwards the building was demolished to make way for a new theatre, announced originally as the Pandora Theatre, but finally opened with the name it has borne ever since, the Empire.[5]

The troubled history of the Empire's early years might well have been taken as an indication that there was no demand for a second theatre in Leicester Square. It opened on April 17, 1884, under the management of Alexander Henderson, with H. J. Hitchins, who was to be associated with the theatre for many years, as acting manager. Hervé's operetta, *Chilpéric*,[6] was billed as the opening production, and A. Bertrand, who had previously worked at the Alhambra, supplied three ballets to specially composed music by John S. Hiller - *Daphne et Corydon*, a *divertissement rustique*; a Spanish ballet called *La Corrida de Toros*; and, to conclude, a 'grand barbaric military ballet', *Les Amazones*. For this last ballet Trouvé of Paris provided some novel electric lamps, three being carried by each of the dancers 'with the most startling and gorgeous effect'. The principal dancers taking part were Marie Laurent and Julie Hofschüller, supported by Mlles Aguzzi, Louie and Sismondi. Before *Chilpéric* was taken off at the end of July the first star ballerina had danced on the Empire boards in the person of Emma Bessone, who electrified the audiences with a wonderful display of power and virtuosity in the Spanish ballet.

Bertrand's services seemed not to have been very much in demand as summer faded into autumn, but after a series of burlesques featuring Nellie Farren, Connie Gilchrist and Phyllis Broughton from the Gaiety Theatre, he set to work on a version of *Coppélia*[7] which was given with a *corps de ballet* of sixty dancers on November 8, 1884. Although created at the Paris Opéra more than fourteen years before, on the eve of the Franco-German War,[8] this ballet had not yet been seen in London. Bertrand's version was condensed into a single scene, and since he had danced in the *corps de ballet* at the first performance in Paris, it is likely that he incorporated some of Saint-Léon's original choreography in this production. London's first Swanilda was Alice Holt, and her sweetheart Franz was played *en travesti*, as was the tradition in Paris, by Mlle Sismondi. The Coppélius was W. Warde, of whose performance the *Era*

5 There was also a project to open there a theatre called the Alcazar. H. J. Hitchins claimed to have chosen the name Empire, which was apparently preferred at a late stage to that of the Queen's. Bruce Smith, the scene painter, was commissioned to design scenery for the Empire's first production, *Chilpéric*, on note paper headed 'Queen's Theatre, Leicester Square'.

6 Originally produced at the Folies-Dramatiques, Paris, on Oct. 24, 1868.

7 The advertisements announced that the music was by 'Léon', but the reviews make it clear that Delibes' score was in fact used.

8 The first performance took place before Napoleon III on May 25, 1870.

wrote: 'For that horrid, painted epicene thing, the male ballet dancer, we entertain nothing but disgust; but there is nothing offensive about Mr Warde, who, indeed, shows pantomime talent of no mean order.'[9]

Coppélia was quickly followed by a production of *Giselle*,[10] also by Bertrand, presented in its two scenes on December 24. The cast was as follows:

Giselle	Miss Alice Holt
Loys	Mlle Sismondi
Queen of the Wilis	Mlle Louie
Princess Bathilde	Miss G. Scott
Prince of Courlande	Mr D. Rowella
Wilfrid	Mr Risson
Hilarion	Mr W. Warde

Though it had been successfully produced in London on several occasions over the previous forty years, *Giselle* did not make much stir at the Empire. 'Pantomimic action,' wrote *The Times*, 'is all but an extinct art, and it would not have been easy last night to comprehend the story without the aid of a few analytical remarks.'[11] In all probability the ballet was very heavily cut.

The Empire was proving a very difficult theatre to launch, and its managements, for there seem to have been a succession of them in these first few years, were struggling to take a page out of the Alhambra's book by presenting light opera and extravaganza. Ballet formed an essential, although somewhat subservient, element in the programmes. Delfina Zauli from Florence was featured in the light opera, *The Lady of the Locket*, in 1885 before being replaced by Emma Bessone, and at the end of that year a 'grand military pantomime and ballet in two acts' called *Hurly Burly* was presented. In March 1886 Bertrand arranged two ballets to music by F. Stanislaus for a drama called *Round the World*, based on the story by Jules Verne. Featured in them was the former favourite of the Alhambra, Erminia Pertoldi, who also appeared in the Moorish Ballet and the Lace Ballet which Bertrand produced for the extravaganza, *The Palace of the Pearl*, in June. The billows of lace which enveloped her did not entirely conceal her considerable *embonpoint*, but *The Times* gallantly allowed that she danced 'as nimbly as ever, notwithstanding her physical ponderosity'.[12]

The run of *The Palace of the Pearl* was cut short in August when Daniel N. de Nicols, the founder of the Café Royal, foreclosed on his mortgage. Some days later he opened the theatre on his own account with an English version of Adam's *Le Postillon de Longjumeau*,[13] which was such a fiasco that it had to be drastically revised before being given a second time. Ill fortune still dogged

9 *Era*, Nov. 15, 1884.

10 Created at the Paris Opéra on June 28, 1841, and first shown in London at Her Majesty's Theatre on Mar. 12, 1842.

11 *The Times*, Dec. 27, 1884.

12 *The Times*, June 19, 1886.

13 First produced at the Opéra-Comique, Paris, Oct. 13, 1836.

it, for at this second performance the conductor inadvertently played the National Anthem before the final ballet, which consequently had to be given with another conductor. This did not augur well for the future, and indeed de Nicols closed the theatre a few weeks later with the intention of converting it to a music hall, but his plans were thwarted when the Alhambra Theatre successfully opposed his application for a music and dancing licence. Having learnt his lesson, de Nicols then called in some men of experience, and a company, the Empire Palace Ltd, was formed with a capital of £15 000. The principal shareholders, in addition to de Nicols himself, were George Edwardes, the lessee and manager of the Gaiety Theatre, who became managing director, and Augustus Harris. With these men at its head the Empire Theatre entered at last a period of prosperity.

It was accepted from the beginning that if the Empire was to survive as a music hall, it would have to accept the conditions established by the Alhambra, and so it too offered its male patrons the amenities of a promenade. Nevertheless, it so managed its affairs that it acquired the reputation of being the more select and distinguished of the two establishments, as was recalled by a writer in *The Times* long after both music halls had disappeared:

> To its Victorian or Edwardian patrons, men about town, gallants from Ouida or Kipling, the Empire Theatre was the most celebrated rendezvous in the world. It bordered on Bohemia and was almost a club. Its social amenities, if such they could be called, included the notorious promenades where ladies of the town consorted with the dandies of the time and shocked the entire nation.[14]

Of course this was an over-statement, but the women who, reasonably discreetly, plied their trade at the Empire were 'several cuts above their sisters at the Alhambra'.[15]

The existence of the promenades certainly offended a significant section of the public, and in 1894, when the Empire's licence came up for renewal, a determined offensive was launched by a fierce champion of morals, Mrs Ormiston Chant, to force the London County Council to grant the application only on condition that the promenade was removed and converted to additional seating. There was a violent outcry, but unexpectedly it came not so much from the habitués as from the trade unions, and the hapless lady and her friends found themselves ridiculed as 'Prudes on the Prowl'. As a result a compromise was reached; the promenade could remain, but it was to be separated from the auditorium by a trellis, which turned out to be so flimsily constructed that it very soon began to fall to pieces and was eventually removed, seemingly without any fuss. It was not until 1916, when a more serious mood prevailed at the height of the Battle of the Somme, that the famous promenade disappeared.

No history of the Empire Theatre would be complete without a glance at the women who paraded in its promenade. Their beauty and elegance

14 *The Times*, May 27, 1961.
15 Macqueen Pope, 182.

lingered in many memories, and in later years the eyes of former habitués would gleam as they recalled those visions of their youth. Even that staid scholar of the ballet, Cyril Beaumont, was strangely stirred. In his youth he was taken once or twice to the Empire by his father. Its ballet interested him little, but to the end of his days he retained a vivid image of the temptresses of the promenade, whose faces, he recalled, 'enhanced by make-up, presented a most fascinating appearance, at times seductive and occasionally sinister and mysterious like certain drawings by Aubrey Beardsley'.[16]

16 Beaumont, *Bookseller at the Ballet*, 82.

VIII

Katti Lanner

The new management began its work auspiciously by engaging Katti Lanner as ballet-mistress. Already well known to the London public as both dancer and choreographer, Lanner was now to embark upon the most prolific phase of a career which had opened in 1845, the year of the famous *Pas de Quatre*, and was to close not long before her death in 1908. During her reign at the Empire, she produced no fewer than thirty-six ballets, some being revised in 'second editions', and the first thirty-four, produced between 1887 and 1905, being consecutive additions to the repertory.

Katharina Josefa Lanner was born on September 14, 1829, the daughter of a famous father, Josef Lanner, one of the waltz kings of old Vienna.[1] Evincing a desire to study dancing from a very early age, she entered the school of the Vienna Court Opera as a child and received her first lessons from the ballet-master, Pietro Campilli. Her father died before she was fourteen, but the reputation that clung to the name of Lanner was soon to be carried on by his daughter, who, on July 17, 1845, made a successful début on the stage of the Court Opera in a *pas de deux* inserted in Antonio Guerra's ballet, *Angelica*.

Under the guidance of Isidore Carey, father of the dancers Edouard and Gustave Carey, Katti Lanner polished her technique and developed her gifts as a mime. Her natural musicality, inherited from her father, gave her dancing a distinctive quality, which earned her recognition as one of the most promising young dancers in the company. She also attracted the attention of two celebrated ballerinas who visited Vienna during the eighteen-forties, Fanny Elssler and Fanny Cerrito, both of whom prophesied that a brilliant future lay ahead of her. It was not long before she was given the opportunity of proving her worth. On August 29, 1847, she appeared in the important mime rôle of the dumb girl Fenella in Auber's opera, *Die Stumme von Portici*, and on September 23 of the same year she played the title-rôle in Victor Bartholomin's ballet, *Elina*, replacing at short notice the American ballerina, Augusta Maywood, who had fallen ill.

The ensuing years saw her reputation grow. She played Myrtha, Queen of the Wilis, in *Giselle* on June 28, 1852, and the following year, on February 7,

1 Josef Lanner was born in the Parish of St Ulrich, Vienna, on Apr. 12, 1801. He married, on Nov. 28, 1828, Franciska Jahns, daughter of August Jahns, a glover, and Katharina Mutzbauer. Katti Lanner, who was born in the Paris of Laimgrube (now part of the Maria Hilf district), had one sister and one brother: Josefa Augusta, born at Laimgrube on Dec. 21, 1831, and August Joseph, born on Jan. 23, 1834. Josef Lanner died on Apr. 14, 1843, and his son on Sept, 27, 1855.

appeared in Paul Taglioni's production of *Die verwandelten Weiber* (*Le Diable à quatre*) as the Countess. Another opportunity followed in 1854 when the Danish choreographer, August Bournonville, visited Vienna and chose her to play the leading rôle in his revival of *Der Toreador*, produced on July 15.

Had her mother and her brother not died within a short time of one another, Katti Lanner might have remained in Vienna until the end of her career and become the established star of the Court Opera ballet. But this double bereavement left her with a desire to escape from a city which held so many poignant associations with her beloved family, and not even a tempting offer from the Director could shake her resolve to leave. She went first to Berlin, making a triumphant début in the title-rôle of *Giselle*, which she played for the first time in her career on December 9, 1856. Then she visited Dresden, and from there went to Munich, where she was personally complimented by the King of Bavaria, Maximilian II.

Katti Lanner's career as a choreographer began in 1862 when she was engaged as ballet-mistress and ballerina at the Stadt-Theater, Hamburg, where she produced her first ballets. These included *Uriella, der Dämon der Nacht* (September 10, 1862), *Die Rose von Sevilla, oder Ein Abend bei Don Bartolo* (October 1, 1862), *Sitala, das Gaukler-Mädchen* (January 28, 1863), *Asmodeus, oder Der Sohn des Teufels auf Reisen* (November 17, 1863), and several Christmas productions which were performed by her pupils between the ages of seven and twelve.

In time the urge to travel came upon her again. She went to dance in Scandinavia, and in October 1869 made her first appearance in France, at the Grand-Théâtre, Bordeaux, leading her own company, the Viennese Ballet Company. Bordeaux had a long and distinguished tradition as a centre of ballet, and the title of 'the Taglioni of the North' which was bestowed upon her there was a compliment she greatly appreciated.

By now her fame had spread as far abroad as New York, where James Fisk had set his heart on securing her services for his newly-opened Grand Opera House. He had tried in vain to negotiate terms by correspondence, but being a determined man, he refused to admit failure and sent his secretary over to Europe specially to treat with her. Persuaded at last to cross the Atlantic – no mean journey in those days, when the crossing took more than three weeks – Katti Lanner made her American début at Fisk's theatre on July 11, 1870, in *Giselle* with Giuseppe Venuto de Francesco[2] as Albrecht and Bertha Linda as Myrtha. During its short season the company also presented *Hirka*, *Sitala* and *Uriella*.

The scene of her next triumph was Lisbon, where she and her company appeared at the Teatro São Carlos during the season of 1870–71. The richer by a gift of diamonds from King Luis I, she left Portugal to fulfil an engagement in London. Deeply conscious of the important position which London had

2 Katti Lanner was very fond of de Francesco, and left directions in her will for the tending of his grave as well as those of her mother and brother. The watch she always carried on her person in her later years at the Empire had belonged to de Francesco.

held in the eighteen-forties, the halcyon years of the Romantic Ballet, Katti Lanner regarded her English début as the realisation of a long-cherished ambition. Engaged by Colonel Mapleson as ballet-mistress at Her Majesty's Opera, Drury Lane, she made her first appearance on the boards of Old Drury in *Giselle* on April 22, 1871, again supported by de Francesco and Bertha Linda. After the London season she visited Baden in the late summer of that year, obtained triumphs in Belgium during the following winter, and on May 9, 1872, appeared for the first time in Paris, at the Théâtre Italien, dancing a *grand pas de deux* with de Francesco in Rosina Penco's benefit performance.

Her energy and vitality was a constant source of wonderment. In later years her friend, S. L. Bensusan, wrote:

> In some of the great cities Madame Lanner has visited, I have listened to the reminiscences of musicians and stage-managers. They have two stories to tell, one of the extraordinary enthusiasm that prevailed among the distinguished audiences that the announcement of Katti Lanner's presence never failed to gather, the other of the long hours spent at practice in the morning, when the auditorium was empty and the stage belonged of right to the stage-carpenter and his ruthless myrmidons, the shifters of scenes. Born with a talent that was exceptional, Madame Katti Lanner polished it until it became genius by dint of long work from which our modern English girls [the dancers of 1901] would revolt.[3]

The indefatigable Katti Lanner crossed the Atlantic a second time in the summer of 1873. Accompanied by a group of dancers known as the Kathi Lanner Coreographic Combination (*sic*), she appeared at Niblo's Garden, New York, in a pantomimic spectacle called *Azrael*, sharing the honours of the dancing with Giovannina Pitteri. She remained in America for two years, touring the States and making occasional visits to New York. Her children's ballet for Augustin Daly's production of *A Midsummer Night's Dream* at the Grand Opera House in August 1873 came at an unfortunate moment, for the country was in the throes of the financial crisis known as the Great Panic, but in the summer of the following year she was warmly received at the Stadt-Theater, a German playhouse in the Bowery, where she danced the part of the Abbess in Meyerbeer's opera, *Robert le Diable*. In February 1875 she was back at Niblo's, dancing in *Tom and Jerry*, and she ended her second American visit at the Grand Opera House in *Ahmed*, a poor spectacle-show with a good ballet in which she was accompanied by Giuseppina Morlacchi, an Italian ballerina who had settled in the States and married the famous scout of the Far West, Texas Jack.

When she returned to Europe in the summer of 1875 with an engagement with Colonel Mapleson, Katti Lanner made London her permanent home. She bought a house overlooking Clapham Common – No. 40 Northside – where she settled with her husband, Johann Alfred Geraldini,[4] who had been the director of the Viennese Ballet Company, and their three daughters, Sofia, Katharine and Albertina. Mapleson was at that time presenting seasons

3 'The Evolution of a Dancer', in the *Sketch*, Mar. 13, 1901.

4 They were married at Kl. Michaelskirche, Hamburg, on Feb. 11, 1864.

of opera at Her Majesty's Theatre, and for five years in succession – from 1877 to 1881 – she held the post of ballet-mistress, producing *Les Nymphes de la forêt* (July 10, 1877, and revived in 1879), *Une Fête de pêcheurs à Pausilippe* (July 24, 1877, and revived in 1878) and *Les Papillons* (May 17, 1878) with music by Hansen.[5] Her career as a dancer was drawing to a close, for she was now approaching fifty. One of her last stage appearances was in *Robert le Diable* at Her Majesty's on July 16, 1878.

One of the reasons for her settling in London was no doubt Colonel Mapleson's decision to place the National Training School of Dancing, which he had established in 1876, under her direction. Situated at No. 73 Tottenham Court Road, this school was to become for many years the nursery from which scores of dancers were trained for the Empire *corps de ballet*, as well as being used as a rehearsal room. Dance teaching in London had reached a pitiful nadir in 1880, but an improvement was soon evident after the arrival of Katti Lanner. 'Ballet-dancing received a stimulus,' wrote Bensusan,

> and the dance-loving public hastened to support the fairy pantomimes and ballets under Colonel Mapleson, Carl Rosa, and others at Her Majesty's, the Alhambra, the Crystal Palace, and elsewhere. In 1880 she was working for Augustus Harris, and continued to arrange ballet for the Italian Opera, the Drury Lane pantomimes, and the provincial productions of Augustus Harris and Oscar Barrett. The Crystal Palace pantomimes, the delightful open-air ballets – who will forget the *Midsummer Night's Dream* with Mendelssohn's music? – were all produced by Madame Lanner, whose artistic development was proceeding steadily, while her resources remained unaffected by her own retirement from public performance. She gave to her pupils some of the grace and charm that had marked her own work in dance and pantomime; perhaps I may remark, without indiscretion, that in recent years I have seen her show how a piece of work should be done in a manner suggesting that what the Training School has gained the stage has lost.[6]

5 Possibly a version of *The Butterflies*, which the Kathi Lanner Coreographic Combination were giving in Pittsburg and Cincinnati in Oct. 1873. The composer Hansen (given as F. P. Hansen in the *Era*, May 26, 1878) may possibly be identified with G. P. Hansen, who was listed as the ballet-master of the company while at Lisbon in 1870–71.

6 *Sketch*, Mar. 13, 1901.

IX

The Empire becomes the home of ballet (1887–91)

London had barely finished celebrating Queen Victoria's Golden Jubilee when the Empire reopened as a theatre of varieties on December 22, 1887, with Katti Lanner as ballet-mistress. The importance given to the two ballets produced by her for the opening programme foreshadowed the theatre's claim to be 'the home of ballet', a claim that understandably caused no little irritation to the Alhambra. With its smaller stage, the Empire could never hope to rival the scale of the Alhambra productions, nor was its *corps de ballet* ever to approach the standards of its neighbour's company, but in one area, that of stage design, it was to assert an undisputed superiority. This was due to the influence of C. Wilhelm, who designed the costumes for one of the two ballets presented on the opening night in 1887 and over a period of nearly thirty years was gradually to assume a dominant position in the production of the Empire ballets.

An Englishman despite his German-sounding professional name, Wilhelm was a ship-builder's son from Northfleet in Kent, where he had been born on March 21, 1858. Considering perhaps that his real names of William John Charles Pitcher hardly befitted a budding artist, he adopted the name of C. Wilhelm at the outset of his career. A self-trained draughtsman, he obtained his first commissions after Gustave Planché had introduced him to E. L. Blanchard, who in turn brought him to the notice of Augustus Harris and other influential figures in the theatre. By 1887 he had already designed two ballets for the Alhambra – *The Golden Wreath* and *Diona* – as well as the Empire's opening production of *Chilpéric* in 1884. During the many years he would work for the Empire, he was to indulge to the full his remarkable flair for colour schemes, which he considered as the all-important element in his work. 'Colour,' he maintained, 'is the life-blood of my art, for, under the furnace-glare of the limelight from every direction, there can be, of course, no artistic light and shade into (*sic*) drapery except by the employment of colour.'[1] His elaborate designs were prepared with the minutest regard for detail, and no costume made from a design of his was ever worn in performance without being most clearly scrutinised by him. On this he insisted, his quiet voice and

1 *Sketch,* Mar. 8, 1893.

manner belying the firmness of his will. His was indeed the iron hand in the velvet glove, for he demanded absolute submission to his authority.[2]

The third member of the team engaged to produce the ballets at the Empire Theatre was the celebrated French operetta composer, Hervé. Today unjustly neglected, Hervé was then approaching the close of his career. In 1887 he was sixty-two and had only five more years to live. Virtually the founder of the operetta style that reflected the carefree gaiety of Parisian life during the Second Empire, he had long brought delight to thousands with the fluent, infectious melodies of his scores and the brilliant nonsense of his libretti. His genius was recognised by people of almost every taste, even by the sombre Wagner, who, on his return to Germany in bitter mood after the fiasco of *Tannhaüser* at the Paris Opéra in 1861, would condescend to say only this when asked about French music: 'One French musician astonished, charmed and captivated me, and that was Hervé.'[3] Hervé was in fact a practised craftsman. He had studied composition and harmony under Auber, and Adolphe Adam, the composer of *Giselle*, had so admired an early piece of his that he produced it at the Opéra-National. Offenbach, who worked in the same field, was another admirer of Hervé, not only as a composer but also as a comic performer, and begged him to play the rôle of Jupiter in the 1878 revival of *Orphée aux enfers*. The last years of the Second Empire had rung with Hervé's music for *L'Oeil crevé*, *Chilpéric* and *Le Petit Faust*, and after the Franco-German War he had shown that his muse had not deserted him by composing a series of pieces for Anna Judic, the most successful of which was *Mam'zelle Nitouche*.

London knew his work well. The Prince of Wales had been so amused by his performance in *Chilpéric* when he saw it in Paris that he encouraged him to learn English for the express purpose of playing his part in London. Thereafter several of his operettas were applauded on the English stage, and in 1874 he composed and wrote the words for a dramatic symphony called *The Ashantee War*, which was played at a Promenade Concert.

The team of Lanner, Wilhelm and Hervé inaugurated their collaboration by providing the highspot of the Empire's opening programme as a music hall. This was the ballet *Dilara* (December 22, 1887),[4] a somewhat conventional work set in an Eastern port and a Caliph's palace, and featuring two internationally renowned dancers, Adelina Rossi and Enrico Cecchetti. Wilhelm's contribution to this ballet was specially remarkable. 'The effects of colour in the first scene,' recorded the *Era*, 'are produced by the admixture

2 In addition to his activity at the Empire, Wilhelm did much work for other theatres. He collaborated in many Drury Lane pantomimes. He designed the costumes for the original productions of *The Mikado* (the men's costumes) and *Ruddigore* (the Ancestors' costumes), Imre Kiralfy's gigantic productions of *Nero* and *Ancient Venice*, *Peter Pan*, *Tom Jones* and *The Arcadians* (the Arcadians' costumes). He also designed several of Genée's later ballets – *A Dream of Roses and Butterflies*, *La Camargo*, *La Danse*, *The Dancer's Adventure*, *Spring*. He was elected to the Royal Institute of Painters in Watercolours in 1920, and died in London on Mar. 2, 1925.

3 Schneider, 52.

4 Katti Lanner had danced in a ballet by Domenico Ronzani called *Dilara, oder Ein europäisches Ballfest in Tunis* in Vienna on Nov. 20, 1847. She played the part of Elise, a sea captain's daughter.

of sea-green and chocolate, crimson and white, and blue and purple costumes. There is an entry of Amazons in shining helmets, and a pretty dance by *coryphées*, each bearing on her wrist a white cockatoo, and an entry of juvenile black slaves playing on silver bells. Bronze and pale green, light green, cream colour and gold, dark blue and brown are mingled with exquisite effect in the second tableau.'[5]

Wilhelm had no part in the other ballet included in the opening programme. *The Sports of England* (December 22, 1887) was a topical *divertissement* which foreshadowed the emergence of the up-to-date type of ballet, later to become such a feature at both the Empire and the Alhambra. In a series of numbers it depicted cricket at Lord's (with female representatives of the M.C.C. and Australian elevens), yachting on the Solent (a *pas du 'mal de mer'*), football at Kennington Oval, polo at Hurlingham, hunting at Melton Mowbray, boating at Hammersmith, boxing, and Derby Day at Epsom.

From that evening on the Empire never looked back, and the struggles of its early years became only a memory. Two new ballets were created in 1888, which also saw the appearance of a succession of brilliant dancers from Italy – Carlotta Brianza, who in 1890 was to create the rôle of Princess Aurora in *The Sleeping Beauty* at St Petersburg, Maria Giuri, Elena Cornalba, Angelina Spotti, Emma Palladino, Luigi Albertieri, foster-son of Cecchetti and in future years to become a distinguished teacher in America, and last but not least, a dancer who was to remain for many years a pillar of the Empire ballets, Malvina Cavallazzi.

Rose d'Amour (May 19, 1888) was to be remembered as 'one of Mme Katti Lanner's greatest triumphs', and 'rather opened the eyes of Londoners as to the possibilities of the art of Ballet'.[6] It had a slender plot about a fairy being driven from her realm by a malignant elf, to be finally rescued by Cupid. Rossi and Cecchetti were the leading dancers, the latter making quite a character study out of the rôle of the elf and astonishing the audience with his dazzling pirouettes. Katti Lanner was as prodigal with her dances as was Wilhelm with his costumes, and packed into her choreography not only a Hungarian wedding, but a flower *divertissement* containing a minuet danced by girls representing lilac and carnations, a quaint Chinese dance of tea-flowers, and, with Wilhelm's collaboration, a remarkable group of colour achieved at the end by massing all the flowers in one gigantic bouquet.

Later that same year another creation followed – *Diana* (October 31, 1888), a slight arcadian *divertissement* based on an idea suggested by Wilhelm. Apart from a dance for the moon and stars in which the latter wore tiny electric lamps in their hair, it was remarkable for the appearance of Emma Palladino, a ballerina who had already gained many admirers in London during engagements at Her Majesty's, Drury Lane and the Alhambra. To judge

5 *Era*, Dec. 24, 1887.
6 Perugini, 279.

from the description of her left by Edouard Espinosa, she was a true 'dancer's dancer':

> It was not I but the whole choreographic world, who named her 'The Complete Palladino'. She had every quality a *première danseuse* should possess: (1) perfection of technique *in* a terrific execution; (2) power and elevation; (3) magnificent *batterie*; (4) *pointes de fer*; (5) fine *pirouettes*; (6) perfect placing throughout; (7) an excellent little figure; (8) delightful appearance, charm and expression . . . It was in [*Diana*] that I saw Palladino execute a *diagonale* which has always lived in my memory. Here is the *enchaînement*: she commenced at the top left corner of the Empire stage, placed in a perfect *arabesque ouverte*, the back leg at hip level, the heel clearly visible below the instep. She executed a series of *relevé*, *arabesque*, *cabriole derrière*, sixteen times, travelling down to the lower right corner. No arm waving up and down – the back leg never lowering – a clear-cut beat by the lower leg, rising to beat the top leg and sending it higher – perfect placing throughout – and *on one leg all the time*! If that is not enough to prove the quality of Palladino's execution then I am an old fool.[7]

Early in the New Year Paul Martinetti presented his pantomime, *The Duel in the Snow* (January 28, 1889), in an expanded version with dances arranged by Katti Lanner and a new score by Hervé. The original mime sketch had been inspired by a duel which had taken place in the Bois de Boulogne in the 'fifties between two carnival revellers who had not troubled to change their fancy dress.[8] Lanner's dances – polkas, boleros, gavottes, jigs, tarantellas, minuets, sabot dances – enlivened the opening scene of a masked ball at the Paris Opéra, while the rest of the ballet was devoted to the drama, culminating with the tragedy of the duel.

The ballet company had meanwhile been strengthened by the engagement of Malvina Cavallazzi, who made her first appearance at the Empire in November 1888. The wife of the operatic impresario, Colonel Charles Mapleson, Mme Cavallazzi was a much travelled ballerina who was as well known in New York as she was in London. For many years she had danced at Her Majesty's Theatre during her husband's opera seasons, and when the Metropolitan Opera House, New York, had opened in 1883, she had been its first prima ballerina. Before that she had begun her career on the smaller stages of Italy in the days when fire was an ever-present hazard for the dancer, and an incident at Cremona when she was still a girl had given her a fear of that element that was to haunt her all her life. She was waiting to be let down to the stage from the 'flies' when a careless stage-hand, after lighting the limelight, dropped a burning match on her costume. Fortunately he at once saw what had happened and promptly smothered the flames with his coat. Though shocked, she was able to make her descent and perform her *pas*, though omitting all the turns, for the back of her costume had been largely burnt away.

7 Espinosa, 'A Forgotten Dancer, Emma Palladino' (*Ballet*, 3, 1 (Jan. 1947), 17).

8 This duel became a sort of legend in Victorian times. See 'The Wintry Duel: a Victorian Import' by Coleman O. Parsons in *Victorian Studies*, Indiana University, June 1959, 317–22. Martinetti's mime sketch had been given elsewhere before the Empire production, which the *Era* of Feb. 2, 1889, describes as a revival.

Cavallazzi's appearance in *Diana* was to mark the last occasion on which she danced in public in ballet-skirts, for thereafter, until her retirement in 1899, she devoted herself entirely to mime rôles with a success that eventually overshadowed her earlier triumphs as a ballerina. 'The art of Madame Cavallazzi,' wrote S. L. Bensusan, 'is not, nor has it ever been, the laboured art of the schools. Certain conventions she has accepted, as in duty bound; but behind them is a wealth of individuality, a keen grip of every dramatic possibility a story affords, great knowledge of technique, and a clear insight that reveals the *nuances* of expression and makes the trained eye glad.'[9]

These great gifts were first revealed in Katti Lanner's *Cleopatra* (May 20, 1889), in which Cavallazzi appeared as Anthony to Maria Giuri's Cleopatra. Inspired by Rider Haggard's novel, which was at that time being serialised in the *Illustrated London News*, the plot of the ballet was superficial, going little further than to show Cleopatra charming Anthony with her dancing and being warned in a vision of her approaching death. The dramatic effect had in fact been sacrificed to the spectacle, which was magnificent indeed, with the stage filled with a colourful throng of Roman soldiery, Nubians, Egyptians and Greek slaves.

Cleopatra and the next ballet, *The Paris Exhibition* (September 26, 1889), were Hervé's last scores for the Empire Theatre. 'Clearly one of the briskest, brightest "balletrettes" that have been produced here or at any other London theatre for some time,'[10] as one critic described it, *The Paris Exhibition* was little more than a *divertissement* introducing a number of character dances, and set in a rather idealised Champ de Mars, with fountains and the Eiffel Tower – the great Parisian landmark which had been erected that very year for the Universal Exhibition – being illuminated as twilight fell. It was not an important work, but it pointed to the double trend that was to characterise the Empire's future ballet policy – that of interspersing its more conventional productions, in which dramatic effect would assume considerable importance until Cavallazzi's retirement, with up-to-date ballets inspired by topical themes and introducing a wider selection of dancing. The aim was to preserve the classical dance, and at the same time, with an eye on the music-hall public, to create a new formula with roots in contemporary entertainment. It was of course a compromise, but it was to endure until Diaghilev produced a better solution.

It was in 1889, after Hervé's retirement, that the triumvirate which was to rule the Empire in its finest period was completed by the engagement, as musical director, of Leopold Wenzel. Born in Naples on January 31, 1847, Wenzel had studied at the Royal Conservatoire there. Drawn to the theatre early in his career, he served a useful apprenticeship at the Alcazar in Marseilles before obtaining a similar post at the Alcazar in Paris. He was soon composing for the stage, and his first important work was the score for the three-act ballet, *La Cour d'Amour*, produced at the Eden-Théâtre, Paris, on October 2, 1884, with Elena Cornalba in the leading rôle.

9 'Madame Cavallazzi Bids Good-bye to the Empire' by S. L. Bensusan, *Sketch*, Feb. 15, 1899.
10 *Era*, Sep. 28, 1889.

During his engagement at the Empire Theatre, Wenzel was to prove a fluent and versatile composer and a strong-willed musical director, perhaps to the extreme of being intractable. His importance was recognised in the appreciation which S. L. Bensusan contributed to the *Sketch* on his retirement:

> Leopold Wenzel has brought to the making of ballet gifts that have not failed to express any note in the gamut of emotions. He is a master of passion and of sentiment, no dance rhythm can baffle him, he has humour, and his knowledge of the full resources of the modern orchestra makes his scores glow with a wealth of colour that would surely have delighted Berlioz himself. In the latest vein of fancy he gave us the music of *Katrina*, only saved from the worst penalties of popularity by the many difficulties it offered to the brazen amateur; in the vein of sparkling musical comedy he wrote the scores of *Round the Town* and *Old China*, while for more serious work that rose to the highest level of achievement the score of *Monte Cristo* will happily remain in evidence. Whatever the mood of the ballet, he has interpreted it for us until the splendid spectacle has seemed to find a response to his guiding hand.[11]

Wenzel's first score for the Empire was for the ballet *A Dream of Wealth* (December 23, 1889). Its theme was the satisfaction to be derived from charity and benevolence, and its central character, played by Cavallazzi, was an old miser who turns a deaf ear to the appeal of a needy widow. In a vision his eyes are opened by the vanity of wealth, until finally he becomes a reformed character and is filled with the spirit of Christmas. Cavallazzi's dramatic performance was matched by the brilliance of Emma Palladino's technique as the Spirit of the Jewel Casket and by the furious energy which Luigi Albertieri displayed as the Demon Avarice. Seldom had Palladino appeared to greater advantage, and 'two of her steps', recorded the *Era*, 'a wonderfully graceful advance with the arms folded, and a lively "prancing" movement, elicited special applause'.[12] Wilhelm had dressed the *corps de ballet* to represent precious stones, banknotes, and gold and silver coins, and *The Times* summed up by predicting that 'the spectacle [would] . . . appeal to a wider circle than the ordinary clientèle of the theatre'.[13]

Maria Giuri returned to the Empire in April 1890, and on May 20 created the title-rôle in Lanner's *Cécile*. It was 'a light pretty thing'[14] about a young girl who is abducted by a Rajah and finally rescued from his palace by English troops. Giuri, whom Perugini described as 'a dancer of exquisite finish and singularly *élégante* style, as well as a most able mime',[15] was 'delightfully refined and graceful' as Cécile, and Cavallazzi played the Rajah with 'boldly

11 *Sketch*, Apr. 6, 1904. The four scores cited by Bensusan were among the manuscripts which became the property of the Paris Opéra after Wenzel's death at Asnières in Aug. 1925. The other scores preserved there are *La Cour d'Amour*, *Attila*, *A Dream of Wealth*, *Cécile*, *Dolly*, *Orfeo*, *By the Sea*, *Nisita*, *Versailles*, *The Girl I Left Behind Me*, *Under One Flag*, *The Press*, *Alaska*, *Les Papillons*, *Our Crown*, *Vineland*, *The Milliner Duchess* (musical scheme only), and *Papillon d'or* (a later work, dated 1910, made up of fragments from earlier ballets).

12 *Era*, Dec. 28, 1889.

13 *The Times*, Dec. 24, 1889.

14 *Era*, May 24, 1900.

15 Perugini, 280.

dramatic expressiveness'. In spite of the naïvety of the story, the ballet was a distinguished production, thanks in large part to Wilhelm who gave full play to his talent for colour schemes. 'The general impression ... may be described as pink,' wrote the *Era*. 'There is creamy pink in the skirts of the young ladies in the first tableau, and there is also – veiled in gauzy folds which "half conceal, half reveal" the rose-coloured fleshings beneath – pink in the costumes of the Nautch girls of the second tableau.'[16] Wilhelm had set the first scene in the Louis XVI period, and for the scene in the Rajah's palace had devised 'a colour scheme of almost one tone, composed of white and silver and mother-of-pearl'.[17]

After the opera season Palladino returned to the Empire to replace Giuri and was featured in the next novelty, *Dolly* (December 22, 1890). Its *raison d'être* was a *divertissement* of toys, but as *The Times* observed, 'the ballet-master is not content nowadays to be artistic; he must be didactic as well'.[18] So the plot retailed the varying fortunes of a poor toy-maker and a hard-hearted rich merchant who in the course of the action loses his fortune and friends and is reduced to wandering with his family on snow-covered Blackheath until Dolly, the Fairy of the Toys, releases him from his misery. It was an agreeable, but not very original, entertainment. As the toy-maker Cavallazzi gave another distinguished character study, and an unusual touch was provided by the appearance of Aenea, the Flying Fairy.[19] Palladino was in time succeeded in the rôle of Dolly by Maria Giuri, who later shared it with Adelina Rossi.

The next new ballet, *Orfeo* (May 25, 1891), was a work on a much more serious level.[20] Conceived by Wilhelm, who was now gradually imposing himself as the dominant partner in the triumvirate, it ran for many months. Perugini called it 'an impressive example of classic ballet',[21] and it provided Cavallazzi with one of her finest rôles, that of Orfeo. Shortly before this ballet entered the Empire's bill, Gluck's opera had been produced at Covent Garden with Giulia Ravogli, whose rendering of 'Che farò' still rang in the ears of those who had heard her. Cavallazzi, of course, could make no vocal appeal, but thousands flocked to see her and many judged her to be the equal, as an interpreter, of the great contralto. Her acting, wrote one critic, 'became supremely dramatic at the moment where Orfeo ... with a gesture of disdain throws his cloak round Eurydice, and with calm dignity conducts her from Hades'.[22] Playing Eurydice was Ada Vincent. The cast also included Adelina Rossi and Enrico Cecchetti. Cecchetti left the Empire in August 1891, and was replaced by Nicolà Guerra, the future ballet-master of the Paris Opéra, who in turn was to be succeeded, a month later, by Vittorio De Vincenti.

16 *Era*, May 24, 1890.
17 Perugini, 280.
18 *The Times*, Dec. 23, 1890.
19 See note 23 on p. 33.
20 See Appendix G for scenario.
21 Perugini, 281.
22 *Era*, May 30, 1891.

X

The emergence of the up-to-date ballet (1891–97)

In the atmosphere of the music hall, where topicality gave spice to the variety turns, the emergence of the up-to-date ballet was almost inevitable. *The Paris Exhibition* having pointed the way, the formula was repeated on August 31, 1891, when the curtain rose on *By the Sea* to reveal Margate beach almost to the life, thronged with excursionists, bathers, minstrels, costers, children, shrimpers and fisherfolk; only the ozone seemed to be lacking. Wilhelm's costumes for this ballet were a mass of colour, and Katti Lanner had arranged such a variety of striking dances that her one concession to tradition – a *pas seul* for Emma Palladino in conventional ballet costume – appeared rather as a skeleton at a feast alongside the coster dance and the bathing ballet, which, as *The Times* recorded, was 'the most remarkable feature of the performance and the nearest approach to the shocking which an observance of the Lord Chamberlain's rules allows'. Wenzel's music struck just the right note of 'somewhat riotous and irresponsible holiday-making',[1] introducing a number of characteristic melodies such as 'Little Annie Rooney' and 'The Bogie Man'.

Bernard Shaw saw the second edition of this ballet in April 1892, when Maria Giuri – in his opinion 'a really brilliant dancer' – had succeeded Palladino, and he was interested to see that she 'condescended to frank step-dancing in a scene set to national airs, which, however, included one brief variation on Yankee Doodle which the most exclusive pupil of the grand school need not have disdained'.[2]

Nisita, the Christmas ballet, marked a return to the old tradition. Its first performance was announced for December 22, 1891, but that evening London was swathed in one of the worst fogs in its history. It was so thick that the drop curtain could not be seen from the third row of the stalls. The performance had to be cancelled, and the ballet was not given until two days later. Shaw saw this ballet too, which had an Albanian setting and introduced a Revel of the Fairies. He thought that Cavallazzi was 'nobler than ever' in it, while Palladino 'hid her defects and made the most of her qualities with her usual cleverness'. De Vincenti, however, for whom he had a very great admiration, seemed to him out of his element. 'I am afraid,' he wrote sadly,

1 *The Times*, Sep. 1, 1891.

2 Shaw, *Music in London*, II, 69–70.

'he is rather lost in Leicester Square, where the audience, capable of nothing but cartwheels, stare blindly at his finest *entrechats*.'[3]

Bernard Shaw's exacting standards found *Versailles* (May 23, 1892) much more satisfying.[4] The conception of this ballet was originally Wilhelm's, and he set about recreating the splendours of Louis XIV's court with his customary minute attention to detail. He constructed his scenario around the King's passion for Louise de la Vallière, who in the final tableau appears in nun's habit, about to enter a convent. Cavallazzi portrayed the majestic Louis XIV, and the dancers in the cast were headed by Sofia Coppini, Bettina de Sortis and Vittorio De Vincente. There were a number of changes of cast during the course of the ballet's run. Palladino replaced Coppini after the second performance, and was in turn succeeded by Cornalba a week later, while for eight weeks in the summer Enrico Cecchetti took the place of De Vincente.

It was Cavallazzi, not De Vincente, who impressed Shaw. 'The other evening,' he wrote,

> I went to the Empire, where I immediately found myself, to my great delight, up to the neck in pure classicism, siècle de Louis Quatorze. To see Cavallazzi, in the Versailles ballet, walk, sit, and gesticulate, is to learn all that Vestris or Noblet could have taught you as to the technique of doing these things with dignity.
>
> In the stage management too – in the colouring, the costuming, the lighting, in short the stage presentation in the completest sense – an artistic design, an impulse towards brilliancy and grace of effect, is always dominant, whether it is successful or not; and in some scenes it is highly successful. Now is it not odd that at a music hall to which, perhaps, half the audience have come to hear Marie Lloyd sing Twiggy voo, boys, twiggy voo? or to see Mr Derby jump a ten-barred gate, you get real stage art, whereas at the Opera the stage is managed just as a first-rate restaurant is managed, with everything served up punctually in the most expensive style, but with all the art left to the cook (called 'prima donna'), helped by the waiters (otherwise the chorus).
>
> Wagner noticed long ago that the supremacy of the ballet-masters, who are all enthusiasts in the ballet, made it the most completely artistic form of stage representation left to us; and I think that anyone who will compare Versailles at the Empire with Orfeo at Covent Garden from this point of view will see what Wagner was driving at.[5]

Historical romance, as typified by *Versailles*, was a genre after Wilhelm's heart. For the up-to-date ballet, on the other hand, he had little enthusiasm, but he was too conscientious an artist to allow his repugnance to affect his work, as he showed when he designed *Round the Town* (September 26, 1892).[6] This was an up-to-date ballet with a London setting, the five scenes being linked by the character of a schoolmaster showing some of his pupils the sights of the town – Covent Garden market, the Royal Exchange, the Thames Embankment, and lastly, of course, the Empire Theatre itself, which gave

3 Shaw, *Music in London*, II, 69–70.
4 See Appendix G for scenario.
5 Shaw, *Music in London*, II, 177–8.
6 See Appendix G for scenario.

EMPIRE THEATRE
LIGHTED BY

PROGRAMME,

Subject to alteration at

1	March "Ra-Fla-Fla" (*L. Wenzel*) - Orchestra
2	BLACK SWAN TRIO Vocalists.
3	SEVERUS SCHAFFER Juggler.
4	D. J. McCARTHY Comedian.
5	BOISSETS Gymnasts.
6	HENDERSON & STANLEY QUARTETTE.

7 **By the Sea,**

OR, FUN ON THE SANDS.
A Ballet Divertissement, in One Tableau,
By Madame KATTI LANNER.
Music specially composed and incidental Music arranged by Mons. L. WENZEL.
Scenery by T. E. RYAN.
Costumes Designed by WILHELM, and executed by Miss FISHER and Madame AUGUSTE & CIE. Wigs by CLARKSON.

CHARACTERS.

Mr. Tardy .. .. Mr. J. CAZALY
Mr. Sharp .. .. Mr. J RIDLEY
Mr. Jones .. .. Mr. F. ARTELLI
Mrs. Jones .. .. Mr. C. BERTRAM
Mabel, their daughter } a runaway couple .. Miss E. SLACK
Albert, her husband } .. .. Miss R. JOHNSTONE
Antonio, Fiancee of Marietta } An Italian Troupe AND Signor V. de VINCENTI
Ernestine .. .. .. Miss A. VINCENT
Julietta .. .. .. Miss L. VINCENT
Rosina .. .. .. Miss A. VINCENT
Peppino .. .. Mdlle. CORA
Marietta .. .. Mdlle. EMMA PALLADINO

Supported by Misses BANNISTER, CLERC, CURGNICO, HERBERT, KAYGILL, PASTON, SHORROCKS, WATKINS, BARKER, COURTLAND, HIND and TREE, and Messieurs VINCENT, PERKINS, LEWINGTON, F. WHITE and GRIFFITHS.

DANCES.

Dance of Fisher Boys and Shrimp Girls, Corps de Ballet. Entrance of Bathers, the Coryphees. Merry Waltz, by the Children. March and Arrival of Passengers, Coryphees and Corps de Ballet. Variation, Miss A. VINCENT. Entrance of Italian Troupe, Coryphees and Corps de Ballet. Solo Mdlle EMMA PALLADINO. Adagio, Mdlle. EMMA PALLADINO and Signor V. de VINCENTI. Variation, Signor V. de VINCENTI. Variation, Mdlle. EMMA PALLADINO. Tarantelle, Mdlle. EMMA PALLADINO, Signor V. de VINCENTI, Mdlle. CORA, Coryphees, and Corps de Ballet. Galop Tem.ète. Misses E. SLACK and JOHNSTONE, Coryphees, Corps de Ballet, and Children. Scotch Dance, Misses L. and A. VINCENT. Dance Cosmopolite. Mdlle. EMMA PALLADINO. Costermongers, Corps de Ballet. American Minstrels, Corps de Ballet and Mr. PERKINS. Finale Excentrique, Mdlles. EMMA PALLADINO, Miss A. VINCENT and CORA, Misses L. and A. VINCENT, E SLACK and JOHNSTONE, Coryphees, Corps de Ballet and Children.

A. "Ciel et Enfer" (Valse)—*L. Desormes.*
B. "March des 13 Jours"—*E. Spencer.*
C. "Furioso" (Galop)—*A. Corbin.*

GOD SAVE THE QUEEN.

Acting Manager ... C. DUNDA
Stage Manager ... Mr. CHARLE

OF VARIETIES

ELECTRICITY.

Monday, Sept. 28th, 1891, and Every Evening, at 7.50

e discretion of the Management.

8 THE SCHAFFERS Acrobats.

9 Mdme. JUANA Operatic Vocalist.

10 Valse 'Melancolie" (O'Metra) - Orchestra

11 THE MARVELLOUS CRAGGS.

12 "ORFEO,"

A New Mythological Ballet Divertissement in 2 Tableaux.
Designed by WILHELM.
The Ballet invented and produced by Madame KATTI LANNER.
Music Specially Composed by Mons. LEOPOLD WENZEL.

Scenery by TELBIN. Costumes Designed expressly by WILHELM, and executed by Miss FISHER and AUGUSTE & Cie. Wigs by Clarkson. Properties by J. R. MOYNHAM. Limelight by W. KERR. Gas Engineer, FRANK SMITH. Machinist, W. BRUNSKILL. Floral Decorations by GATTI & Co.

CHARACTERS:
MORTALS.

Orfeo ... ... Signorina MALVINA CAVALLAZZI
Eurydice ... ... Miss ADA VINCENT
Melita ... ... Miss L. VINCENT
Malignity ... ... Signor V. de VINCENTI
Hymen ... ... Mdlle. CORA
Pluto ... ... Mr. J. CAZALY
Proserpine ... ... Miss LOUISE ALLEN
AND
The Spirit of Fascination... ... ... Signorina ADELINA ROSSI

A Demon, Miss L. VINCENT; Friends of Orfeo, Misses R. JOHNSTONE and M. PASTON; Pupils of Orfeo, Misses BANNISTER, E. JONES, HERBERT, and KAYGILL; Companions of Eurydice, Misses CLERC, CURONICO, SHORROCKS, and WATKINS; Priest, Demons, People, &c., &c. Supported by Messrs. ARTELLI, BERTRAM, and J. RIDLEY.

1st Tableau.—ARCADIA—A Sacred Grove before the Temple of Hymen.
1. Hymeneal Dance, Miss L. VINCENT, Coryphees, Corps de Ballet, and Children. 2. Variations, Miss L. VINCENT. 3. Idyllic Waltz, Miss L. VINCENT, Coryphees, Corps de Ballet, and Children. 4. Appearance of Hymen, Mdlle. CORA.

2nd Tableau.—HADES—The Realms of Pluto.
Entrance of Pluto's Guards. 2. Revels of the Demons, Miss L. VINCENT, Corps de Ballet, and Gentlemen of the Ballet. 3. Entrance of the Spirit of Fascination, Signorina ADELINA ROSSI. 4. Appearance of Malignity (Solo), Signor V. de VINCENTI. 5. Dance of Proserpine's Guards, Corps de Ballet. 6. Grand Adagio, Signorina ADELINA ROSSI, Signor V. de VINCENTI, Misses L. VINCENT R. JOHNSTONE, M. PASTON, Coryphees, and Corps de Ballet. 7. Variations, Signor V. de VINCENTI. 8. Variations, Signorina ADELINA ROSSI 9. Bacchanale, Signorina ADELINA ROSSI, Signor V. de VINCENTI, Misses L. VINCENT, R. JOHNSTONE, M. PASTON, Coryphees, Corps de Ballet, and Gentlemen of the Ballet. 10. Grand Tableau Finale.

PRICES OF ADMISSION:
Private Boxes, 1 to 3 Guineas. Fauteuils (Numbered and Reserved), 6s.
Box Stalls (Unreserved), 5s. Stalls, 3s. Grand Circle, 3s.
Pit Stalls, 2s. Pit, 1s. Gallery, 6d.
BOX OFFICE OPEN FROM 10 A.M.

ATER
VILSON

Empire Theatre programme, September 28, 1891.

Wilhelm the opportunity of bringing the ballet to a close in a blaze of colourful pageantry with the tableau, 'The Daughters of the British Empire'. Cavallazzi had an unusual rôle as a drunkard who is reformed in the course of the ballet by the schoolmaster, and Willie Warde made such a hit as an 'Oofless Swell'[7] that his part was later expanded by the addition of an eccentric Salvationists' dance, which he performed with Katie Seymour, 'one of the very neatest dancers that ever trod the London boards'.[8]

The Times called the ballet 'a curious production' which attained 'at least the honours of a *succès de curiosité*, though the sombre attire of its modern *personnel* compares unfavourably with the purple and fine linen of the ordinary ballet'.[9] Bernard Shaw was frankly dissatisfied, finding it 'mostly mere drill and topical spectacle', relieved only by the performances of Cavallazzi and Warde. He was saddened to see that De Vincente had 'given up the British public in despair, and now [treated] them to unlimited cartwheels and teetotums instead of to the fine classic dancing he used to give us', and he was bored stiff by the end 'through the spinning-out of the final scenes by mechanical evolutions involving repeats in the music beyond endurance'.[10]

Since the first edition of *Round the Town* ran for eight months, it could not have lacked entertainment value. Arthur Symons, that self-confessed student of frivolity who found an evening at the Empire the most satisfying way of spending his leisure time, knew every moment of the first edition by heart:

> It amuses me sometimes, to sit at the back of the promenade, and, undistracted by my somewhat too agreeably distracting surroundings, to follow, by the sound of the music, every movement of the ballet on the stage, which I see only in my mind's eye. Now, I say to myself, the Volunteers are marching on to the sound of that haunting bit of march music ... Now Miss Elise Clerc, Captain of Volunteers, comes down on her heels with that odd little jerk which brings her into position at the head of her men. Now the swell ladies are dancing to the bootblacks' tune, and the soft hair of that Italian girl who smiles so prettily is flapping up and down on her forehead as it always does. Now Mdlle Cora, in white, circles seriously on her toes in front of the writhing line of Nautch girls. I know just how she will spread out her hands in the conventional bow that she makes so personal, so winning. And now it is the dainty disorder of the Lottie Collins dance, and in my mind's eye I look from face to face along the two lines, resting, perhaps, on a particular oval, out of which two great, serious eyes smile strangely. And now, I know, Miss Lizzie Vincent, with her look of good-humoured ease, is doing that difficult, delightful leaping dance on one foot across the stage; now Miss Ada Vincent, in her white and pink finery - resolute not to smile - stands, with beautiful severity, for England.[11]

The second edition of *Round the Town* contained a new scene in Trafalgar Square, with more up-to-date songs for the shoe-blacks, and more *fin de siècle*

7 'Oofless': slang word meaning temporarily impecunious. Derived from oof, an abbreviated form of the East End (Yiddish) term, ooftish, meaning money.

8 Perugini, 281.

9 *The Times*, Sep. 27, 1892.

10 Shaw, *Music in London*, II, 179.

11 *Sketch*, June 7, 1893.

costumes for the ladies. A grotesque dance by Fred Flexmore and a mild can-can were added, and the last scene was rearranged for two ballerinas - the French Marie Savigny, and the Italian Felicita Carozzi, who, to Symons's eyes, had the defects without the qualities of Cerale.

Luigia Cerale was an Italian ballerina who a short while before had created the title-rôle in Lanner's *Katrina* (January 20, 1893). This inconsequential *divertissement* was introduced by a short mime scene in which a young student - played by Cavallazzi - was shown falling asleep over his books and dreaming that his cat is transformed into a mischievous girl whom he chases out of the window and over the rooftops. The second scene was a *divertissement* set in the Kingdom of Cats, with a décor invented by Karl Lautenschläger, in which skilful use was made of glass and electric light. Although Cerale created an excellent impression with her strong technique, her engagement was brief, and at the end of March Emma Palladino returned to the Empire and took her place.

With George Edwardes and Augustus Harris on the Board of Directors, it was only to be expected that the Empire would adopt a policy for its ballets that paralleled trends on the London stage generally. Katti Lanner's next ballet, *The Girl I Left Behind Me* (September 27, 1893), was a study in the kind of realism which Harris was producing at Drury Lane, and merely by the addition of dialogue it might have become a typical Drury Lane drama of the period. It told the story of a young man who is ruined on the turf and enlists in a Highland regiment which is on the point of sailing for Burma. His fiancée, braving her father's anger, vows to be true to him and rejects the advances of the villain who has been responsible for the hero's downfall. In Burma the young soldier is awarded the Victoria Cross, and is finally forgiven by the heroine's father. With 'big guns going off behind the scenes, big horses prancing about in front, fire-escapes, sea-sickness, virtuous workmen, and vicious baronets',[12] the ballet had every ingredient of realistic drama. The scenes at the Epsom races and of the regiment's embarkation were such that 'only such a daring *metteur-en-scène* as Sir Augustus Harris [had] hitherto attempted',[13] and contrasted strongly with the ballet's more conventional moments - a vision scene, and the Burmese scenes at the end, on which Wilhelm lavished his brilliant palette:

> Colours clash like discords, resolve into startling and satisfying harmonies of tone; violet, maize, red, green, and gold, with a rim of tin and tinsel, gold and silver, in the trotting children, like little heathen idols. Banners, all flowers, wave in the air, advance, retreat, like a moving forest of feathery trees. It is a carnival of colour, of movement, of gaiety. Lines flow and undulate, curving into circles, become rigid, and cross and re-cross in file, melt into cunning caprices, and twine into exquisite arabesques.[14]

12 *Sketch*, Oct. 4, 1893.
13 *The Times*, Sep. 28, 1893.
14 *Sketch*, Oct. 4, 1893.

The leading rôles of the girl and the young hero were played by Ada Vincent and May Paston with typical British restraint, while Cavallazzi gave a more expansive portrayal of the villain. The new ballerina, Héva Sarcy, who danced as the Spirit of Gambling in the dream scene, was 'somewhat inclined also to a certain kind of exaggeration in movement', but Katie Seymour, in the rôle of the heroine's maid, danced with 'sheer effervescent gaiety',[15] flitting across the stage like a bird.

Héva Sarcy did not remain long at the Empire, being replaced in November by Carlotta Brianza. The following April saw another change of cast, when Isabella Brambilla arrived to make her English début. Brambilla, a Milan-trained ballerina with triumphs to her credit in Bucharest and Naples, was allowed to insert a *pas* from her personal repertory into the last act and obtained a decided success. She was featured shortly afterwards in a new ballet by Lanner, *La Frolique* (May 21, 1894).[16] Leopold Wenzel had left the Empire, temporarily as it was to turn out, and the score for this ballet was composed by Ernest Ford, whose music was found pleasing enough, although lacking distinction in its dance rhythms.[17] There was little plot in this gay and lively little work, which opened in a *jardin publique* and closed in a law court, where a dancer who has dared to perform the forbidden *chahut* is acquitted and finally has all the legal luminaries dancing with her. By all accounts the *chahut* in this ballet was a very innocent version of that dance. Florence Levey played La Frolique, and Isabella Brambilla and Vittorio De Vincenti were the classical dancers, while a part was also found for the Spanish dancer, Candida, who performed a 'haughty and defiant' dance with 'curious pawing and prancing movements and strokes at the ground'.[18]

Another up-to-date *divertissement* by Lanner followed, *On Brighton Pier* (October 10, 1894), which again had a score by Ford that was mainly a characterless setting of popular melodies. In a realistic scene representing the well known sea-side resort, troops of nursemaids, lady cyclists and schoolchildren filled the stage. Two threads of human interest were woven into the action: Cavallazzi was a mother who discovers her long-lost daughter appearing in a minstrel troupe, while the love problem of a young American girl provided the excuse for a vision scene. This introduced yet another newly-engaged ballerina, Bice Porro, whom Symons considered to be, 'in company with Legnani, the most charming and accomplished dancer that we have had in London for a long time'. She had, he continued, 'several graceful and intricate dances in the dazzling scene of the vision; a veritable queen of sirens, she floats and curves, and is enticing and elusive, among a miraculous group of sea-nymphs, who, with their glowing and fainting colours, from the palest

15 *Sketch*, Oct. 4, 1893.

16 This ballet was possibly inspired by Katti Lanner's burlesque ballet, *Der Cancan vor dem Tribunal*, produced at the Stadt-Theater, Hamburg, on Oct. 15, 1865.

17 Ernest Ford (1858–1919) was a pupil of Edouard Lalo, composer of the ballet, *Namouna*, and had conducted the orchestra at the first performance of Sullivan's opera, *Ivanhoe*.

18 *Sketch*, May 30, 1894.

of greens to the warmest of reds, leap suddenly, in a sort of watery Inferno, into the frivolous, flirting worldliness of Brighton'.[19]

One of the highlights in this ballet was Will Bishop's masher dance. Bishop, who had recently joined the Empire and was to remain a stalwart member of its company for many years, was the very antithesis of a classical dancer. Coming from an old theatrical family, he had been taken under the wing of Tom Ward, the 'champion dancer of the world', with whom, as a boy, he had toured the country music halls, giving exhibitions of the various styles of clog-dancing. He thus represented a typically English tradition of the dance.

Early in 1895 the Empire engaged Elena Cornalba, who danced in the year's only ballet creation, *Faust* (May 6, 1895).[20] Wilhelm, whose influence presaged a return to a more traditional policy, not only designed the costumes, but wrote the scenario and was responsible for the *mise-en-scène*. Credit for the score was shared by Meyer Lutz, who composed the first two scenes, and Ford, who wrote the rest; Joseph Harker and Glendenning collaborated with Karl Lautenschläger in producing the scenery; and Katti Lanner arranged the dances. Goethe's story was skilfully arranged, the ballet being, in the opinion of *The Times*, 'as praiseworthy from the dramatic point of view as . . . from that of effective stage grouping and elaborate dancing'.[21]

It closed with a most effective apotheosis, in which Marguerite was seen, clad all in white, standing on a golden staircase, at the head of which were groups of angels. To reach their lofty position the girls who were cast as the angels had to climb a steep ladder back-stage, and the sight of them doing so moved a poet to write some verses, which he entitled 'An Earthly Paradise', and which were published in the *Sketch* over the initials J.M.B.:

A crystal stair, and in the air
  The angels hover round,
With tapering wings; their presence brings
  A sense of peace profound.
The music rises soft and low
The while they soar aloft, as though
  They ne'er had touched the ground.

There's Marguerite, and at her feet
  Poor Faust repentant lies,
While, far above, each angel-love
  Looks down with pitying eyes.
So innocent and pink each elf,
That one would almost think oneself
  Transported to the skies.

19 *Sketch*, Oct. 17, 1894.
20 See Appendix G for scenario.
21 *The Times*, May 7, 1895.

It's hard to climb at any time,
For Heaven is, oh, so high!
And then the road is never broad,
It often makes one sigh.
Behind the scenes, so steep the stairs
The angels cannot keep in pairs
In mounting to the sky.

Nor long they soar, it soon is o'er,
The curtain tumbles down;
And in a trice the paradise
Has vanished - harp and crown;
No more the angels deck the sky -
Those angels hail from Peckham Rye,
From Bow or Kentish Town.[22]

In the rôle of Faust, Cavallazzi gave an impressive performance, and Ada Vincent, though she had little to do, made a charming Margaret. Francesca Zanfretta, a newcomer to the Empire whom many Londoners remembered from her appearance a few years before in the mime play, *L'Enfant prodigue*,[23] was a 'fascinating' Mephistopheles, giving the impression of 'a snake-like spirit of evil'.[24] Cornalba played no rôle herself, but appeared merely to dance classical *pas*, which formed a strong contrast to the eccentric dance performed by Will Bishop.

The Empire's long search for a permanent ballerina among the many gifted Italians it had engaged had so far proved fruitless, and the management now turned its attention to a different quarter. On November 4, 1895, Lydia Nelidova, a Moscow ballerina, took over Cornalba's part in *Faust* with considerable success. Her light, graceful movements were much appreciated, as also were her *ports de bras*, which were found to be more flowing than those of the Italians. She could only remain in London for a short while and all too soon had to be replaced. She was succeeded, not by an Italian, but by a German ballerina, Martha Irmler, who had had considerable success in New York, where she had danced for several years.

It was for Irmler that Katti Lanner arranged the *divertissement*, *La Danse* (January 25, 1896). In a series of numbers illustrating the history of the dance from Sallé to Kate Vaughan, Irmler appeared as Taglioni in a representation of the famous *Pas de Quatre*. 'However, the true value of *La Danse*,' according

22 *Sketch*, Jan. 1, 1896. Might the author be J. M. Barrie, who was writing verse of a mediocre quality at the time? His tribute to R. L. Stevenson had appeared in 1895, and *Jane Annie* not long before that. Barrie has several associations with the ballet. His novel, *My Lady Nicotine*, inspired Lucia Cormani's ballet of the same name, produced at the Alhambra in 1905, and he was the author of a play called *The Truth about the Russian Dancers*, produced at the Coliseum in 1920 with Tamara Karsavina. He also wrote the scenario for *The Origin of Harlequin*, which Edouard Espinosa produced at a charity performance in 1917.

23 See note 17 on p. 70

24 *Sketch*, May 15, 1895.

to one critic, '[lay] in the concerted pieces admirably performed by the splendidly dressed ladies of the ballet. It is noteworthy,' he remarked, 'that during the past few years the standard of dancing of the rank-and-file has wonderfully improved; their work used to be a weak point at the Empire, and now that is altogether changed. I wonder whether men could be taught to do the complicated manoeuvres which seem to give so little trouble to the ladies. I doubt.'[25]

The year 1896 marked the welcome return as musical director of Leopold Wenzel, who proved how invaluable he was by his score for *Monte Cristo* (October 26, 1896).[26] His music, wrote Bensusan, was 'like a grand opera score, and no movement on the stage is without its accompaniment in the orchestra'. *Monte Cristo*, which marked the resumption of the Lanner-Wilhelm-Wenzel partnership, was the most outstanding success the Empire had so far achieved. In it, Bensusan declared, 'ballet attains the highest point of development ... It marks all that perfect taste, extraordinary talent, and unlimited expenditure can accomplish.' Bensusan's own words give a vivid description of the beauties of this work:

> There is no need to deal with the scenario; the story is too well known. It is more pleasant to dwell upon the most delightful details of the performance. The wedding procession of Dantès and Mercedes is the gem of the first tableau, a procession of tiny bridesmaids carrying boughs of orange-trees, and tripping to some of the sweetest music that ever flowed from Wenzel's fluent pen. The second scene, in the cells of the Château d'If, gives Madame Cavallazzi such an opportunity as seldom comes to an actress, and is never more brilliantly taken. Two scenes later, Haydée, in the pretty person of Ada Vincent, strikes a sweet tremulous note in the great human symphony; and then comes the *divertissement*, a dream of wealth with animated precious stones and metals. Imagine for a moment a luminous vision of rubies, sapphires, and emeralds, chrysoprases, pearls, amethysts, turquoises, and opals, with diamonds to complete the picture. And, when these living jewels move towards the front, strange gleams of electric colour in harmony with their own break into shining flowers above, as though some charm of melody or movement had inspired the very genius of light. Finally, the many jewels move together in long lines of variegated colour to the suggestion of a *valse* that flatters the ears, and the very apotheosis of *divertissement* is reached in a climax of glowing pearls and radiant diamonds.
>
> The interval of eight minutes offends nobody; it is a relief ... Before any feeling of impatience can arise, the music is resumed, the curtain rises upon the grounds of Monte Cristo's château, where his guests are dancing in the rich light of early evening; dancing in the glow of sunset under the flowering chestnut-trees, amid the scent and colouring of lilac-blossoms; dancing to the subtle melody of a gavotte with whose strains the plaint of a fountain mingles delightfully. It is a triumph of stage-management. There is a moment of passion and anger when Dantès reveals his identity, a sense of one predominant personality at whose side all others fall to insignificance, and a final touch of something akin to sadness as the Count and his love, a slave no longer, pass through the ranks of the guests and pause for a brief

25 *Sketch*, Feb. 5, 1896.

26 See Appendix G for scenario.

> moment in the attitude of benediction on the steps leading to the château. There is all the strength of dignity and unconventionality in this exit, with which the ballet ends.[27]

Never was Cavallazzi more magnificent than in her interpretation of the rôle of Dantès. She dominated the ballet, acting with heart, brain and body. 'The ballet stage,' declared Bensusan, 'has never seen a better performance than hers.'[28] It 'thrilled the house through and through; it was tragedy, strong, intense and virile'.[29]

Monte Cristo drew great crowds to the Empire in the year of Queen Victoria's Diamond Jubilee, which was celebrated by a *divertissement d'occasion* by Katti Lanner, *Under One Flag* (June 21, 1897). This patriotic ballet, a pageant of the British Empire at its height, of course took pride of place at the end of the programme, and *Monte Cristo* had to be curtailed. One further claim to fame, however, was still in store for *Monte Cristo*, for in the darkening days of November one of its scenes was to be chosen as the framework for the London début of Adeline Genée, the ballerina whose appearance was to bring to an end at long last the Empire's quest for a star of its own.

27 *Sketch*, Nov. 4, 1896. Another important description of this ballet is to be found in 'The Art Movement, Costume Designing for the Ballet', by C. Wilhelm in *Magazine of Art*, 1897, pp. 162–4.
28 *Sketch*, Nov. 4, 1896.
29 *Sketch*, Feb. 15, 1899.

XI

The Genée years (1897–1908)

There was a certain amount of luck, allied with a measure of justice, in the fact that when Adeline Genée came to London, it was to dance at the Empire. For the Empire had been the first to notice this young dancer, and had offered her a short engagement during the Diamond Jubilee celebrations. The director of the Hoftheater in Munich, where she was then appearing, was willing to grant her three months' leave so that she could accept the Empire's offer, but only on condition that she remained at Munich as prima ballerina for a further five years. This her uncle and guardian, Alexander Genée, would not allow and the negotiations came to naught. Alfred Moul, the manager of the Alhambra Theatre, was the next to approach her. The terms he offered were very tempting, but at the last moment he had the misfortune to offend the dancer's very touchy guardian. The way then became clear for the Empire to renew its approach. The moment was propitious, for not only had Alexander Genée's desire to arrange a London engagement for his niece been whetted by these two failures, but the Empire's second offer arrived when the young ballerina was uncommitted.

Adeline Genée came to London with an engagement for only six weeks, but she was to stay for ten years, becoming one of the foremost and most popular figures of the Edwardian theatre. She was to enable the Empire to acquire a prestige that outshone that of the Alhambra, while her own achievement went far beyond filling the houses. She was to contribute very largely towards removing the social stigma that clung to the dancer's profession, and thus she helped to pave the way for that great awakening of interest in ballet as a serious art which was to follow later in the twentieth century. During her long spell at the Empire she built up a reputation that justly placed her among the great ballerinas of all time. She became a star of a magnitude to which no other dancer in London had been able to aspire since the days of Taglioni, Elssler and Cerrito sixty years before, and although the artistic quality of the ballets she appeared in did not approach the high level of the productions which Diaghilev was to bring to London, her talents were so outstanding that the great Russian impresario wished, though in vain, to attach her to his company.

Adeline Genée was not quite twenty when she made her début at the Empire Theatre in the Treasure Island scene from *Monte Cristo* on November 22, 1897, but she had much more experience behind her than her youthful appearance suggested. She had been dancing with her uncle's own company ever since she was a child, and more recently had held the position of prima ballerina at the opera houses of Berlin and Munich. The directors of the Empire were delighted by her success on their stage, and having extended her contract, they presented her in a new ballet, *The Press*, on February 14, 1898. This was a conception of Wilhelm's, a spectacular ballet rather of the type which the Italian ballet-master Luigi Manzotti had been producing a decade or so before. Its theme was the development of the newspaper press, and after a series of scenes in which Caxton and Edward IV were represented, the stage was given over to dances, arranged by Katti Lanner, in which the company was dressed to represent the papers and magazines of the day.

On October 12 of the same year Genée further consolidated her position when she took the purely dancing rôle of Fairy Good Fortune in Katti Lanner's next ballet, *Alaska*. Suggested by the Klondike gold rush, the ridiculous plot was redeemed by the splendour of the ballet's setting. After a mime scene depicting a quarrel between two gold-seekers - one played by Cavallazzi, whose last rôle this was - the spectacle itself opened with the appearance of

> the snow-fairies, an event which gives occasion for a most auspicious display of the Aurora Borealis, and a dance. This scene is extremely attractive, the white diaphanous garments of the dancers being illumined in the prettiest way by electric glow lamps; and a finishing touch being put to the composition by the sudden blaze of a thousand stars in the sky. It is, however, but a curtain raiser for the next scene, which is a most dazzling arrangement in tones of gold. The background of ice and snow gives place to a glowing scene from which pour all the resources of the Empire and of Madame Katti Lanner in dazzling variety of costumes of gold, brightened and illumined by gold nuggets, through which shine the rays of electric glow lamps. The effect is indescribably dazzling and gorgeous; and if the real Klondike had half such solid attractions there are but few who would not go to seek it.[1]

Dazzling was obviously the word for the spectacle, but the real attraction of the ballet in the eyes of many connoisseurs was the dancing of Adeline Genée.

The management had still not decided whether to engage her as the Empire's permanent star, and for a few weeks in the beginning of 1899 they brought over Cecilia Cerri to alternate with her in *Alaska*. The contest was soon decided, beyond all doubt, in Genée's favour, and from that moment until her departure from the Empire she shared her supremacy with no one. When Arnold Bennett visited the Empire on a winter evening to see *Alaska* he chanced upon one of the nights when Cerri was appearing, and it was therefore the mature Italian ballerina and not the young Danish star of whom he wrote in his Journal:

> The hypnotised audience crowded tier above tier of the dark theatre, held itself strained and intent in its anxiety not to miss one gyration, one least movement, of the great dancer - that dancer who had enslaved not only New York and St Petersburg but Paris itself. Swaying incorporeal, as it were within a fluent dazzling envelope of endless drapery, she revealed to them new and more disturbing visions of beauty in the union of colour and motion. She hid herself in a labyrinth of curves

1 *Daily Graphic*, Oct. 14, 1898.

which was also a tremor of strange tints, a tantalising veil, a mist of iridescent light. Gradually her form emerged from the riddle, triumphant, provocative, and for an instant she rested like an incredible living jewel in the deep gloom of the stage. Then she was blotted out, and the defeated eye sought in vain to penetrate the blackness where but now she had been . . .

It was a marvellous and enchanting performance. Even the glare of the electric clusters and the gross plush of the descending curtain could not rob us all at once of the sense of far-off immaterial things which it had evoked in our hearts. We applauded with fury, with frenzy; we besieged the floor with sticks and heels, and clapped till our arms ached . . . At length she came before the footlights, and bowed and smiled and kissed her hands. We could see she was a woman of thirty or more, rather short, not beautiful. But what dominion in the face, what assurance of supreme power! It was the face of one surfeited with adoration, cloyed with praise.

While she was humouring us with her fatigued imperial smiles, I happened to look at a glazed door separating the auditorium from the corridor. There, pressed against the glass, was another face, the face of a barmaid, who, drawn from her counter by the rumour of this wonderful novelty, had crept down to get a glimpse of the star's triumph.

Of course I was struck by the obvious contrast between these two creatures. In a moment the barmaid had departed, but the wistfulness of her gaze remained with me as I listened to legends of the dancer – her whims, her diamonds, her extravagances, her tyrannies, her wealth. I could not banish that pale face; I could not withhold it from my sentimental pity.

Later I went up into the immense gold refectory. Entrenched behind a magnificent counter of carved cedar flanked on either side by mirrors and the neat appearance of bottles and bon bons, the barmaid stood negligently at ease, her cheek resting in the palm of one small hand as she leaned on the counter. I noticed that she had the feeble prettiness, the voluptuous figure, the tight black bodice inexorably demanded of barmaids, In front of her were three rakish youths whom I guessed to be of the fringe of journalism and the stage. They talked low to her as they sipped their liqueurs, frankly enjoying this brief intimacy. As for her, confident of her charms, she was distantly gracious; she offered a smile with a full sense of its value; she permitted; she endured. These youths were to understand that such adulation was to her an everyday affair.

In the accustomed exercise of assured power her face had lost its wistfulness, it was the satiated face of the dancer over again, and so I ventured quietly to withdraw my sentimental pity.[2]

So far Genée had been featured only as a classical ballerina, but the Empire public was to be given a foretaste of her versatility on May 8, 1899, when she appeared in the rôle of Lizette, a French maid, in *Round the Town Again*. This marked a return to the up-to-date type of ballet, a note of topicality being

2 *Journals of Arnold Bennett*, I, 88–90. A footnote, appended after Bennett's death by his editor, purports to identify the dancer as Genée, but the description obviously fits the more mature Cerri. If Bennett visited the Empire on the date of the entry, Saturday, Jan. 28, 1899, he would have seen Cerri, but the entry for the previous day suggests that he may have been writing of an earlier visit, a few days before, when, as he describes, he and three friends went home on top of an omnibus in a gale. Reference to the weather reports fixes their visit beyond any doubt as having taken place on Saturday, Jan. 21, when the weather was squally and rainy with southerly and south-westerly gales. Cerri was also dancing on that evening.

struck at the very rise of the curtain when the interior of Charing Cross Station came into view, with troops arriving from the recently reconquered Sudan. Ensuing scenes took the audience to Bond Street, Hyde Park, and finally to a brilliant masked ball at Covent Garden. To add realism, guardsmen from Wellington Barracks were used to augment the *corps de ballet*, and eight dancers who were cast as drummer boys were given lessons beforehand by Pat Murray, the drummer of the Empire orchestra. Genée had her classical *variation* at the end of the ballet, but in earlier scenes she appeared in high-heeled shoes. She was, wrote the *Era*, 'very arch and lively, and her *pas seuls* both in "up-to-date" attire and in short skirts [were] positively bewitching in their finish and grace'.[3] For the music, Wenzel had put together a selection from various well known musical comedies, and Katti Lanner had arranged a variety of dances introducing some of her child pupils in the Hyde Park scene. The ballet proved so popular that a new edition was produced in January 1900, and was not taken off until the two editions together had run for well over a year.

The next new ballet, *Sea-side*, did not enter the programme until September 10, 1900. This was another up-to-date work, inspired by the success of the earlier ballet, *By the Sea*. With Bexhill replacing Margate as the setting, the new ballet had little plot to speak of, but Will Bishop contributed a brilliant comic character study as a detective, while Genée once again delighted the audience with a series of charming dances. She was now assuming greater authority in the theatre, and it was during the rehearsals of this ballet that she had the temerity to cross swords with the redoubtable Wenzel over the selection of music for her variation. In the battle of wills that followed it was the dancer who had her way in the end.

The Empire's *corps de ballet* was usually used only in the ballets, but on November 29, 1900, it was featured in an effective sketch entitled *The Phantom Guards*, which *The Times* described as

> really in the nature of a ballet, in which some new and striking effects are obtained; and if these are not quite as 'creepy' as the mind is prepared to expect, they are certainly pretty and very ingeniously arranged. With proper regard for ghostly convention, the appearance of the 'Phantom Guards' is heralded by the footlights turning blue; and while the orchestra plays 'soft music' in a minor key, the curtain is lifted upon a pitch-black stage. From the darkness, and in the far distance, presently arises a line of white motionless figures illuminated with a special radiance. When they have come to full view, the figures advance slowly, and then pass downwards out of sight. Again they rise, and again advance and disappear, still apparently in the distance; but, at the next moment, they are suddenly 'discovered' in the front of the stage. It is only distance which has lent terror to the view, however, for the 'Phantom Guards' are now recognisable as ladies of the ballet, clad in white from head to foot, the costumes, which are extremely effective, being after the pattern of a military uniform of the last century. As though confessing that disguise is no longer possible, the Captain of the Guards, resplendent in gold lace, and quite innocent

3 *Era*, May 13, 1899.

32 The Empire Theatre in 1895. PHOTO: George Newnes Ltd.

33 The interior of the Empire Theatre in 1887.

34 LEFT: C. Wilhelm.

35 BELOW: Katti Lanner and some of her pupils, in their costumes for her *Faust* (1895). PHOTO: Martin & Sallnow. (*Sketch*, March 13, 1901)

36 RIGHT ABOVE: Lanner's *Orfeo* (1891). An impression of Scene II by C. Wilhelm.

37 RIGHT BELOW: Lanner's *Versailles* (1892), with Malvina Cavallazzi as the King and Ada Vincent as Louise de la Vallière (inset: Leopold Wenzel). Drawing by J. Jellicoe. (*Illustrated Sporting and Dramatic News*, June 4, 1892)

M. L. WENZEL

TABLEAU 3.

38 Left: Malvina Cavallazzi as Edmond Dantès in Lanner's *Monte Cristo* (1896). Photo: Alfred Ellis. (*Sketch*, February 15, 1899)

39 Right: Francesca Zanfretta in Lanner's *Round the Town Again* (1899). Photo: Alfred Ellis & Walery. (*Sketch*, February 28, 1900)

40 Lanner's *Round the Town* (1892). An artist's sketches. (*Illustrated Sporting and Dramatic News*, October 15, 1892)

41 'Facing the House'. An impression of a ballet of the 1890s, as seen from the back of the stage. (*Sketch*, August 15, 1894)

42 Left: Martha Irmler as Taglioni in Lanner's 'Pas de Quatre' section of *La Danse*. Photo: Alfred Ellis. (*Sketch*, May 6, 1896)

43 Below: Antonietta Ferrero. (*Tatler*, November 12, 1902)

44 Above: Lanner's *Monte Cristo* (1896), Scene I.

45 Right: Adeline Genée in Lanner's *Alaska* (1898).

46 Lanner's *Sea-Side* (1900). Sketches by Sydney Higham. (*Daily Graphic*, September 13, 1900)

47 ABOVE: Adeline Genée in Lanner's *Old China* (1907).

48 LEFT: Adeline Genée in Lanner's *The Milliner Duchess* (1903). PHOTO: Hana.

49 Left: Adeline Genée in Lanner's *High Jinks* (1904). Photo: Hana.

50 Right: Adeline Genée and Dorothy Craske in Farren and Genée's *Cinderella* (1906). Photo: Campbell & Gray.

51 Alexander Genée's *Coppélia* (1908), Act I, with Adeline Genée as Swanilda and Dorothy Craske as Frantz. PHOTO: Dover Street Studios.

52 Adeline Genée's return to the Empire Theatre in 1908. Sketches by Ralph Cleaver. (*Daily Graphic*, June 12, 1908)

53 Lanner's *The Debutante* (1906), Scene I, with Dorothy Craske and Bessie Trevissick. PHOTO: Dover Street Studios.

54 Lanner's *The Debutante* (1906), Scene III, with Fred Farren as the Sultan and Adeline Genée in the ballet within the ballet. PHOTO: Dover Street Studios.

55 Right: Lydia Kyasht in Farren's *A Day in Paris* (1908). Photo: Alfred Ellis & Walery.

56 Left: Phyllis Bedells in Farren's *A Day in Paris* (1908). Photo: Alfred Ellis & Walery.

57 Left above: Alexander Genée's *Roberto il Diavolo* (1909), with Adeline Genée and Noel Fleming (tenor). Photo: Alfred Ellis & Walery.

58 Left below: Lydia Kyasht and Fred Farren in *The Faun* (1910). Photo: Alfred Ellis & Walery. (*Illustrated London News*, October 29, 1910)

59 Above: Farren's *Sylvia* (1910), with Fred Farren as Pan, Lydia Kyasht as Sylvia and Unity More as Amyntas. Photo: Alfred Ellis & Walery. (*Play Pictorial*, 1910, No. 109)

60 Right: Phyllis Bedells in Farren's *Ship Ahoy!* (1910). Photo: Alfred Ellis & Walery.

61 Espinosa's *The Dancing Master* (1914), with Edouard Espinosa and Phyllis Bedells (centre).

62 Farren's *The Vine* (1915), with Carlotta Mossetti (wearing animal skin), Phyllis Bedells (holding grapes) and four coryphées.

> of any phantasmal suggestion, now walks on from the wings and puts her company through a series of elaborate evolutions, beguiled with song. Against the impenetrable darkness of the stage, the intricate manoeuvring of the white figures gives a very pretty effect, which is cleverly enhanced by the sudden illumination of tiny electric lamps arranged in rows down the tunics and around the hats of the Guards.[4]

A shift in the Empire's policy became evident with the next creation, *Les Papillons* (March 18, 1901). Now that Wilhelm, who had never looked on the up-to-date ballet with much favour, was becoming the predominant figure in the Empire's ballet-making team, and Genée was establishing herself more and more as a popular star, a return to a more conventional type of ballet was inevitable. Katti Lanner had staged a ballet with the same title in America and at Her Majesty's Theatre in London during the eighteen-seventies, but the Empire production was an original work rather than a revival, for both Wilhelm's scenario and Wenzel's score were new. The plot was very slight, the ballet's main interest centring on the dances in the Butterflyland scene, in which Genée was very prominently featured. Wenzel enjoyed a special success. 'He has entered into the spirit of the fairy-story so completely,' wrote the *Illustrated London News*, 'that bees, flower-elves, butterflies, glow-worms, and the rest of the fanciful creation are as effectively treated in the orchestra as on the stage; the story of fairy-land is set to music that maintains the illusion from start to finish; Mme Katti Lanner's daintiest devices never fail to find support. M. Wenzel is without doubt the greatest living master of ballet-music.'[5]

After spending many hours at the Natural History Museum in South Kensington, Wilhelm had produced for this ballet a portfolio of costume designs that would have satisfied even the most fastidious lepidopterist, but to some critics this preoccupation with accuracy in every detail highlighted a common artistic fault in many of the Empire's ballets of this time: a lack of simplicity and breadth in their treatment. Professor Selwyn Image pointed this out in an article he wrote for the *Saturday Review*, noting it as a facet of a trend that was infiltrating into every branch of theatrical art:

> Speaking of its various scenes in general, one is not impressed in them by any splendour or even interesting effect of imaginative colour, but only of a shifting, distracting, and really ineffective jumble of colours. On the whole and throughout there is far too great a crowd of performers all on the stage at once, restlessly interweaving themselves, damaging one another's effectiveness, overdazzling and perplexing the spectator to distraction ... These lepidopterous costumes are altogether over-elaborated and frittered away in insignificant, worrying details ...
>
> Simplicity and grace, genuine effects of carefully studied imaginative colour, and room for the dancers to exhibit their delightful art easily, room in a word to dance, not merely to run about and form figures – that is what made these two ballets [*Les Saisons* and *The Swans*, two early Alhambra ballets he had been referring to] so delightful, and keeps the memory of them fresh. What has come to us that we are

4 *The Times*, Dec. 1, 1900.

5 *Illustrated London News*, Mar. 23, 1901.

no longer given such performances? That we are all gone crazy after crowds, and jumble, and properties, and frippery? . . .

How much we have suffered ever since [Sir Augustus Harris's] dictatorship in the matter of over-elaboration on our boards, of mere monstrosities in scenery and costume and grouping and properties fit only to set a vulgar and jaded audience agape with stupid wonderment! . . . Why should [the Empire management] not try their skilled and patient hands on a ballet that sought not to amaze us by lavishness but to enchant us by pure grace and a kind of classical simplicity?[6]

This was a voice crying out from the wilderness, and on November 6, 1901, the Empire, knowing well what pleased its public, presented a new production, *Old China*, for which Wilhelm had turned his energies to making an exhaustive study of old porcelain. Some china pieces come to life as the mantelpiece clock strikes midnight, and in the space of a brief hour a Chelsea beau flirts with a pretty Dresden shepherdess in a Watteau-like Arcadia. To heighten the effect of the scene, Wilhelm had arranged for the stage to be painted a delicate shade of pink, orders being given to cover it with a cloth to preserve its colour whenever the ballet was not being performed. 'It is not in Dresden china to be humorous or passionate or deeply racked by human distresses,' wrote G. E. Morrison;

its only business is to be pretty. And nothing prettier than *Old China* has ever been seen . . . The dresses . . . have the pure unobtrusive hues, patient yet persevering, that come only with the collaboration of time. There is hardly a design that does not catch something of a legendary charm. So mindful did one become of these fragile remembrancers of the past that when, their dancing done, they herded close together one trembled for their slender crooks, their brittle brocades.[7]

It was altogether an appropriate vehicle for a dancer with such innate delicacy and perfection of style as Adeline Genée, who was seen for the first time with a male dancer - Amedeo Santini - partnering her in an *adage*.

In the summer of Coronation year, 1902, on May 28, a new *divertissement* called *Our Crown* was produced to mark the occasion by the tried team of Wilhelm, Lanner and Wenzel. The first part consisted of twelve tableaux. Five of these showed events in the reigns of the former King Edwards: Edward I presenting his son, the future Edward II, to the people of Wales at Caernarvon Castle; Edward III at the siege of Calais; Edward IV visiting Caxton; Edward V and his little brother imprisoned in the Tower; and Edward VI founding the Bluecoat School. For this last tableau Wenzel used some songs and carols of the period which he had unearthed in the British Museum. Then followed a scene showing the Messenger of Peace (Genée) summoning the Colonies to contribute their resources to fashion a new Imperial Crown for Edward VII, and the remainder of the ballet was devoted to these contributions: gold from Australia, rubies from Burma, sapphires from India, pearls from Ceylon, diamonds from Cape Colony, and ermine from Canada, culminating in a brilliant blaze of colour with a coronation

6 *Saturday Review*, Apr. 13, 1901.

7 *Morning Post*, Nov. 7, 1901.

festival, 'The Roses of England'. This last scene afforded Wilhelm the opportunity to work out an impressive colour scheme ranging from the palest pink to the deepest damask, with all the shades perfectly balanced. After Genée had danced her variation she was joined by forty dancers of the *corps de ballet* in a grand adagio. Then, to a stirring trumpet march, the ballet closed with a procession of Coronation officials – gold and silver sticks-in-waiting, beef-eaters, choristers, heralds – who set the final seal on of the brilliant spectacle.

A few months later Genée was granted a few weeks' leave of absence to appear as guest artist at the Royal Theatre, Copenhagen, and in her absence her place at the Empire was temporarily filled by Antonietta Ferrero, a native of Turin who had enjoyed considerable success in Italy. The London public's affection for Genée, however, was by now so deeply rooted that Ferrero's reception was apparently, to her mind, rather disappointing. 'Mlle Ferrero,' wrote the *Tatler*, 'does not understand English, and thinks that it is just as well, for she laughingly remarks that London critics do not regard dancing as such an important branch of stage art as do their *confrères* of France and Italy.'[8]

The Empire was in fact complacently confident in possessing Genée as its ballerina, and the Directors certainly felt no qualms when another dancer, quite as great in her very different sphere, was allowed to slip through their fingers. It was the custom to hold a band rehearsal every Monday, when new turns were rehearsed and auditions held, and at one of these at about this time a striking American girl came on to dance in a loose pink costume and bare feet. She was not engaged, but one dancer in the Empire company was sufficiently impressed to recognise the girl's portrait on posters when she paid a visit to Germany some time later. She then learnt that her name was Isadora Duncan.[9]

When Genée returned to the Empire, a new ballet on a modern theme, *The Milliner Duchess*, went into rehearsal without delay, and was given its first performance on January 14, 1903. It was a slight work, costing the theatre only about £3000, or a fifth of what might be expended on one of the more spectacular productions. Nevertheless it proved to be one of Genée's greatest successes, being described by Perugini as 'the first of what may be called essentially the Genée ballets – ballets, that is, which seemed more particularly than before infused with the personality of this accomplished dancer'.[10]

Genée played the rôle of a young country girl who is employed in a fashionable West End millinery establishment, and eventually wins the heart of a young Marquis. In the course of the ballet she had to develop the character of her part from a naïve little creature dressed in her country best and clutching a large umbrella and a straw basket, to a lady of polish and distinction. One of the highlights of the ballet was the passage, which Genée

8 *Tatler*, Nov. 12, 1902.
9 Interview with Miss Theresa Heyman, Aug. 31, 1957.
10 Perugini, 287.

arranged herself, when the heroine is left alone in the shop and cannot resist trying on all the hats. Genée's 'fine artistic appreciation of the *nuances* of comedy' came as a revelation, for in her earlier ballets she had had little opportunity to reveal her ability as a mime. In the way she conveyed the charms of country life, described Perugini, 'so clever and so perfect was the combination of mime and dance that a positive illusion was created; and only at the close did one realise, suddenly, that it was veritably a song without words. A step, a gesture, a little glance, and one could have sworn one heard a poet's lines! Popular as the dancer had already made herself, her work in this particularly charming ballet confirmed the growing opinion that here was a dancer who was supreme in her art as a dancer-mime; one to be reckoned among any gallery of the great artists of the past.'[11]

The music of *The Milliner Duchess* was largely an arrangement by Wenzel of airs from musical comedies, one of Genée's dances being performed to Lionel Monckton's 'Captivating Cora'. As for Wilhelm, who had written the scenario, the absence of spectacle did not hamper his imagination, for he seized the opportunity of introducing a splendid fashion parade.

Realising that they now had a star of the first magnitude, the Empire persuaded Genée to dance in two ballets on the same evening. So throughout the summer of 1903 she appeared in both *The Milliner Duchess* and a revival of *The Duel in the Snow*, in the latter work dancing a *pas de deux* arranged by Alexander Genée in which she was partnered by a male dancer, Paul Sundberg, whom the Empire had rather grudgingly engaged at a salary of £5 a week. At the end of June there was a spell of very hot weather, and G. E. Morrison, after remarking on the plentiful supply of palm-leaf fans, went on to add: 'But even more cooling and refreshing is the dancing of Mlle Adeline Genée, whose charm was never so great as now, and in the exquisite effortlessness and delicious precision of whose art one is transported for a while from a world of failure and fatigue.'[12]

On September 26, 1903, another ballet by Wilhelm, Lanner and Wenzel appeared in the programme. *Vineland* was a suite of four scenes, each inspired by a different beverage. Old England was the setting of the first, the second took place in a beergarden overlooking the Rhine, in the third the audience was transported to a quayside at Oporto, and for the fourth the scene changed to the Champagne country. *Vineland* was a charming work of its kind. 'It has not much body,' wrote Morrison, 'but it is bright, has sparkle, is beautiful of colour, and of exquisite bouquet.' And for Genée there was the superb Champagne Dance, which she gave with all 'her exhilarating ease, her extraordinary brightness and grace, and her joyful vivacity'.[13]

As its title suggested, the next novelty, *High Jinks* (March 9, 1904), was an up-to-date ballet. Wilhelm's idea was to present a house party, not in the dreamlike, suggestive manner that Nijinska and Marie Laurencin were to

11 Perugini, 288.
12 *Morning Post*, June 30, 1903.
13 *Morning Post*, Sep. 28, 1903.

adopt in *Les Biches* two decades later, but in a realistic mode.[14] It opened with the guests returning from a hunt, and closed with a burlesque performance of *Faust*.[15] In between there was much opportunity for comic business, and Fred Farren, who was made up to represent a certain well-known literary figure, excelled himself as the author of the burlesque and danced a brilliant eccentric dance. Genée, of course, was the star, and one of the dances in this ballet, the Hunting Dance, performed to the music of 'John Peel' was later to become the most popular of her solos. Arranged by herself from her own observations of circus horses and her memory of the Jockey's Galop which her aunt, Antonia Zimmermann, used to perform, it carried the dance

> as far in the direction of high spirits, of exhilaration unmixed with passion, of sheer delight in the physical fact of life, as it can possibly go. The spirited little horsewoman in black riding-habit, that clings to the lines of her gay and lithe figure, has an air at once of fragility and vigour; she is borne through the air on her dashing leaps, she curvets, she caracoles, the slender steely limbs make nothing of the weighty burden of skirt and boots – and yet all is done with such a whirl and wind of enthusiasm that the motive force appears to be not muscular activity, but merely a fever of the blood. All the jollity, all the glorious high spirits, all the high-heartedness, all the intoxication of delight, in all the hunting mornings that ever were, are concentrated in that swaying, swirling, leaping, laughing figure.[16]

This was not the only delight which *High Jinks* had in store for the audience, for she then changed into a ravishing afternoon dress to dance a Cake-walk, and finally appeared as Marguerite in the *Faust* burlesque, 'Merry Marguerite'. Never before had she displayed such versatility. As one critic put it:

> The most noticeable individual performance is that of Mlle Genée. One must write of her work in terms of highest praise. The great dancer is drawn into the picture; she must perforce discard the traditional costume associated with her art, and accept her share of the limitations that have been imposed upon composer and ballet-mistress. Like all truly great dancers, Mlle Genée has adaptability, and her modern, up-to-date work is hardly less fascinating than the more difficult and delicate developments of the Italian school, of which her last *pas seul*, the subtle *brisé* that in one form or another has drawn all Italy to the feet of great dancers, may be noted as a remarkable example.[17]

The score for this ballet – an arrangement from many sources – was Wenzel's last work as musical director of the Empire. Katti Lanner, too, was growing old, but her choreography for *High Jinks* was full of variety and originality.

14 Wilhelm's scenario for this ballet, preserved with the Wenzel papers in the Bibliothèque de l'Opéra, Paris, is printed in full in Appendix H. This is presumably the sketch of the action prepared for submission to the Directors of the Empire Theatre. It will be observed that in this early version, the guests return to the house from a shoot, not a hunt.

15 Because of objections to the liberties taken with Gounod's *chef d'oeuvre*, the burlesque had to be replaced during the summer by a *divertissement* called 'Pan and Pierette'.

16 Flitch, 180–1.

17 *Illustrated London News*, Mar. 10, 1904.

Her 'skill in arranging the series of modern dances is bewildering', wrote one critic. 'She seems to have taken from them everything that jarred upon the eye elsewhere. Perhaps it is the long experience of her pupils that enables them, with her aid, to extract a charm from cakewalks and other aberrations of the modern dance.'[18]

For the next creation a ballet with an existing score was chosen. *The Dancing Doll* (January 3, 1905), was a version of a popular Viennese ballet, *Die Puppenfee*,[19] with its original score by Josef Bayer arranged by the conductor, Cuthbert Clarke, but with completely new choreography by Katti Lanner. The action took place in Professor Marvel's toyshop on Christmas Eve. Alderman Pompous enters with his family, and the professor shows them his dolls. Finally he brings out his masterpiece, Bébé, but the mechanism fails and the Pompous family stalk out. The professor is heart-broken, but when midnight strikes, the Christmas Fairy descends from the Christmas tree and brings all the toys to life. Genée, of course, played Bébé and danced a whole series of enchanting numbers: a Dance of Animation, a Pas Militaire with the *corps de ballet* as toy rabbits, a Sailor's Hornpipe, a Danse Coquette, and finally a *pas seul*, 'La Folie'.

This was Katti Lanner's last ballet before her first retirement. Her successor at the Empire was to be Fred Farren, who was primarily a character dancer by training. He had made his stage début as a boy in the Drury Lane pantomime of 1885, and had been a member of the Empire company since 1904. Adeline Genée did not consider him sufficiently competent to choreograph for her, and the programme for his first ballet, *The Bugle Call* (October 9, 1905), credited her dances to her uncle, although they were devised largely by herself. There had also been a change in the musical direction in 1905, and this ballet had a score by the new holder of that post, Sidney Jones. It was an unpretentious piece, set in a Normandy orchard during the late eighteenth century and telling of a bugler boy who dresses up in his sweetheart's clothes to teach his colonel a lesson for showing the girl too much attention. Adeline Genée played the bugler boy. 'Besides her bewitching dancing,' wrote G. E. Morrison, 'Mlle Genée is rapidly becoming a very fine and subtle pantomimist . . . She played with the archest humour, and her roguish antics were hugely relished by a crowded audience.'[20]

It was not a part, however, that appealed to all her admirers, but no one was to be disappointed by her next rôle. *Cinderella* (January 6, 1906) was devised by Wilhelm. Sidney Jones composed and selected the music, and Fred Farren arranged the dances, again with the exception of Genée's own. Being originally staged to be given at matinée performances during the Christmas holidays, it proved so popular that it was taken into the evening bill a month after its first performance. Genée was, of course, Cinderella, with Dorothy

18 *Illustrated London News*, Mar. 19, 1904.

19 *Die Puppenfee* was first performed at the Court Opera, Vienna, on Oct. 4, 1888, with choreography by Josef Hassreiter. Camilla Pagliero was the first 'Puppenfee'.

20 *Morning Post*, Oct. 10, 1905.

Craske playing the Prince *en travesti*, Zanfretta making an imposing Fairy Godmother, and Fred Farren himself taking the part of Cinderella's stepmother.

Wilhelm found the subject one after his own heart. '*Cinderella*,' he wrote,

> the most charming, as it is assuredly the most popular of all fairy-tales, has been so often and so variously re-told as to make it difficult to present it afresh without introducing many conventions grown familiar by repetition, but alien to the spirit of the romance. In view of the limitations imposed by 'dumb-show', I have felt it desirable to treat my version of this delightful story as simply and directly as possible, and have endeavoured to preserve something of the atmosphere of the Fairy-tales of Perrault and Mme d'Aulnoy, instinct as they are with dainty and delicate fancy. To emphasise this treatment I have selected the picturesque period of Louis Quinze, associated for all time with the graceful fantasies of Watteau, Lancret and Fragonard, and have sought inspiration from their 'Fêtes Champêtres', with ladies, gallants, and pages footing it on the greensward to the strains of lute and guitar. Students of the period will note that the Court Dancing Master pirouettes to a contemporary melody by Rameau and may recognise in the little black page, attached to the person of Cinderella's vain and frivolous stepmother, a characteristic fashion of the time. Our heroine goes to a State Ball in a sedan chair, attended by link-boys, as was the mode; and the names of the characters figuring in the story are adapted from Contes des Fées. In devising the schemes of colour and composition for the scenic artists and costumiers I have attempted to reflect something of the fragile, porcelain-like quality - occasionally a little bizarre - of the Arts of the period, with an added suggestion of the elusive fragrance that hangs about the old phrase - 'Once upon a Time'.[21]

It was one of the Empire's most successful productions, and the audience took away with them many delightful memories of Genée's 'fairy dancing . . . over flowers and ferns and amid lamp-lit glades'.[22] Hers was a flawless performance. The celebrated theatre critic, A. B. Walkley, penned a delightful description of her in this ballet:

> See her, when Cinderella is left alone in the kitchen, after the others have gone to the ball. At first she sits forlorn; then the picture of the ballroom takes hold of her and her face beams with delight at the idea of improvising a little ballroom scene all to herself. Up she jumps, plucks a couple of feathers from her broom and sticks them in her hair, snatches up the table-cloth to make a train, and whirls round with her broom for an imaginary partner. The dainty grace with which she makes believe to eat an ice, to bow to her partner, to yield to a pressing invitation for just one dance more! To every little endearing detail she brings some quaint touch of humour, some ingenuity of invention. As to technical skill, we called it wonderful. It is dancing without the slightest trace of effort, every step - in reality, no doubt, calculated to a hair's breadth and assiduously practised - having the air of a happy improvisation.[23]

21 *Theatrical Souvenir No.* 4: the Empire Theatre, 1906.

22 *Illustrated London News*, Jan. 13, 1906.

23 *The Times Literary Supplement*, Feb. 16, 1906.

MONDAY, MAY 22nd, 1905, **EMPIRE**

Subject to alteration at the discretion of the Management. →✱ **PROGR**

1 **OVERTURE.**

Overture . "Ivanhoe" . *A. Sullivan.*

2 LEONA THURBER and her Coons, in their Original Act.

3 THE EARLE TRIO. A Musical Novelty.

4 MASTER RALPH MOORE, The Boy Patti.

5 THE HADJI MOHAMED TROUPE of Arab Tumblers.

6 **SELECTION.**

Selection "The Orchid" ... *Caryll & Monckton.*

7 THE ORIGINAL BICYCLE-POLO TEAM.

8 BAILEY AND MADISON, Eccentric Comedians.

9 MISS EDITH HELENA, Wonderful Soprano.

10 THE MARCONI SYSTEM OF WIRELESS TELEGRAPHY, Demonstrated by CAPTAIN BLOOM.

11 **SELECTION.**

Selection ... ... "The Casino Girl" ... ... *Englander.*

NEW EDITION OF

12 **THE DANCING DOLL,**

A Fairy Divertissement.

(*Suggested by the Viennese Ballet, "Puppenfee."*)

Under the Direction of Mr. GEORGE EDWARDES.
The Entire Production Designed and Supervised by Mr. WILHELM.
The Action and the Dances arranged by Madame KATTI LANNER.
Music by Herr JOSEF BAYER, with additional numbers composed and selected by Mr. CUTHBERT CLARK.
Scenery by Mr. JOSEPH HARKER

The Costumes executed by Miss HASTINGS and MORRIS ANGEL & SONS. The Properties by F. LABHART and A. SKELLY. Machinist, W. BRUNSKILL. Electrician, Mr. WALTON Wigs by W. CLARKSON. Stage Manager, Mr. GEORGE CAPEL.

In accordance with the requirements of the London County Council,

The Public may leave at the end of the Performance by all Exit and
The Fireproof Screen to the Proscenium Opening is lowered at least on
All Gangways, Passages, and Staircases must be kept free from Chairs

PRICES OF ADMISSION.—Private Boxes, 1 to 3 Guineas. Fauteuils, 7s. 6d,
Unreserved, 2s. F

RESERVED SEATS can be Booked in Advance fo

Box Office open from 10 a.m. to 10 p.m.

Manager, Mr. H

THEATRE. and every Evening at 8.0.

AMME.

Subject to alteration at the discretion of the Management.

Professor Marvel .... Signor AMEDEO SANTINI.
Bertha (his Daughter) .... Miss E. BADHAM.
Apprentices .... Misses ROULLRIGHT, DAWSON, SHEPHERD & G. EDWARDS.
Shop Girls .... Misses G. TREE, RUBY, GUEST & C. CRASKE.
Alderman Pompous and Percy Pompous .... Mr LEWINGTON & Mr. A. YOUNG.
Mrs. Pompous .... Miss M. PASTON.
Old Farmer and his Wife .... Mr. PERKINS & Miss BANNISTER.
Nursemaid .... Miss ADA VINCENT.

DOLLS.

Noeline (the Christmas Fairy) .... Miss JANETTA MICHAELS.
Topsy (a Piccaninny Doll) .... Miss B. TREVESICK.
Sambo (a Nigger Doll) .... Mr. TOM VINCENT.
Hansel and Gretel (Tyrolese Dolls) .... Miss D. CRASKE & Miss G. THOMAS.
Mariquita (a Spanish Doll) .... Mlle. F. ZANFRETTA.
The Bridal Doll .... Mlle. MARJORIE
Punchinello .... Mons. P. SUNDBERG.
Jack-in-the-Box .... Mr. F. FARREN.
The Toy Soldier .... Mr. F. WALTON.
Clown .... Mr. BENNETT.
Dutch Dolls .... Mr. W. VOKES & Miss OSMOND.
Humming-Tops .... Misses ADA VINCENT, E. TREE, D. CRASKE, G. THOMAS & E. BADHAM.
Lady Dolls (living in the Dolls' House) Misses E. McFarlane, Bunyon, Shaw, & E. Banbury.
Boy Dolls (Visitors to the Dolls' House) Misses L. Collier, Courtland, Kaygill, & Swanton.
Doll Housemaid .... Miss E. COLLIER.
French Dandy Doll .... Miss F. JENKINS.

AND

BÉBÉ .... (The Dancing Doll) .... Mlle. ADELINE GENÉE.

Shopmen—Commissionaires—Jugglers—Clowns—Animated Dolls of various types—Toy Rabbits—Polichinelles—Wooden Soldiers—Gollywogs—Puppets and Fairies, by the Ladies and Gentlemen of the Corps de Ballet—Children—And Stedman's Choir of Boys.

SCENE—PROFESSOR MARVEL'S EMPORIUM OF TOYS AND GAMES.

DANCES, &c.

Visit of the Pompous Family to Professor Marvel's Emporium—Exhibition of various Dolls—Breaking of the "Bébé" Doll—Despair of Professor Marvel—Appearance of the Christmas Fairy.

Valse of Animation .... Mlle. ADELINE GENÉE
Danse des Poupées .... By the CORPS DE BALLET
Tea Party at the Dolls' House .... By the SECONDES.
Pas Militaire .... Mlle. GENÉE and the TOY RABBITS (CORPS DE BALLET)
Review of the Wooden Soldiers .... Mr. F. WALTON & STEDMAN'S BOYS.
The Jack-in-the-Box and the Toy Soldier Mr F. FARREN & Mr F. WALTON.
Coon Dance .... Miss B. TREVESICK, Mr. TOM VINCENT and CORPS DE BALLET.
Les Boulonnaises .... Miss F. JENKINS and CORPS DE BALLET.
Dance of the Bridal Doll .. Mlle. MARJORIE, Miss F. JENKINS & CORPS DE BALLET.
Sailor's Hornpipe .... Mlle. GENÉE.
Little Mary and the Woollamaloo .... Miss E. CLERC & Mr. F. FARREN.
Humming-Top Dance .... Misses A. VINCENT, E. TREE, D. CRASKE, G. THOMAS, and E. BADHAM.
Dutch Scene .... By the CHILDREN.
Eccentric Dance .... Mr. W. VOKES and Miss OSMOND.
Les Polichinelles .... By the CORYPHÉES.
Marionette Dance .... Mr. F. FARREN & CORPS DE BALLET.
Spanish Dance .... Mlle. ZANFRETTA and CORPS DE BALLET.
Danse Coquette .... Mlle. GENÉE and Mons. SUNDBERG.
Grand Ensemble .... By the COMPANY.
Pas Seul—"La Folie" .... Mlle. ADELINE GENÉE.

GRAND VALSE AND GALOP FINALE.

13 THE BIOGRAPH.

ntrance Doors, which must open Outwards.
during every Performance to ensure its being in proper working order.
any other obstructions, whether permanent or temporary.

Box Stalls, 5s. Stalls, 3s Grand Circle, 3s. Pit Stalls—Reserved, 2s. 6d.,
s. Gallery, 6d.

all parts of the Theatre (except Pit and Gallery).

Telephone No. 3527 Gerrard.

. HITCHINS.

Empire Theatre programme, May 22, 1905.

It had long been Adeline Genée's desire to persuade the management to stage one of the classical ballets for her, but they had shown a most persistent obstinacy, objecting to *Giselle* because it lacked a happy ending and *Coppélia* because it was too old. She was to have the last word, however, for in 1905 her contract became due for renewal, and she refused to discuss the matter until she had been given an assurance that *Coppélia* would be produced for her by her uncle.

It was to be her greatest triumph. London first applauded her in the rôle of Swanilda, which she had danced before in Munich and Copenhagen, when Alexander Genée's two-act version was presented at the Empire Theatre on May 14, 1906. Her wonderful lightness and almost incredible timing made her dancing a joy to behold, while her expressive acting as the mischievous village girl had a superb foil in Fred Farren's very moving portrayal of Coppélius. D. L. Murray long remembered 'the pathetic derangement of the aged Coppélius amid the wreckage of his automata' at the end of the ballet.[24]

Max Beerbohm went to see Genée as Swanilda, and came away enchanted:

> Perfect though she is in the *haute école*, she has by some miracle preserved her own self. She was born a comedian, and a comedian she remains, light and liberal as foam. A mermaid were not a more surprising creature than she – she of whom one half is that of an authentic ballerina, whilst the other is that of a most intelligent, most delightfully human actress. A mermaid were, indeed, less marvellous in our eyes. She would not be able to diffuse any semblance of humanity into her tail. Madame Genée's intelligence seems to vibrate to her very toes. Her dancing, strictliest classical though it is, is a part of her acting. And her acting, moreover, is of so fine a quality that she makes the old ineloquent conventions of gesture tell their meaning to me, and tell them so exquisitely that I quite forget my craving for words.[25]

Cinderella had by then been taken off, but its opening scene seemed too good to waste. So Wilhelm devised a new Watteau *divertissement*, using the same set but with different music, selected and arranged by the conductor, C. J. M. Glaser. Entitled *Fête Galante*, it went into the bill on August 6, 1906, with Dorothy Craske and Fred Farren.

It made a deep impression on Mark Perugini:

> To see the *Fête Galante* was itself a liberal education in the art of stage effect. It was an ideal realisation of the art of Watteau, Lancret and Fragonard. The very spirit of the period was caught, and it was as if all that one had learnt at secondhand of the people, the dress, the manners, dances, arts and music of the 'Grand Century' in France had suddenly awakened into life, and become a living reality of which one was a living part. Yet, paradoxically, it was strangely dream-like still, even as are Watteau's pictures.
>
> The scene represented a garden such as you see in so many of his paintings . . . A minuet was in progress. All was stately and dream-like, made the more so by the music.

24 *The Times*, May 9, 1956. Obituary notice of Fred Farren.
25 *Saturday Review*, May 19, 1906.

> For all the gaiety of the huntsmen's entrance, it was gaiety demure, as if restrained by an inherent sense of fitness with stately surroundings; and so with the troupe of dancers, introduced for the diversion of the Marquise Belle Etoile, and the Court ladies and courtiers grouped about her. The mood of all, demurely gay, or gaily demure, was suffused with a stately languor, a dream-like grace that found an echo in the subtle colour-harmonies of the old-world garden in which the people moved.
>
> And when the opera-dancer, L'Hirondelle, and Passepied, the master of the revels, began their *pas de deux*, the climax of exquisite illusion was reached, and Camargo was before us - the Camargo of Lancret's famous picture, with the soft, full white skirts, trimmed with garlands of small pink roses and falling almost to the ankle; Camargo with the red-heeled, red-rosetted shows; with blue shoulder-knot and powdered hair adorned with pale blue ribbons.
>
> As the fête drew to a close the picture mellowed in the amber light of a waning day; and, amid fallen leaf and chestnut bloom, slowly marquise and prince, Court lady and courtier, dancer and page, began in stately fashion to dance, their shadows lengthening in the failing light, the music growing slower and dreamier as, little by little, the picture was re-formed into the likeness of the opening scene, and the falling curtain brought one back into the world of living things today.[26]

Wilhelm's imagination then took a leap into the age of Romanticism, to the Paris of Taglioni, and being anxious that the style of the dances should be reproduced with the greatest possible authenticity, he persuaded the Directors to beg Katti Lanner to come out from her retirement and produce the new ballet. Out of friendship for Wilhelm, whose artistic aims she had always appreciated, the old lady agreed. The resultant ballet, *The Débutante* (November 15, 1906), was one of her greatest successes.

In his scenario Wilhelm recreated the backstage atmosphere of the Paris Opéra which is described so vividly in Albéric Second's spicy volume, *Les Petits Mystères de l'Opéra*, published in 1844. A temperamental ballerina refuses to play a new rôle, and is replaced by a brilliant young dancer. This is the débutante herself, who has a great triumph in the ballet, which is a piece of Romantic Orientalism about a slave-girl who fascinates a sultan in order to obtain the release of her lover. Cuthbert Clarke wrote the music for the first scene, and the rest of the score was the work of C. J. M. Glaser.

Age had in no way diminished Katti Lanner's powers of invention, and among the details which impressed themselves on the spectators were the charming arm movements she devised for the *corps de ballet*. 'The linked arms are very effective', wrote G. E. Morrison, 'and we do not remember to have seen the arm converted to such fascinating uses at the Empire before.'[27] In the rôle of the débutante, Genée dominated the ballet from beginning to end, dancing and miming brilliantly. It was a work replete with period charm, and a great ovation was reserved for Mme Lanner when she came before the curtain at the end in her plain dress to be presented with a bouquet quite as large as herself.

26 Perugini, 290–1.
27 *Morning Post*, Nov. 16, 1906.

Such was the success of this ballet that Katti Lanner was persuaded to stay on and produce another work. This was *Sir Roger de Coverley* (May 7, 1907). It had a scenario by Adrian Ross[28] about an eighteenth-century elopement, and the music was by Dr Osmond Carr, who introduced many old English airs. The ballet closed with a recreation of a fête at Vauxhall, for which Wilhelm took a large share of the credit for designing the scene. Genée was the heroine and Dorothy Craske her suitor, while among the smaller parts Tom Walls made his first London appearance as Ensign Ruffler.

Sitting in the circle on the first night was an excited little girl called Phyllis Bedells, who carried away a vivid memory of the final ovations. 'At the end,' she wrote, 'the ballet mistress, Katti Lanner, took many curtain calls. With this dear old lady was my adored Genée. The contrast between the two was very amusing. They did not come on together; but Genée, with her merry little face, flitted across to the footlights, and Katti Lanner followed her, stumping along with a not very straight back, swinging her bouquet upside down like a market-bag.'[29]

This was, alas, to be the last memory that her public was to have of Mme Lanner, for she did not emerge from her retirement again. She died at her home on Clapham Common just eighteen months later, on November 15, 1908, the second anniversary of *The Débutante*.

After a series of excursions into the past the directors now considered it time for something up-to-date, and Wilhelm dutifully complied by devising a *divertissement* set in Covent Garden market in those early hours when revellers made their way home from a fancy dress ball at the Opera House. It was given the title of *The Belle of the Ball*, and was first performed on September 30, 1907, to an arrangement by Cuthbert Clarke of popular airs of the previous half-century, from 'Villikins and his Dinah' and 'By the Side of the Zuyder Zee' to selections from *La Grande Duchesse*, *La Fille de Madame Angot*, *Véronique* and – loud and boisterous by comparison – *The Belle of New York*. This was to be Genée's last new ballet before her first American tour on which she was to embark early in the New Year. In the *Véronique* passage she entered riding a small donkey, and for full measure she also danced her famous Hunting Dance. The little girl who not long before had been applauding Genée from the circle was now making her stage début, playing the Demon Dwarf in the *Rip Van Winkle* scene, and later appearing as a little coster girl dancing to a barrel-organ. In a few years this child, Phyllis Bedells, would be occupying the famous No. 1 Dressing Room, which Genée was about to vacate.

With the imminence of Genée's departure the close of an era was now at hand, for over the ten years that she had danced on the stage of the Empire, attracting devotees in hundreds of thousands not only from London but from every corner of the British Empire, she had become established as one of the

28 Adrian Ross was the pseudonym used by Arthur Reed Ropes, the lyric writer and librettist who contributed to many famous musical comedies, including *San Toy*, *A Country Girl*, *The Dollar Princess*, *Our Miss Gibbs*, *The Quaker Girl*, *The Count of Luxembourg* and *Lilac Time*.
29 Bedells, 19.

greatest artists of the London theatre of her time. Not even the advent of the Diaghilev Ballet with all its exotic brilliance was to dim the lustre of her fame. Crawford Flitch, who was a passionate admirer of the Russians, declared:

> If there is such a thing as a physical genius for the dance, independent of the qualities of the spirit, that genius is hers . . . But whereas many dancers might have relied almost entirely on this natural genius, which is hers by right of birth, Genée has added to it a training which in severity, conscientiousness and thoroughness perhaps few dancers have equalled . . . he has fulfilled to the letter Ruskin's affirmation that an artist must submit to a law which it was painful to obey, in order that she may bestow a delight which it is gracious to bestow. In proficiency in the strict, classical school of ballet-dancing, it is possible that Madame Genée has never been surpassed and perhaps never even equalled.[30]

* * *

During the years when Genée was the star of the Empire, her admirers may have spared little thought for the *corps de ballet* subserviently toiling in her shadow. But they were nevertheless part and parcel of the evening's entertainment, and no history of the Empire ballet would be complete without a glance at that humble and today virtually anonymous band. In 1907, and for many years before that, the structure and the numerical strength of the Empire *corps de ballet* remained more or less unchanged. Apart from the stars its dancers were exclusively British. The main *corps de ballet* proper, the 'house ballet' as it was called, were on individual contracts, but they were frequently augmented by pupils apprenticed to Mme Lanner, who hired out their services when required, deducting a proportion of their fees as her commission. Most of the dancers in the house ballet came from lower-class families, only a sprinkling being from the middle class, for while Victorian prejudice against the dancing profession was beginning to erode, the old attitudes still prevailed. The social stigma that marked the profession of the dancer was founded on prejudice and, probably more often than not, was unjustified. Many of the girls of the Empire ballet in late Victorian and Edwardian days were industrious and respectable, even if some of their colleagues had joined the company for the opportunities offered of making the acquaintance of a wealthy 'stage-door Johnny'. By the standards of the time they were not inadequately rewarded. Dancers in the house ballet could expect between £12 and £18 a month if they merely had a pretty face and a good figure, from £20 to £25 if they possessed some talent in addition, and more if they undertook rôles. As for the children, when their services were required, they were paid one or two shillings a performance, while a few senior pupils could expect to be more generously treated, receiving from £4 to £8 a month.

The training was far from rigorous by today's standards. The house ballet was not obliged to attend class, and indeed nothing very much was required of them beyond punctual attendance and mastery of a few simple evolutions. They were not expected to perform *pointe* work; in fact it was only when

30 Flitch, 179–80.

Alexander Genée produced *Coppélia* in 1906 that the practice began of arranging *pointe* work at all for any but the prima ballerina. Consequently it was not very difficult for a reasonably proficient girl to secure a place in the front row, for the back rows tended to be filled by the hangers-on and the dependents of the profession – cousins of the carpenters, or daughters of the door-keepers or the firemen.

Even Katti Lanner had to admit that the training she gave to her pupils fell short of what she herself had received in her youth. On the other hand, although technical standards were low, strict discipline was enforced in the theatre, for the Empire merited its reputation as a well managed house. Dancers were not allowed out of their dressing rooms between the two ballets in the programme, and unpunctuality and negligence were punished by fines, the accumulated penalties being distributed among the well-behaved at Christmastime. The result of this discipline was to be seen in the professional efficiency with which the large stage staff, under the silk-hatted stage manager, realised productions that were complicated enough by any standards.

XII

The final phase (1908–15)

After more than ten years' uninterrupted engagement as the Empire's prima ballerina Adeline Genée sailed from Southampton, on New Year's Day 1908, to conquer fresh fields in the New World. As if unable to believe that she would not return, even though she had made it plain to them that she intended to bind herself to no particular theatre for the moment, the Empire's directors at first made no serious attempt to replace her. Her most recent creation, *The Belle of the Ball*, was not taken off, but was revised by Fred Farren to feature Topsy Sinden.

Topsy Sinden, who had made her first appearance at the Empire as a child in 1889, in the ballet, *The Paris Exhibition*, performing a Lancashire clog-dance with her brother Bertie, was in no sense a classical ballerina. By training she belonged to what was then called 'the English school'. This was the term that comprised the tap-dancing and skirt-dancing that were so popular on the late Victorian and Edwardian musical comedy stage, and which had produced such famous exponents as Kate Vaughan, Letty Lind, Alice Lethbridge and Sylvia Grey.

Well received though she was, Topsy Sinden could not hope to replace the classically trained Genée in the hearts of the Empire audience, and a vociferous welcome lay in store for the Danish ballerina when she returned for a short season the following summer. On the night of June 10, 1908, the house was packed almost to overflowing, and when she first came into view as the curtain rose on *Coppélia*, the audience burst into a roar of welcome that continued for nearly a full minute. *Coppélia* remained in the bill for several weeks, with Francesca Zanfretta playing opposite Genée as Franz. Fred Farren repeated his success of the year before as Coppélius, but, falling ill during the run, was replaced for a few performances by Alexander Genée himself, who had not appeared before the public for more than ten years.

Before the close of this short summer engagement, Genée was to realise one of her ambitions. On September 7, 1908, she appeared in the pastoral fantasy of *The Dryad*, which had been written and composed by her great friend, Dora Bright. It was a haunting, tranquil little ballet which gave Genée an opportunity, in the words of J. Crawford Flitch, 'for displaying not only her marvellous technique, but also a perhaps half-unsuspected power of raising and expressing emotion. It afforded scope for the range of her feeling and revealed the actress beneath the dancer'.[1] There were only two characters in

1 Flitch, 177.

SEPTEMBER 7th, 1908.

EMPIRE

PROGR

Subject to alteration at the di

OVERTURE ... "Fingall's Cave" ... ... *Mendelssohn.*

1 **Emma Francis and her Arab Boys.**

2 **Warren & Brockway.**

3 **Mlle. Lydia Kyaksht,**
Premiere Danseuse, from the Imperial Theatre St. Petersburg, in Selections from her Repertoire
Supported by **Mons. Adolf Bolm.**

4 **Velanche's Dogs.**

5 **Vernon Davidson.**

6 "THE DRYAD."

A Pastoral Fantasy in Two Tableaux.

By Miss DORA BRIGHT.

The Action and Dances by ALEXANDER GENÉE.

THE DRYAD .... **Mlle. ADELINE GENÉE.**
The Shepherd .... **Mr. Gordon Cleather.**

Ten Years are supposed to elapse between the Tableaux.

A certain Dryad, the fairest of the Wood Nymphs, subdued all mortals to her by her loveliness and the magic of her dancing—whom the implacable Aphrodite caused to be imprisoned in an oak tree, only granting her freedom to come forth once in every ten years between sunset and sunrise until she should find a mortal faithful to her during the allotted term. A Shepherd, passing through the wood on the night of her freedom, sees her dancing beneath the moon, and is lured to love her, and vows eternal constancy. When the dawn breaks she bids him farewell and re-enters the tree, which closes around her. After ten years have passed away, the Dryad comes forth again, seeking to allay the longing she has kindled, but her lover has not been constant, and the wood is empty. She dances through the night, deluding herself with hope till the hour of her doom returns, and she is compelled to re-enter her prisoning tree. When the dawn breaks the Shepherd is seen wandering through the grove, but he is oblivious of his love, and her footprints have vanished from his memory.

SELECTION ... "The Fortune Teller" ... ... *Victor Herbert.*

7 "AFTER THE OPERA."

A Dramatic Episode in Three Scenes.

Adapted from the French of E. Reibrach and G. Docquois by **NORAH KEITH.**

By arrangement with **Mr. ARTHUR BOURCHIER.**

LAWRENCE DEVAS .... **Mr. ROBERT PATEMAN**
Captain GORDON FOLLETT .... **Mr. VERNON STEEL**
An INSPECTOR .... Mr. GEORGE BARRON
A BURGLAR .... Mr. TOM WALLS
MARIE .... Miss E. CLERC
LADY LULU DEVAS .... **Miss EVELYN D'ALROY**

Time—The Present Day—A Night in Winter.

Scenes 1 *and* 3.—Lady Lulu's Boudoir at Devas's House in Park Lane, *R. McCleery*
Scene 2.—Outside the House, under the Boudoir Window ... .. *R. McCleery*

The Directoire Gown worn by Miss D'Alroy designed by Mr. REVILL, and executed by REVILL & ROSSITER, Ltd., 15, Hanover Square, W.

Incidental Music composed by CUTHBERT CLARKE.

Stage Director, SPENCER BARRY.

8 **Ray Wallace.**

FINALE MARCH ... ... "St

Floral Decorations by ROBERT GR

In accordance with the requirements of the London County Council,
The Public may leave at the end of the Performance by all
The Fireproof Screen to the Proscenium Opening is lowered
All Gangways, Passages, and Staircases must be kept free fr
Gentlemen are politely informed that Pipes
The Management earnestly trust that Ladies will very kindly rei

Musical Director—**Mr. CUTHBERT CLARKE.**

PRICES OF ADMISSION.—Private Boxes, 1 to 3 Guineas (all Box Tickets admit to
Box Circle, 5s. (first three rows Numbered and Reserved). Grand Circle (fir
No Re-A

Box Office (*Mr. J. E. Pickering*) **open**
Daily from 10 to 10.

Manager, Mr. H.
Acting Manager, I
Treasurer, N

THEATRE. and every Evening at 8.0.

.AMME.

scretion of the Management.

9 . **COPPÉLIA.**

A BALLET IN TWO SCENES BY CH. NUITTER AND A. SAINT LEON.

Produced and Dances arranged, by ALEXANDER GENÉE.

Music by LEO DELIBES.

Scenery by JOSEPH HARKER.

Costumes designed and supervised by C. WILHELM.

The Dresses executed by Miss HASTINGS and MORRIS ANGEL & SONS. Machinist, W. SHELDON.

Properties by P. GRIEVESON. Electrician, C. WINTER. Wigs by CLARKSON.

SWANILDA (a Village Girl) .... **Mlle. ADELINE GENÉE**

FRANZ (her Sweetheart) .... Mme. ZANFRETTA

COPPÉLIUS (an Eccentric Inventor of Mechanical Figures) .... Mr. FRED FARREN

IRMA (the Betrothed of Laszlo) .... Miss E. CLERC

COPPÉLIA (a Doll, Coppelius's Masterpiece) .... Miss E. COLLIER

LASZLO (a Slovak Pedlar) .... Mr. B. FORD

The Burgomaster and his Wife .... Mr. JAMESON and Miss M. PASTON

Innkeeper .... Miss SHEPHERD

FRIENDS OF SWANILDA .... Misses BANKS, BOSETTI, HILL, PETERS, PAVER ARRIGONI, OSMOND, and RUSHTON

CZARDAS and MAZURKA DANCERS, VILLAGERS, MUSICIANS, &c. — Misses TREVESICK, DAWSON, KAYGILL, EDWARDES, ROULLRIGHT, LYONS, B. COLLIER, L. PIACENTINI, B. ARIGONI, E. McFARLANE, and the Ladies and Gentlemen of the Corps-de-Ballet.

Scene I.—A VILLAGE ON THE BORDERS OF GALICIA.

VALSE .... Mlle. ADELINE GENÉE

MAZURKA .... THE CORPS DE BALLET

PAS COMIQUE (Slovak) .... Miss E. CLERC and Mr. B. FORD

GRAND BALLET (Slav Theme, with Variations) — Mdlle. ADELINE GENÉE, Misses PAVER, PETERS, B. HILL, L. OSMOND, and BOSETTI

CZARDAS (Hungarian National Dance) .... Mme. ZANFRETTA, Miss E. CLERC, Mr. FORD, and CORPS DE BALLET.

The scene opens with Swanilda, on the morning of the Burgomaster's golden wedding, discovering a life-like doll in the window of Coppelius' house; as she gazes at it her lover Franz kisses his hand to the mechanical figure. Swanilda becomes jealous under the impression that the doll is a living girl; the doll-maker issues from his house and is seized upon by a crowd of students headed by Franz; he drives them off, but in his excitement drops his door key; this is picked up by a friend of Swanilda, and she and her maidens determine to explore the mysterious workshop. Prior to doing so the Burgomaster and his wife arrive, and are treated to a Czardas by a Slovak Pedlar and Irma, while Swanilda puts her lover to the test of an Ear of Corn, accompanied by a Valse on Hungarian Themes.

During the Entr'acte of Three Minutes Leo Délibes' celebrated "MARCHE DES CLOCHES" *will be played.*

Scene II.—THE WORKSHOP OF COPPÉLIUS.

AUTOMATON DANCE .... Mdlle. ADELINE GENÉE, Mme. ZANFRETTA, Mr. F. FARREN, and CORYPHÉES

VALSE COPPÉLIA, ADAGIO, BOLERO .... Mdlle. ADELINE GENÉE

GRAND GALOP AND FINALE .... Mdlle. ADELINE GENÉE, Mme. ZANFRETTA, CORYPHÉES, and CORPS DE BALLET.

This scene begins with the entrance of the girls, led by Swanilda, who sets all the automatic figures to work, and generally make hay in the workshop. They are disturbed by the return of Coppelius and all fly, except Swanilda, who secretes herself behind an arras and takes the place of Coppelia the doll: while the doll-maker is putting the place in order Franz, bent on solving the mystery of the doll, clambers through the window and is seized by Coppelius. At first inclined to punish him for his trespass, the old man decides to make use of him, gives him a sleeping potion and, while insensible, endeavours to transfer the life from Franz to the supposed doll. Swanilda humours the old doll-maker, and he imagines that, following the instruction of a book of magic, he is making the doll do everything but talk. The arrival of Swanilda's friends and the Burgomaster cruelly dispel the illusion; Franz awakens; the lovers are reconciled; and a purse of gold compensates Coppelius for the damage done to his figures.

---

10 **THE BIOSCOPE Special and Exclusive Pictures.**

(Photographs by THE WARWICK TRADING CO., LONDON.)

The Battle of Salisbury (The London Territorials in Action).

The Marathon Race from Start to Finish.

LAST WEEK OF

Mlle. GENÉE'S PRESENT ENGAGEMENT.

..uss" ... ... *Mezzacapo.*

..N, Ltd., Crawford Street, W.

..it and Entrance Doors, which must open Outwards.

..t least once during every Performance to ensure its being in proper working order.

..n Chairs or any other obstructions, whether permanent or temporary.

..re not allowed in the Stalls or Box Circle.

..ve their Hats (if so desired) and thus add to the comfort of all.

Stage Director—Mr. SPENCER BARRY.

..Parterre). Stalls (Numbered and Reserved), 7s. 6d. Parterre (Unreserved), and .. row Numbered and Reserved, 3/-), Unreserved, 2s 6d. Amphitheatre, 1s. ..mission.

J. HITCHINS. ***Telephone No. 3527 Gerrard.***

..r. A. ALDIN.

.. J. DAVIS.

Empire Theatre programme, September 7, 1908.

the ballet, the dryad, played by Genée, and the shepherd, a sung rôle taken by the baritone, Gordon Cleather. The scenario told of a dryad who is confined within an oak tree, from which she is permitted to emerge during the space of one day only once in ten years until she should find a mortal who will remain faithful to her throughout the intervening period. Perugini called the work 'one of the most perfect gems yet seen in the historic gallery of Ballet'.

> The Dryad [he described], afire with joy at being released from the imprisoning tree, and discovering the beauty of the sunlit, flower-strewn forest glade; joyous in her love of the handsome shepherd and her love returned; her sorrow at parting to return to the tree; her deeper joy on her renewed release; her alternating hope and fear as the concluding moment of the ten-year tryst draws nigh; her eager search for her lover; the shuddering tremors of doubt as she finds him not; her triumphant happiness as she hears his voice; the heart-wringing suspense, and then the overwhelming despair, as she finds he has forgotten her for another love and passes on his way, leaving her solitary and doomed to be imprisoned yet again within the tree, desolate amid autumnal desolation; these, and a thousand more *nuances*, expressive of poetic emotion, were conveyed with a sureness, a sensitiveness, a depth of instinctive dramatic genius that astonished, delighted and enthralled.[2]

Some weeks before *The Dryad* was given, the Empire bill had included, among the variety numbers, the names of two Russian dancers from St Petersburg's Maryinsky Theatre, Lydia Kyaksht and Adolph Bolm, who performed a *pas* from *The Little Hump-backed Horse*.[3] They were the vanguard of what was very soon to become a veritable invasion of Russian dancers. Their quality was never in doubt, and in September Lydia Kyaksht took over the rôle of Swanilda in *Coppélia*.

Kyaksht, who held the rank of *première danseuse* in the Russian Imperial Theatres, had been approached in St Petersburg by an agent acting on behalf of the directors of the Empire, and had accepted a month's engagement at £40 a week. When it became known, her intention to leave the Imperial Theatres created quite a stir. As she herself recalled,

> I was made to feel my action was almost in the nature of a crime . . . The Tsar was extremely displeased with me when I wished to retire. His principal cause of complaint was that the Empire was a music hall, and not an opera house, and in his Imperial estimation quite outside the pale. At length a satisfactory compromise was arrived at by my agreeing to take a year's holiday from the Imperial Ballet, during which period I was to fulfil my engagements at the Empire. When the year had expired I was able to prove that I had kept strictly to the traditions of the Imperial Ballet, so the Tsar allowed me to resign.[4]

2 Perugini, 296–8.

3 Ballet by Arthur Saint-Léon to music by Pugni, first performed at the Bolshoi Theatre, St Petersburg, on Dec. 3/15, 1864.

4 Kyasht, 150–1. According to M. Borisoglebsky, *Materials for the History of Russian Ballet* (Leningrad, 1937–39, II, 159), Kyasht was granted leave without salary until the end of 1908, which was later extended to Sep. 1, 1909, and was struck from the list of the St Petersburg ballet company when she did not return.

The headline which the *Sketch* chose to accompany Kyaksht's photograph in its issue of August 19 – 'The Genée of St Petersburg' – was prophetic, for she met with approval and was offered a year's engagement as the Danish ballerina's successor at an increased salary of £75 a week. At the same time the spelling of her name was simplified to Kyasht so that her English admirers could pronounce it.

It was not long before she was seen in a new ballet. *A Day in Paris* (October 19, 1908), was a lively, up-to-date entertainment written by Lt-Col. N. Newnham-Davis and produced by Fred Farren to a score composed and arranged by Cuthbert Clarke. Its five scenes were set in the Place de l'Opéra, the Quais, the Champs-Elysées, outside the Moulin Rouge, and finally inside that famous music hall, where the ballet closed with a scene, designed by Wilhelm, of an Artists' Ball. Kyasht had three dances to perform, all arranged by Alexander Genée – two *pas seuls* and a *pas russe* – and a minor sensation was created by the *Danse des Apaches* by Fred Farren and Beatrice Collier, which the theatre historian, W. Macqueen-Pope, described many years later as if he had seen it but the evening before:

> The cold, compelling cruelty of everything he did, the calculated brutality to the girl who adored him for it, was a thing of great artistry, because the passion of the man for the girl he half strangled and threw about, was allowed to throb through in the most subtle and amazing way. Every movement, every poise, every piece of seeming brutality registered and was from the miming and dancing point of view, a work of art. The music, by Archibald Joyce, was also perfection and full of the right atmosphere. Its delineation and interpretation by Freddie Farren and Beatrice Collier was in the best tradition of Ballet; such things come but once in a lifetime and the Apache Dance filled the Empire for months and still glows in the memory.[5]

The realism of *A Day in Paris* was almost too much for Max Beerhohm:

> My sole object to it is that one might almost imagine oneself in Paris. Paris itself – I mean, of course, the cispontine part of it – has become so much less like a city than a stage 'set'. All reality seems to have gone out of it, leaving only a hard artificial glare for the bedazzlement of tourists. Fifteen years ago, there were still in the centre of Paris many remnants of reality, of quietude, of a local and exquisitely civilised life. But these remnants are gone, and I cordially detest the place. If the Empire ballet produced an *absolute* illusion, I should be much oppressed. Luckily, the dancers intervene, and save the situation. The dances are more than usually well invented and well done.[6]

In the summer of 1909 Adeline Genée returned to the Empire, but again only for a season of a few weeks. The performances she gave were in fact to be her

5 Macqueen-Pope, 230.
6 *Saturday Review*, Oct. 31, 1908.

last at the theatre where she had built up a reputation unparalleled in London since the days of Taglioni. It was a happy choice, therefore, to present her in a part which that great Romantic ballerina had been the first to dance nearly eighty years before – the Abbess in the 'Ballet of the Nuns' from Meyerbeer's *Robert le Diable* (July 3, 1909).[7] This revival was staged by Genée's uncle in a production designed by Wilhelm. It was too good to drop when Genée departed, and she was succeeded in the leading rôle by Lydia Kyasht.

These were the early days of the cinema, and Fred Farren's next ballet, *Round the World* (October 9, 1909), seemed to owe not a little to that as yet infant art. As its title suggested, it was a variant on the classical fantasy by Jules Verne, the scenario being written by Newnham-Davis and Wilhelm, who was also the designer. To win his wager, the hero, Captain Jack Beresford, has to travel round the world in a month, and the six scenes showed his progress from the grounds of the Monaco Club, by way of Red Square, Moscow, the Siberian Railway, the Garden of a Thousand Joys in Tokyo, and One-eyed Jack's Saloon in San Francisco, to the foyer of the Empire Theatre. Adventures, attacks, and hair-breadth escapes followed fast and furious, but dramatic though the ballet was, the dances were, by general consent, too few and far between. The Moscow scene, a superb scene of stage-realism, which in a way foreshadowed *Petrushka*, included a rousing Cossack dance, as well as solos for Phyllis Bedells, Fred Farren and Lydia Kyasht, who danced a *Danse Tsigane* to music by Brahms. These three dancers also appeared in the Japanese scene, in which Wilhelm had obtained 'some beautiful effects of shaded lights and graduated colouring'.[8] Despite its shortcomings the ballet proved to be so popular with the public that a second edition, entitled *East and West*, was presented nearly six months later with a new *pas de deux* by Kyasht and Bolm entitled 'Les Papillons de l'Orient', inserted in the Tokyo scene.

London was now making the exciting discovery of Russian ballet. Tamara Karsavina had come over to the Coliseum in the summer of 1909 after the end of the Diaghilev Ballet's first Paris season. Ludmilla Schollar and Lydia Kyasht's brother, Giorgi Kyaksht, had followed a few months later to fulfil an engagement at the Hippodrome, and 1910 had brought Anna Pavlova and Mikhail Mordkin to the Palace, Karsavina to the Coliseum, and Olga Preobrazhenskaya to the Hippodrome.

In this fabulous summer of ballet the Empire had to struggle to preserve its prestige as a centre of the dance. Having decided to inject a dose of Russian ballet into their programme, the directors engaged Adolph Bolm, who happened to be free during the summer of 1910, as assistant ballet-master to Fred Farren. Bolm produced a series of dances which were presented under the

7 *Robert le Diable* was first performed at the Paris Opéra on Nov. 21, 1831. The Ballet of the Nuns was originally produced by Taglioni's father, Filippo Taglioni, against a magical setting by Ciceri showing a ruined cloister by moonlight. The spectral effect of this *divertissement* started the vogue for the supernatural in ballet, which was to be so brilliantly exploited in the age of Romanticism in such ballets as *La Sylphide* and *Giselle*.

8 *Daily Graphic*, Oct. 11, 1909.

titles of *Dance Ideals* and *Fantaisie Chorégraphique*, the principal number being 'The Princess and the Slave', which skilfully contrasted Kyasht's poetic dancing with Bolm's tempestuous energy. The series was 'remarkable for that high-voltage dancing, that volcanic energy and rapidity yet grace of movement, characteristic of the Russian school',[9] but it was not the answer to the Empire's predicament.

The complacency of the Empire's board had only been slightly shaken, for they soon showed they had no intention of meekly surrendering to the vogue for Russian ballet. For the next new production looked back to the days before the exotic visitors from the East had arrived. *The Dancing Master* (July 25, 1910), was an adaptation of Genée's earlier success, *The Débutante*. Fred Farren, who was responsible for the production, played his old rôle of the dancing master. Lydia Kyasht, who was cast as the débutante, remembered:

> I shall never forget his wonderful make-up in that particular part, or his long tight-fitting trousers, and the pair of remarkable-looking striped socks he wore. His wig was a triumph to the art of Willie Clarkson, and was the most realistic-looking shock of hair. It fell around his face in stray locks, and gave just the character touch that the impersonation required. Mr Fred Farren made up his eyebrows that night in a style which has since been made famous by George Robey.[10]

When she appeared as the débutante Lydia Kyasht was on the point of leaving for her annual holiday, and on August 8, the day before her seventeenth birthday, Phyllis Bedells moved into the No. 1 dressing room and took over the rôle.

On Kyasht's return from Russia a few weeks later a new ballet at once went into preparation. *The Faun* (October 10, 1910) was another poetic fancy by Dora Bright. In it Lydia Kyasht played the part of an Italian flower-girl who, in the shimmering noonday heat, playfully sprinkles water on a statue of a faun and falls asleep, unaware of the local legend that the waters possess a magic power of giving life for an hour to any inanimate form. The part of the faun was one of Fred Farren's most remarkable character studies. Slowly he began to stir.

> His fingers move over his pipes, he stretches himself in the bright sunlight, and finally descends from his pedestal with wondering steps, and awakens the sleeping girl. She is startled, of course, and thinks she is dreaming, but although she shrinks from him when she recognises his features, she soon succumbs to his fascination and strange piping, and dances with him. Then she realises that it is no dream at all, and that in order to free herself from his spell she must regain the girdle he has snatched from her in a passionate embrace. The allotted hour of enchantment is gradually expiring, and the rapidly-stiffening faun has laboriously resumed his pose over the fountain before she tears it from his grasp. At that moment the pipes fall to the ground and are broken, and the sound of the organ from the village church brings comfort to the terrified girl, who falls fainting upon the church steps. When she recovers, the villagers, coming from Mass, treats her story as a day-dream, but the

9 Perugini, 301.
10 Kyasht, 154.

> sight of the broken pipes recalls to their minds the tradition of the fountain, and they offer her shelter and companionship. But she cannot stay at a place where she has had such a terrible experience, and, alone as she came, she takes her departure along the dusty high road once again with her basket of flowers over her shoulder.[11]

A very different kind of work was the next novelty, *Ship Ahoy!* (November 15, 1910), a nautical *divertissement* with a scenario by Wilhelm, who also designed the production, choreography by Fred Farren and music by Cuthbert Clarke. Fun and melodrama on the upper deck of the R.M.S. Empire was its subject, with Fred Farren giving a neat display of tap-dancing and Lydia Kyasht, cast as a French *danseuse*, dancing a *pas de deux* with Jan Zalewski 'somewhat in Pavlova–Mordkin manner'.[12]

It had been the Empire's policy, almost without exception, to present original ballets. The success of *Coppélia*, however, had shown the directors that there were merits still in the best ballets of the past and it was now decided to repeat this experiment. Delibes' music for *Sylvia* had long been well known in London, but the ballet itself had never been produced before in England. In its original version, as presented at the Paris Opéra in 1876, it had comprised three acts, but this was considered much too long for the Empire. A shortened version in one act was therefore prepared, Cuthbert Clarke being entrusted with arranging and supplementing the score and Fred Farren being placed in charge of the production. The plot, too, had to be revised, and this task was given to Wilhelm, who transformed the character of Orion the Hunter into Pan, who pursues Sylvia but is foiled when Eros drives him away after resuscitating the shepherd Amyntas.

Lydia Kyasht, who had the honour of being London's first Sylvia when the ballet entered the programme of the Empire on May 18, 1911, was described by the *Stage* as 'dainty and engaging' and praised for her splendid miming.[13] Unity More played Eros, Carlotta Mossetti made a fine Amyntas *en travesti*, and Fred Farren gave another superb characterisation, 'the primeval craftiness of his rustic Pan lying in wait behind the rock for the nymph Sylvia' expressing 'a whole chapter of intuitively sensed mythology'.[14] It was an instinctive interpretation, for Farren was not versed in the classics and had to ask a friend to explain to him what kind of god Pan was. After listening carefully he saw at once how to play the part. 'He'd be always watching – and listening, wouldn't he?' he said, and the result was a brilliant study in which he seemed to divine the very nature of the ancient Roman God of nature.

On special occasions, such as the nights after the Boat Race or the Varsity rugger match, the Empire audience was traditionally in boisterous mood, and

11 *Stage*, Oct. 13, 1910.

12 *Stage*, Nov. 17, 1910. Anna Pavlova had made her first appearance in London at the Palace Theatre on Apr. 10, 1910. Among the most striking numbers in her programme was *L'Automne Bacchanale*, which she danced with Mikhail Mordkin.

13 *Stage*, May 25, 1911.

14 *The Times*, May 9, 1956. Obituary Notice of Fred Farren by D. L. Murray.

Lydia Kyasht, who was accustomed to the adoring respect of the St Petersburg balletomanes, found this difficult to accept. One evening, when she was dancing in *Sylvia*, she showed her disdain a little too plainly. 'That was fatal!' remembered Phyllis Bedells, who was to take over the title-rôle when Kyasht left for her holiday that summer. 'At the end of one of her solos I had to come on carrying a tribute of fruit which I held at arm's length above my head before kneeling and laying it at her feet. As I was doing this someone in the stalls shouted "Have a banana!" - a popular catch-phrase of the day. It struck me as being apt, and somehow extremely funny. I collapsed with laughter, and so did the *corps de ballet*; and then, in front of the audience, Lydia stamped her foot at me and cried angrily, 'Phyllis, you encourage dem!'[15]

Both in performance and in content the Empire ballets were a strange mixture of the serious and the light-hearted. They ranged over a very wide selection of styles and subjects, as was well illustrated when the mythological *Sylvia* was followed by *New York* (October 10, 1911), an up-to-date ballet inspired by the ragtime craze that was sweeping the London ballrooms. Newnham-Davis's scenario for this rather formless work described junketings on Independence Day, and among the dances which Fred Farren produced for it were the Temptation Rag and the Yankee Tangle. Cuthbert Clarke worked into his score the strident rhythms of jazz, while Wilhelm was able to forget any aversion he might have felt for these modernities by designing an episode of the Pilgrim Fathers and Red Indians.

Lydia Kyasht, who was cast as a Russian ballerina, could hardly have relished appearing in such ballets as this, which afforded her no greater opportunity than to dance one or two isolated *pas*. But there was now to be a change. Fred Farren's engagement as ballet-master was not renewed, and for the next two years Kyasht was to be permitted to arrange her own choreography.

Her first work was *The Water Nymph* (April 2, 1912). Described as 'a dance-idyll', it was performed to music by Cesare Pugni (called 'Pouney' in the programme) with solo variations by Kadletz. The production was designed, as usual, by Wilhelm. Beyond a thread of romance between a naiad and a magician that was suggested in the dance, there was no plot. 'All that has been aimed at,' explained the *Stage*, 'has been to charm the eye with a series of dainty movements and delightful tuneful melodies.'[16] Kyasht, who danced as the naiad, was partnered by Edward J. Kurylo, *premier danseur* from the Imperial Opera House, Warsaw.

Equally unpretentious was her dance episode, *First Love* (September 24, 1912), in which she danced with Alexandre Volinine. From this trifle about crinolined ladies and their elegant beaux in the rose garden of a Russian mansion on the night of a ball, music by Glinka was used, with the addition of a gavotte specially composed by Cuthbert Clarke.

15 Bedells, 50.
16 *Stage*, Apr. 4, 1912.

In *The Reaper's Dream* (February 11, 1913) Kyasht reserved the principal rôle of the Spirit of the Wheatsheaf who appears to the reaper, played by Flo Martell. Phyllis Bedells added to her growing reputation as the Sun Ray. The music was selected from the works of Delibes and Tchaikovsky.

These three works were trifles by comparison with Lydia Kyasht's fourth and last ballet for the Empire, which, in the opinion of Phyllis Bedells, was 'quite the loveliest' of her productions. Wilhelm's name was associated with that of Kyasht on the programme of the 'fantastic choral ballet', *Titania* (October 4, 1913). It was he, of course, who designed the work, which was performed to Mendelssohn's music with additional numbers by Cuthbert Clarke. The ballet was divided into three scenes, the Hawthorn Brake, Titania's Bower, and the Apotheosis of Oberon and Titania. Shakespeare's lines were used for the opening and closing 'tags', spoken by Unity More as Puck, and for the rehearsal episodes, and there were also some interpolated choral numbers. Kyasht fashioned the part of Titania for herself, one of the finest passages being her lulling of Bottom to sleep, which was accompanied by Mendelssohn's 'Spring Song'. Leonide Zhukov appeared as Oberon, and Phyllis Bedells was cast as Philomel.

Scenically the ballet was memorable. 'The opening scene,' described the *Stage*, 'showing a hawthorn brake ablaze with snow-white bloom, is fine enough; but that of Titania's Bower – a flowery woodland dell, with a forest stream and winding upland paths, and the light coming through interlaced foliage in the far distance – is something that will linger long in the memory of all who see it.'[17]

When Kyasht's engagement at the Empire came to an end in December 1913, Phyllis Bedells moved permanently into No. 1 dressing room and succeeded her as Titania. Zhukov, too, left the Empire, being replaced by Alexandre Gavrilov, while Ivy St Helier took over the rôle of Puck.

Times were now changing. The success of the Diaghilev Ballet had not been without its effect on the Empire Theatre, whose policy of importing a Russian ballerina had not, however, succeeded in restoring the prestige of the ballet there to its former level. The younger generation was too dazzled by the visiting Russians to spare much enthusiasm for the Empire ballet, and even the attractions in the promenade seemed to be losing their glamorous appeal. Compton Mackenzie described the predicament which faced the great music halls of the metropolis in the years before the first World War, and which led them to turn more and more to the developing genre of revue:

> Night after night the most comfortable stalls in London – stalls as individually wide and well-sprung as the armchairs of the clubmen who frequented them – grew emptier. Death and illness and age were telling upon the habitués of the older generation, and the younger men of the new generation were not taking their places. The promenade was still full enough; but the hobbled skirts of 1910 had cramped the style of peripatetic harlotry. Large hats, long trains, ample busts, sequins and silk petticoats had been accepted as the standard of a luxury article. When hobbled skirts

17 *Stage*, Oct. 9, 1913.

> came in they might as well have frequented the Leicester Lounge or one of the Cafés nearby; full-rigged whores were going the way of full-rigged ships: the promenade . . . was not what it was.[18]

The dance was not entirely forgotten in the Empire's early revues, but on the whole it was relegated to a relatively minor place. In 1913 Kyasht had arranged a dance episode entitled 'The Gambler' to music by Drigo, which she danced with Pierre Vladimirov in *All the Winners*; early in 1914 Phyllis Bedells appeared as Pavlova in a sketch called 'The Dear Departed' in *Nuts and Wine*; and in the summer of that same year Alexandra Balashova and Mikhail Mordkin came from Moscow to dance in a *divertissement* to music by Glazunov, Tchaikovsky and Schütt, 'The Garden of Flowers', which was a feature of Alfred Moul's *The Merry-go-round.*

For the moment the coming of revue did not entirely oust the production of new ballets. Kyasht's departure had presented the Empire with the double problem of finding both a new prima ballerina and a new choreographer. The solution to the first problem had not been difficult since Phyllis Bedells had on several occasions given proof of her ability to step into Kyasht's shoes, but a new ballet-master had to be sought elsewhere. The choice finally rested on Edouard Espinosa, son of Léon Espinosa and one of the finest teachers in Britain. He was schooled in the direct classical tradition, and his first production for the Empire was a revival of *The Dancing Master* (February 27, 1914) with himself in Fred Farren's old rôle and Phyllis Bedells as the débutante.

For a number of years now the clouds of war had been gathering over Europe, and the conflict which broke out in August 1914 inspired the next new work. Alfred Butt's wish to produce a topical and patriotic *divertissement* was realised in an astonishingly short time, for the new ballet, *Europe* (September 7, 1914), entered the programme of the Empire within five weeks of the declaration of war. The idea for the ballet was Wilhelm's, Espinosa arranged the action and the dances, and the music was selected and composed by Guy Jones. There were three scenes - Dame Europa's Schoolroom ('When the cat's away - '), On the Map (England receives a proposal), and The Heights of Dover (England's answer) - and the cast was headed by Francesca Zanfretta as Dame Europa, Dorothy Craske as Jack, John Bull's Boy, Carlotta Mossetti as Alexis, Stephen Hall, a pupil of Espinosa, as Billy the Bully, and Phyllis Bedells as Mlle Paris. Dorothy Craske of course had to dance a hornpipe, which the *Dancing Times* explained was 'an abridged version of the dance as executed by T. P. Cooke, the greatest hornpipe dancer there has ever been'.[19] By modern standards the patriotic fervour expressed in this ballet might seem exaggerated, but it awoke a deep response at the time when the

18 Mackenzie, 8.

19 *Dancing Times*, Dec. 1914. In his *Technical Vade Mecum*, 1948 edition, 99-100, Espinosa has this to say about the Sailor's Hornpipe: 'The set of this dance, considered Traditional, was compiled by T. P. COOK (*sic*), a British actor who specialised in "nautical" rôles. He visited every port on our coasts and assimilated all the various steps used in different Hornpipes around Britain until he stabilised what may be called a commonsense "Routine and Pattern", which eventually became standardised and accepted as the "CORRECT SAILOR'S HORNPIPE".'

horrors of war and insecurity had not made their full mark on the peoples of Europe. Perugini, writing not many months after it was produced, thought it worthy of the best traditions of the Empire Theatre:

> The choice of such a theme as the condition of Europe, just before and during the greatest war in history, might have been called into question on the score of taste, and in the hands of any but a fine artist might easily have become trivialised. The subject was treated with marked dramatic ability and poetic dignity, and the production, passing from the comparative lightness of the first scene, into the more serious note of the second, attained to a high level of art in the patriotic symbolism of the third, and offered a tableau worthy of the brush of any English painter of historical subjects.[20]

By the following spring the war had lost its novelty, the first battle of Ypres had been fought, and the theatre was beginning to offer an avenue of escape, be it only momentary, into a make-believe world of beauty. *The Vine* (March 22, 1915) marked a return to the dance-idyll style. Fred Farren had been brought back to the fold as choreographer, and Harvey Pinches arranged the music, which was mainly selected from the works of Schumann, Grieg and Debussy. Based on an idea by Wilhelm, who was also the designer, it told of the tempting of a young shepherd, played by Carlotta Mossetti, by the Spirit of the Vine. The latter part was played by Phyllis Bedells, who was glad to have an opportunity for once of playing an evil spirit, and had her long curls cut off specially for the part. A pretty child, named in the programme as Little June, was the Spirit of the Mountain Stream.

Later in the year a Watteau dance-idyll in one tableau called *Pastorale* (September 6, 1915) went into the programme, with dances arranged by A. H. Majilton and music by Harvey Pinches. Phyllis Bedells and Carlotta Mossetti appeared as Giroflée and Narcisse. This was to be the last of the Empire ballets. Discontented because only short ballets had been staged for her, Phyllis Bedells would not renew her contract with the Empire at the end of the year. At her last appearance in *Pastorale* Adeline Genée, who was in the stalls, threw a bouquet at her feet. It seemed not merely a tribute to the young English dancer, but also symbolically a gesture of farewell to the tradition which had been built up at the Empire over three decades.

For although Phyllis Bedells was to return in 1916 in the revue, *Razzle-Dazzle*, when it was transferred from Drury Lane, the Empire could no longer substantiate its claim as the home of ballet. The ballet company had been disbanded, and the dance numbers included in the wartime revues were of minor importance and no more than incidental. Little need be said of the ballet scene, 'A Deserted Garden', with Phyllis Monkman and Serge Morosov in *Hanky-Panky*, or the Jungle Dance which the latter danced with Dithy Tarling in *Topsy-Turvy* in 1917.

After the war the Empire did not reconstitute its ballet company, but it provided the setting for more than one important dance occasion. The Diaghilev

20 Perugini, 306.

Ballet appeared there for nearly three months at the end of 1919 with an impressive line of stars - Karsavina, Tchernicheva, Sokolova, Massine, Idzikowski, Woizikovski and the Cecchettis. Ansermet and Adrian Boult were among the conductors, and the highlight of the season was the first London performance, on November 14, of the Cocteau-Massine-Picasso-Satie ballet, *Parade*. Then, in the autumn of 1924, four Russian dancers were billed in a short *divertissement*: Alexandra Danilova, Tamara Gevergeyeva (or Geva, as she later became), George Balanchivadze (shortly to adopt the name of Balanchine) and Nicolai Efimoff. And hard on the heels of these recent exiles from Russia came Leonide Massine and Vera Trefilova in a programme of dances.

Soon now, the Empire, where only little more than thirty years before, on March 3, 1896, Lumière's Cinématograph had been seen in London for the first time, was to be surrendered to the rapacious new art of moving pictures. *Lady, Be Good*, with the Astaires, was its last production before it closed as a theatre, and the final night, on January 22, 1927, was an occasion to remember. Underlying the enthusiasm of the audience was a sadness felt by all those who recalled the theatre in the days when Genée was its star. Then someone recognised the former ballerina in a box, and the whole audience rose to cheer her. It was an epilogue to a period which had really come to an end many years before. 'Ghosts of the gilded youth of yesteryear,' wrote a reporter of that night, 'haunted the last hours of the old "Empire", roamed round its spacious foyers, crowded its dozen bars, thronged its countless stairways; and as the curtain fell, floated sorrowfully away into the shapes of middle-aged men.'[21]

21 *Weekly Dispatch*, Jan. 23, 1927.

Appendices

APPENDIX A

Ballets produced at the Alhambra, 1860–1912

Date		Title	Choreographer	Composer	Weeks in Programme
10 Dec.	1860	*The Fairy Ambuscade*	J. Lauri		
26 Dec.	1864	*Grand Oriental Divertissement* (Dagger Dance)	Cormack		
20 Feb.	1865	*Royal Alhambra Bouquet Divertissement*			
22 May	1865	*Divertissement Espagnol*	Boleno, Collier		
21 Aug.	1865	*The Skaters*			
26 Dec.	1865	*The Descent of King Dragon Fly and His Cortege of Golden Moths into the Clematis Bowers of Arcadia*	Collier	Hird	
26 Dec.	1865	*Un Ballo in Maschera in the Illuminated Groves of Cleophas*	Collier	Hird	
26 Feb.	1866	*Amore nella Tina*	E. & H. Lauri		
2 Apr.	1866	*Der Teufelspiel*	D'Auban, Warde		
4 Jun.	1866	*The Watteau Fête*	Collier	Hird	
18 Jun.	1866	*The Pearl of Tokay*	Kiralfy, Collier	Hird	
2 Jul.	1866	*The Titanic Cascades and Sports of Diana*	Collier	Hird	
17 Sep.	1866	*The Alhambra Blue Jackets*	Collier	Rivière	
12 Nov.	1866	*Tullochgorum*	Collier	Rivière	
24 Dec.	1866	*The Mountain Gorge*	Milano	Rivière	
24 Dec.	1866	*Where's the Police?*	D'Auban, Warde, Collier	Rivière	
24 Dec.	1866	*The Bullrush Fens and the Silver Stream*	Milano	Rivière	
18 Feb.	1867	*The Merry Devil of Nürnberg*	Collier, Evans		
22 Apr.	1867	*The Village Torment*[1]	Collier, Evans	Lee	
20 Apr.	1867	*The Bower of Pearls*	Collier	Rivière	
24 Jun.	1867	*The Caverns of Ice*	Milano	Rivière	
7 Oct.	1867	*Quicksilver Dick*	Evans, Milano	Lee	
28 Oct.	1867	*May Blossoms*	Milano	Rivière	
23 Dec.	1867	*X.X.X.*	Milano		
23 Dec.	1867	*The Golden Plumes*	Milano	Rivière	
16 Mar.	1868	*Mabille in London*	Milano	Rivière	13
21 May	1868	*The Sprig of Shillelagh*	Milano	Gough	
15 Jun.	1868	*Mammoth Waterfall*	Milano	Rivière	
28 Sep.	1868	*Comeathimifyoucano*	Milano	Gough	
28 Sep.	1868	*The Conscript in Love*			
19 Oct.	1868	*A Strange Dream*	Milano	Rivière	21
26 Dec.	1868	*Fantisticuf*	Milano, Evans	Gough	13
26 Dec.	1868	*The Fairy Acorn Tree*	Milano	Rivière	13

1 Revived on 31 Aug. 1868.

Date		Title	Choreographer	Composer	Weeks in Programme
29 Mar.	1869	*Pepita*	Milano	Rivière	28
17 May	1869	*The Bridge of Mudpen*	Vokes	Gough	11
7 Jun.	1869	*The Spirit of the Deep*[2]	Milano	Rivière	22
2 Aug.	1869	*Pierrot*	H. Boleno		8
27 Sep.	1869	*Coming of Age*	Milano	Rivière	13
4 Oct.	1869	*All's Well That Ends Well*	D'Auban, Warde		
28 Dec.	1869	*Flamma*[3]	Justament	Rivière	23
28 Dec.	1869	*Watnoteenotumnotimo*	Evans		14
7 Mar.	1870	*Les Fleurs du Jardin*	Dewinne	Rivière	35
18 Apr.	1870	*The Terror of the Forest*	D'Auban, Warde	Gough	10
23 Jun.	1870	*Les Nations*	Dewinne	Rivière	19
4 Jul.	1870	*Brown, Jones and Robinson*	H. Boleno		8
29 Aug.	1870	*The Rivals*	Evans	Lee	10
24 Apr.	1871	*The Beauties of the Harem*	Milano	Rivière	23
24 Apr.	1871	*Puella*	Milano	Bottesini	12
29 May	1871	*Something of All Sorts*		D'Auban, Warde	4
26 Jun.	1871	*Fignolet et Entrechat*			1
17 Jul.	1871	*The Sylph of the Glen*	Milano	Rivière	11
16 Oct.	1871	*Fête à la Watteau*	Milano	Gough	10
16 Oct.	1871	*A Chinese Revel*	Milano	Gough	10
16 Oct.	1871	*The Rival Tailors*			10
4 Mar.	1872	*Buttons*	Evans		4
1 Apr.	1872	*Nana Sahib*	Verli	Panizza	9
1 Apr.	1872	*Twiddletumtwist!*	Evans	Lee	9
18 Aug.	1873	*The Enchanted Forest*	Dewinne	Jacobi	18
18 Aug.	1873	*Here, There and Everywhere*	Evans		5
22 Sep.	1873	*Dolly Varden's Lovers*	Kitchen		9
26 Dec.	1873	*Flick and Flock*	Dewinne	Hertel	36
28 Sep.	1874	*Pierrot en Voyage*	Dewinne		
10 May	1875	*Diable de Feu*	J. Lauri		7
26 Jun.	1875	*Cupid in Arcadia*	Dewinne	Jacobi	19
8 Nov.	1875	*The Flower Queen*	J. Lauri	Jacobi	7
8 Nov.	1875	*Love in a Tub*	J. Lauri		7
26 Dec.	1876	*The Fairies' Home*	Justament	Jacobi	18
18 Aug.	1877	*Yolande*[4]	Bertrand	Jacobi	17
20 May	1878	*The Golden Wreath*[5]	Bertrand	Jacobi	17
17 Oct.	1878	*Les Saisons*	Bertrand	Verdi	9
20 Oct.	1879	*Carmen*	Bertrand	Jacobi	9
31 May	1880	*Diona*[6]	Bertrand	Campana	12
27 Dec.	1880	*Hawaia*[4]	Bertrand	Jacobi	13
1 Dec.	1884	*The Swans*	Hansen	Jacobi	49
22 Dec.	1884	*Melusine*	Hansen	Jacobi	47
5 Oct.	1885	*Nina*	Hansen	Jacobi	33
21 Dec.	1885	*Le Bivouac*	Hansen	Jacobi	47
24 May	1886	*Cupid*	Hansen	Jacobi	30
15 Nov.	1886	*Dresdina*	Hansen	Jacobi	26
20 Dec.	1886	*The Seasons*	Hansen	Jacobi	29
16 May	1887	*Nadia*	Hansen	Jacobi	31
11 Jul.	1887	*Algeria*	Hansen	Jacobi	47
24 Dec.	1887	*Enchantment*	E. Casati	Jacobi	36

2 Revived on 11 Oct. 1869. Milano also produced it at the Circo, Madrid, on 13 Aug. 1870 as *El espíritu del mar*.

3 Produced at the Théâtre du Châtelet, Paris on 14 Aug. 1870.

4 Scenario be Alfred Thompson.

5 Scenario by J. Albery.

6 Scenario based on Saint-Georges' *Les Elfes* (Paris Opéra, 1856).

Date		Title	Choreographer	Composer	Weeks in Programme
4 Jun.	1888	*Antiope*	E. Casati	Jacobi	28
3 Sep.	1888	*Ideala*	E. Casati	Jacobi	30
17 Dec.	1888	*Irene*	E. Casati	Jacobi	29
1 Apr.	1889	*Our Army and Navy*	E. Casati	Jacobi	51
8 Jul.	1889	*Astrea*	E. Casati	Jacobi	24
23 Dec.	1889	*Asmodeus*	E. Casati	Jacobi	26
24 Mar.	1890	*Zanetta*	E. Casati	Jacobi	60
23 Jun.	1890	*Salandra*	E. Casati	Jacobi	25
15 Dec.	1890	*The Sleeping Beauty*	L. Espinosa	Jacobi	26
30 Mar.	1891	*On the Roofs*	C. Lauri		18
15 Jun.	1891	*Oriella*	Coppi	Jacobi	27
21 Dec.	1891	*Temptation*	Coppi	Jacobi	25
22 Feb.	1892	*On the Ice*	Coppi	Jacobi	30
13 Jun.	1892	*Don Juan*	Coppi	Jacobi	27
19 Sep.	1892	*Up the River*[7]	Dewinne	Jacobi	28
19 Dec.	1892	*Aladdin*	Coppi	Jacobi	26
27 Mar.	1893	*Chicago*	Grédelue	Jacobi	53
19 Jun.	1893	*Fidelia*	Grédelue	Jacobi	25
11 Dec.	1893	*Don Quixote*	E. Casati	Jacobi	28
30 Mar.	1894	*The Revolt of the Daughters*	H. Agoust, E. Casati	Jacobi	25
25 Jun.	1894	*Sita*	E. Casati	Jacobi	24
24 Sep.	1894	*Monkey Island*	H. Agoust	Slaughter	23
13 Dec.	1894	*Ali Baba and the Forty Thieves*	Coppi	Jacobi	33
4 Mar.	1895	*A Day Out*	H. Agoust		31
30 Jul.	1895	*Titania*	Coppi	Jacobi	20
7 Oct.	1895	*The Gathering of the Clans*	Coppi	Jacobi	43
16 Dec.	1895	*Blue Beard*	Coppi	Jacobi	32
4 Jun.	1896	*Donnybrook*	Coppi	Jacobi	34
29 Jul.	1896	*Rip Van Winkle*[8]	Coppi	Planquette	32
15 Dec.	1896	*The Tzigane*	Coppi	Jacobi	39
25 May	1897	*Victoria and Merrie England*	Coppi	Sullivan	24
4 Jan.	1898	*Beauty and the Beast*	Coppi	Jacobi	14
8 Aug.	1898	*Jack Ashore*[9]	Pratesi	Byng	37
30 Jan.	1899	*The Red Shoes*[10]	Pratesi	Mader, Byng	28
24 Apr.	1899	*A Day Off*[9]	Pratesi	Byng	33
21 Aug.	1899	*Napoli*[11]	Pratesi	Byng	39
11 Dec.	1899	*Soldiers of the Queen*[12]			47
24 Sep.	1900	*The Handy Man*[9]	Rossi	Byng	37
19 Dec.	1900	*The Gay City*[9]	Cormani, Farren	Byng	42
10 Jun.	1901	*Inspiration*[13]	Coppi	Byng	27
10 Oct.	1901	*Gretna Green*[9]	Coppi	Byng	41
23 Dec.	1901	*Santa Claus*	Coppi	Byng	11
21 Apr.	1902	*In Japan*[14]	Coppi	Ganne	38
16 Jun.	1902	*Britannia's Realm*[13]	Coppi	Ronald	46
12 Jan.	1903	*The Devil's Forge*[13]	Cormani	Byng	44
7 May	1903	*Carmen*[9]	Cormani	Bizet, Byng	47

7 Scenario by John Hollingshead.

8 Scenario by Carlo Coppi.

9 Scenario and production by Charles Wilson.

10 Adapted from a scenario by H. Regel and J. Hassreiter.

11 Production by Charles Wilson and Giovanni Pratesi.

12 Scenario by 'A.Sol.Dato' and production by Charles Wilson. Revived on 16 Dec. 1901 as *Soldiers of the King*.

13 Scenario and production by Malcolm Watson.

14 Scenario by S. L. Bensusan, based on his story *Dédé*, and production by Charles Wilson. Revived at the Scala, Milan, on 1 Mar. 1903 as *Nel Giappone*.

Date		Title	Choreographer	Composer	Weeks in Programme
21 Jan.	1904	*All the Year Round*[15]	Cormani, Farren, Rosi	Glover	56
29 Aug.	1904	*The Entente Cordiale*[13]	Curti	Ronald	67
27 Feb.	1905	*My Lady Nicotine*[9]	Cormani	Byng	55
17 Jul.	1905	*Le Rêve*		Byng	7
30 Oct.	1905	*Lucerito*	Rosi (interpolated dances)	de Anduaga, Byng	8
11 Dec.	1905	*Parisiana*[9, 16]	Curti	Glover	61
11 Jun.	1906	*L'Amour*[17]	Curti	Thomé	53
25 Feb.	1907	*Queen of Spades*	Curti	Mario Costa, Byng	31
17 Jun.	1907	*Electra*	Curti	Byng	13
7 Oct.	1907	*Les Cloches de Corneville*[18]	Curti	Planquette, Byng	40
27 Jan.	1908	*Cupid Wins*	Curti	Byng	9
30 Mar.	1908	*Sal'-Oh-My!*		Byng	27
25 May	1908	*The Two Flags*	Curti	Byng	32
12 Oct.	1908	*Paquita*	Curti	Byng	25
14 Dec.	1908	*Narcisse*		Byng	3
4 Jan.	1909	*La Petite Bohémienne*		Thomé	12
22 Feb.	1909	*On the Square*	Clerc	Byng	30
5 Apr.	1909	*Psyche*	Curti	Moul	25
20 Dec.	1909	*Our Flag*	Curti	Byng	23
28 Feb.	1910	*The Polar Star*	Clerc	Byng	12
30 May	1910	*Femina*	Curti	Byng, Valverde	51
1 Aug.	1910	*On the Sands*	Clerc	Byng	22
13 Mar.	1911	*The Mad Pierrot*	Clerc	Byng	11
29 May	1911	*The Dance Dream*	Gorsky	various	22
19 Oct.	1911	*1830*[19]	Agoust, Clerc	Byng	17
24 Jan.	1912	*Carmen*	Berger	Bizet, Byng	18
7 May	1912	*The Pool*		Clutsam	4

15 Scenario and production by Charles Wilson, from a plot suggested by Alfred Sturgess.
16 Second edition presented on 19 Mar. 1906.
17 Production by Charles Wilson, scenario by Mrs T. Hay Ritchie and Charles Wilson.
18 Revived on 9 Aug. 1909.
19 Scenario by Maurice Volny.

APPENDIX B

Light opera divertissements at the Alhambra, 1872–84

Date		Title	Composer (*bal.* = ballet music)	Choreographer	Ballets
3 Jun.	1872	*Le Roi Carotte*	Offenbach	Verli	1. Sabotière and Characteristic Dance; Farandole 2. Grand Ballet 3. Butterfly Ballet
23 Dec.	1872	*The Black Crook*	Jacobi, Clay	Hus	1. Amazonian Bell Ballet 2. The Island of Pleasure: Grand Ballet
16 Aug.	1873	*La Belle Hélène*	Offenbach	Dewinne	La Belle Hélène Quadrille
26 Dec.	1873	*Don Juan*	Offenbach, Lecocq, Clay, Jacobi	Dewinne	1. Dance of Pirates 2. Bolero
18 May	1874	*La Jolie Parfumeuse*	Offenbach	Dewinne	Villagers' Quadrille
7 Sep.	1874	*The Demon's Bride*	Jacobi	Dewinne	1. The Star of Hope 2. Grand Divertissement Carnavalesque
2 Nov.	1874	*Le Roi Carotte* (revival)	Offenbach	Dewinne	1. Sabotière Rustic Quadrille; Farandole 2. The Insect Kingdom: Grand Ballet 3. Monkey Divertissement
26 Dec.	1874	*Whittington*	Offenbach	Dewinne	1. Sailors' Dance 2. Grand Barbaric Ballet 3. Ballet of Peasants and Archers
10 May	1875	*Chilpéric*	Hervé	Dewinne	1. Spanish Divertissement 2. Grand Barbaric Ballet (from *Whittington*)
27 Dec.	1875	*Lord Bateman*	Jacobi	Lauri	Turkish Ballet
12 Feb.	1876	*Don Juan* (revival)	various, *bal.* Jacobi		1. Pirate Ballet 2. Spanish dancers (Casabonas)

Date		*Title*	*Composer (bal. = ballet music)*	*Choreographer*	*Ballets*
22 Dec.	1879	*Rothomago*	*bal.* Jacobi	Bertrand	1. Les Vins Gaulois: Grand Vintage Ballet 2. Memnon: Grand Egyptian Ballet 3. Grand Ballet Céramique, or International Congress of all the Porcelains
19 Apr.	1880	*La Fille du Tambour Major*	Offenbach, *bal.* Jacobi	Bertrand	The Alpine Brigands (first perf. 23 Aug. 1880)
20 Dec.	1880	*Mefistofele II*	Hervé, *bal.* Mendelssohn		The Walpurgis Night Revels
28 Mar.	1881	*Jeanne, Jeannette and Jeanneton*	Lacome, *bal.* Jacobi	Bertrand	1. Endymion 2. Grand Masquerade Ballet
4 Jul.	1881	*The Bronze Horse*	Auber, *bal.* Jacobi	Bertrand	1. Japanese Divertissement 2. In a Star
3 Dec.	1881	*The Black Crook* (revival)	Jacobi, Clay	Bertrand	1. Amazonian Ballet 2. Ballet of Ferns 3. Coral Isle Ballet
8 Apr.	1882	*Babil and Bijou*	Jacobi	Bertrand	1. Grand Ballet of Fish (music: A. Adam) 2. Grand Ballet of the Seasons[1]
16 Oct.	1882	*The Merry War*	Strauss, *bal.* Jacobi	Bertrand	Grand Military Ballet
1 Jan.	1883	*Yellow Dwarf*[2]		Hansen	1. Grand Ballet of Fans 2. Dolls' Quadrille 3. Furies' Orgie
26 Mar.	1883	*A Trip to the Moon*[2] (revival)	Offenbach		1. Grand Ballet des Chimères 2. Grand Snow Ballet
3 Dec.	1883	*The Golden Ring*	Clay	Bertrand	1. Pastoral Ballet and Sailors' Dance 2. Grand Storm Ballet 3. Grand Festival Ballet
12 Apr.	1884	*The Beggar Student*	Millöcker, *bal.* Jacobi	Hansen	1. Grand Ballet of Fair Folk 2. Grand Military Ballet
2 Aug.	1884	*Black-Eyed Susan*	Lee	Hansen	1. Maypole and Morris Dance 2. Hornpipe and Broadsword Combat Dance

1 According to Jules Rivière, Jacobi was responsible for the Spring and Summer numbers only, the rest being composed by le Billemont.

2 Given at Her Majesty's Theatre, while the second Alhambra Theatre was being built.

APPENDIX C

Principal dancers in the Alhambra ballets, 1860–1912

Mmes
Adamovitch, Ekaterina 1911
Adler, Wanda 1893
Agnes 1871
Agoust, Louise 1894–96
Alexia 1907
Anderson, Elizaveta 1911
Aouda 1887
Austin, Esther 1871

Balashova, Alexandra 1911
Balbi, Clotilde 1871
Baratti, Giovannina 1872
Bartoletti, Malvina 1872
Bessone, Emma 1885–90
Bioletti, Ernestina 1865
Blaney, Jacqueline 1902, 1908
Boleno, Emma 1865
Bordin, Maria 1906–07
Britta [Petersen] 1908–10

Campana, Lina 1896–97
Casaboni, Josephine 1896–99, 1903–04
Castelli, Luigia 1871
Cavallazzi, Malvina 1879
Cerri, Cecilia 1894–96, 1898
Clayton, Bessie 1911
Clerc, Elisa 1909–11
Collier, Carrie 1866–67
Colonna 1870
Cormani, Gina 1906–11
Cormani, Lucia 1886–91, 1893–94, 1902, 1905–07
Cossio, C. 1887–89, 1893–94
Cristino 1891
Cyrene 1893

D'Alençon, Emilienne 1898–99
David, Judith 1878
De Gillert, Theodora 1876–81
De La Bruyère, Consuela 1882–83
Delachaux, Anna 1876
De Lorenzi 1888

Earle, May 1906–08
Elia, Carolina 1891–92
Elliott, Topsy 1883, 1887
Espinosa, Judith 1900–01
Espinosa, Ray 1911
Estra 1866–67

Feder, Julie 1868
Ferrero, Antonietta 1891
Finette 1868
Franzioni 1886
Fredericke, Eugénie 1865
Fuensanta, María 1879

Galeotti 1888
Geltser, Ekaterina 1911
Gneroschi, Vanda 1887–88
Grigolatis, Preciosa 1894–95
Grosvenor, Lizzie 1871
Guerrero, Rosario 1899, 1902–03
Gunniss, Lizzie 1871
Gunniss, Tessy 1867

Haupt, Emma 1895
Hoby 1891–92
Holt, Elise 1872

Kiralfy, Aniola 1866

Lauri, Louisa 1860
Lee, Lillie 1886
Leggiero, Rita 1910
Legnani, Pierina 1888–94, 1897
Leonora, La Belle 1908–10
Levey, Florence 1895–96
Linda, Berta 1872–73
Lola la Flamenca 1910
Luna [Lauri] 1878

Macellaro, Margherita 1871
Mari, Alma 1902–03
María la Bella 1903, 1905, 1912
Marianna 1863
Marie 1886–95
May, Jane 1905–06
Moore, Xenia Greville 1911
Morino 1907–08
Mosolova, Vera 1911
Mossetti, Carlotta 1909, 1912
Muller, Marie 1880
Müller, Poldi 1911

Palladino, Emma 1881–82, 1884–88
Paris 1886–87
Passani 1876–77
Pertoldi, Erminia 1874–84
Pitteri, Giovannina 1869–70, 1873–76
Pollini, Palmira 1892–93
Pomponnette 1908
Porro, Bice 1893–94

Rescalli 1890
Rigl, Betty 1875
Roffey 1888, 1890–94
Rokoh, Imra 1879
Rosa [Abrahams] 1876–81, 1884
Rosalind, Amy 1867–70, 1872
Roselli 1879
Rossi, Adelina 1883

Salandri 1909
Salmoiraghi, Elena 1893–94
Sampietro 1884
Sangalli, Rita 1871
Sara [Wright] 1873–74
Saracco, Maria 1889–90
Scotti, Pia 1889–90
Seale, Julia 1890–99, 1907–10
Sidonie 1873–75
Sismondi 1867–69, 1871–72, 1875–80, 1883
Skelley, Marjorie 1903–04, 1908–12
Slack, Edith 1900–06
Sozo, Adelina 1886–87
Spotti, Angelina 1889–91
Sylphe, La 1905–06

Tessi 1878
Thurgate, Minnie 1887–92
Tourneur, Anaïs 1866–67

Valain, Marie 1882
Varasi, Enrica 1906
Vawara 1871
Vergé 1890

Zajah, Enil 1911
Zallio, Adela 1886–87
Zanini, Angelina 1871
Zimmerman 1890–92

MM.
Agoust, Emile 1910–12
Almonti, E. 1901–04
Almonti, G. 1900–04, 1906
André, Jules 1866
André, Victor 1911

Bekefy, Aladar 1871–73
Biancofiori 1891–92

Corge, Eugène 1868–69
Coventry, Tom 1899–1912
Curti, Alfredo 1906

De Vincenti, Vittorio 1889–91
Dewinne, Henri 1870, 1873–74

Evans, Fred 1867–70, 1872–73

Faico 1910
Farren, Fred 1898–1902
Flexmore, George 1894–95
Frielli, Henri 1904–08

Giuseppe 1863
Gobbo, Laurentini 1896–97
Grey, Lytton 1894–1902
Guainazzi 1897

Josset, Alfred 1873–79
Josset, Emile 1875–79

Kiralfy, Bolossy 1866
Kiralfy, Imre 1866
Koslov, Alexis 1911

Lauri, Charles 1891
Lawton, Frank 1909
Lupino, George 1892–93

Macellaro, Delpino 1871
Miralles 1905

Novikov, Lavrenti 1911

Orfeo 1907

Paganini Redivivus 1893
Pratesi, Giovanni 1898–99
Protti 1911

Raymond, Charles 1898–1901, 1910–11
Raymond, J. 1866–67, 1869, 1871
Rimma, Fritz 1898–99
Rosi, Giovanni 1904–09
Rossi, Egidio 1897–98

Santini, Amedeo 1905–08
Saracco, Giorgio 1889–90
Storey, Fred 1892–94, 1896–97, 1900–01

Tikhomirov, Vasili 1911

Vanara 1896–97
Vawara 1871
Volbert 1903, 1909, 1912

Zhukov, Leonide 1911

Troupes
Agoust family 1894–99
Almonti family 1892–99, 1903
Kromo family 1898
Lauri family 1866, 1875
Ri-Tchave troupe 1910
Vokes family 1898

APPENDIX D

Alhambra ballets: selected scenarios

NOTE: Two other Alhambra ballets are described in Cyril Beaumont's *Complete Book of Ballets – Femina* and *The Dance Dream*.

The Sleeping Beauty

Grand Spectacular Ballet in five tableaux. The ballet arranged by Léon Espinosa. The music specially composed by Georges Jacobi. The scenery by T. E. Ryan. The costumes by M. and Mme Alias from designs by M. Gray and Howell Russell. First performed at the Alhambra Theatre, December 15, 1890.

Princess Diana	Pierina Legnani
The King (her father)	Mr Wagner
The Queen (her mother)	Mlle Zimmerman
Prince Hubert	Mlle Marie
Equerry to the Prince	Edouard Espinosa
A Courtier } A Woodcutter }	Mme Roffey
Good Fairies	Teresina Cormani; Mlle Catherine [Kate Brandon]; Pia Scotti
The Evil Geni	Vittorio De Vincenti

TABLEAU I. *Banqueting hall in the Palace.*

The King and Queen are giving, in honour of the fifteenth birthday of the Princess, a grand Reception and Ball, to which all the nobility of the country have been invited, as well as certain Fairies, the Princess's Godmothers, who present her with fairy gifts, such as beauty, virtue, wisdom, happiness, &c.

The Evil Geni, who has been in friendly relations with the King, but is now enraged at not having been invited to the entertainment, enters, and threatens a terrible revenge, which is to take the following shape, *i.e.*, the young Princess is to see a Spinning-wheel which, tempted by curiosity, she will try to work, and the Needle in which will prick her finger and inflict a wound from the effects of which she will die.

The Good Fairies, compassionating the grief of her parents at this dismal prospect, promise to watch over and protect their God-child, and also promise further that, although it is not in their power to completely neutralise the spell, they can and will so modify it that the Princess shall not actually die, but only *appear* to do so, falling, in reality, into a deep sleep and so continuing until a young Prince shall arrive and by his presence awake and release her.

The King orders all the spinning-wheels in the Kingdom to be destroyed, and the Princess making her appearance he desires the Dances to be resumed.

Passepied

Sword Dance and Bacchanalian Dance

TABLEAU II. *An old gallery in the Palace.*

The Evil Geni enters and causes a Spinning-wheel to appear. The Princess approaching, he assumes the guise of an old woman and dances mockingly. When the Princess enters he pretends to be asleep, and she dances round the supposed old woman, who, waking up, applauds her dancing. The Princess admires the Spinning-wheel and at the suggestion of the Geni tries to work it. The needle pricks her finger and he rejoices maliciously at his success. The King and Queen, accompanied by the Fairies, enter, and the fainting Princess falls into their arms.

TABLEAU III. *(20 years later.) The magic wood (night).*

The Geni appears and orders the trees to prevent the Prince from approaching the sleeping Princess. (*Exit.*)

The Prince enters, he has lost his way, and calls for his Equerry, who comes in trembling at the sight of the glow-worms glimmering in the grass. A Woodcutter approaches; the Prince asks him whose castle is that which he sees in the distance. The Woodcutter, in reply, relates the story of the Sleeping Beauty, and says the Princess, like all the other inhabitants of the castle, has slept for 20 years. The Prince thanks and rewards the Woodcutter, who then retires.

The Prince resolves to proceed to the castle and release the Princess from her spell, but Wood-nymphs appear and try to prevent him. (*Slow valse of Wood-nymphs and Glow-worms.*) Being, however, fully determined, the Prince draws his sword and begins to advance, whereupon the Wood-nymphs disappear, the trees vanish, and he makes his way to the castle.

TABLEAU IV. *State bedchamber of the Princess.*

The Princess and some of her attendants are seen asleep, covered by dust and cobwebs. The Fairies then approach and enchant the Air, which gives Love to the Prince when he breathes it. The Prince enters and tries to wake the Princess, who without waking, rises and resumes life in *A Magnetic Dance*, at the conclusion of which the Prince kisses her. Then she wakes and he declares his love; the King and Queen enter, unite the happy pair, and bless their union.

TABLEAU V. *A bridal festival.*
Grand Valse of Lace and Fans
Folly Polka
Grand Galop
Finale
APOTHEOSIS

Don Juan

Ballet in three scenes by Carlo Coppi. Music by Georges Jacobi. Scenery by T. E. Ryan. Costumes designed by Howell Russell. First performed at the Alhambra Theatre, June 13, 1892.

Don Juan ('an up to date Johnny')	Mlle Marie
Leporello (his servant)	G. Lupino
The Commandant (a statuesque person)	Mr Wagner
Anna (his daughter)	Miss Hooton
Elvira (a former love of Don Juan)	Miss Hoby
Max (betrothed to Zerlina)	Mme Roffey
Zerlina (a giddy girl)	Pierina Legnani
Incidental Personages:	
The Four Statues	The three Almontis, F. Yarnold

NOTE: The story of 'Don Juan' came originally, like all stories, from the east, and through the Moors was brought into Spain. From Spain Molière got the plot which formed the basis of his comedy *Le Festin de Pierre*. This piece was adapted for the English market by Shadwell, under the title of *The Libertine*. Shadwell's *Libertine* became a ballet in England about 1790, and was taken up *con amore* by Grimaldi. Played by this great pantomimist, who represented Leporello, it was the only entertainment that stopped, for a single night, the 'OP Riots' at Covent Garden Theatre in the early part of the century. *Don Juan* at the Alhambra has been modernised in the spirit of the present age, and has been dressed in some parts *à la fin du siècle*.

JOHN HOLLINGSHEAD

TABLEAU I. *A Bavarian beer garden. Holiday fête. Drinking, dancing and flirtation.* Leporello makes mischief, and gets a beating. German students cause a riot. They end by dancing. Anna, the Commandant's daughter, escapes from Don Juan. He consoles himself with other ladies until he takes a fancy to Zerlina. At last he has to face the indignant Elvira, his former love. By this time Leporello feels the effect of Lager-beer. Don Juan returns to Anna. The Commandant interferes and challenges Don Juan. The duel takes place off stage, and the Commandant is killed. The people are indignant, and try to arrest Don Juan, but, by the aid of the students, he escapes. The scene winds up with a beer-revel.

Tableau II. *Shows an opera colonnade with dancers coming from a masked ball.* Don Juan is flirting with Anna and Zerlina, watched by Elvira, all masked. Leporello has letters to deliver, but goes to sleep. Elvira reads the letters. Anna and Zerlina do the same. Leporello awakes. The moon lights up the statue of the Commandant. Leporello's fright. Teetotum Dance. Don Juan rebukes Leporello for his carelessness. Leporello points to the statue and Don Juan tells him to ask the Commandant's ghost to supper. Leporello tries to climb up the statue. Don Juan at last invites the Commandant himself and his offer is accepted.

Tableau III. *Don Juan's Palace.*
Grand fête and banquet. Leporello introduces a gipsy band, amongst whom are three ladies (Anna, Elvira and Zerlina). Fortune-telling scene. Don Juan hears his doom, but goes on with the festivities. Danse de Jupon, by Signorina Legnani. A knock is heard: the Commandant enters. He claims Don Juan, and after a wild orgie, secures his victim and is revenged.

Victoria and Merrie England

Grand National Ballet in eight tableaux. The scenario and the ballet invented by Carlo Coppi. Music by Arthur Sullivan. Scenery by T. E. Ryan. Costumes designed by Howell Russell. First performed at the Alhambra Theatre, May 25, 1897.

Genius of Britain (Sc. I) May Queen (Sc. III)	Pierina Legnani
Britannia	Ethel Hawthorne
Robin Hood (Sc. III) Jester (Sc. VI)	Julia Seale
Maid Marian	Josephine Casaboni
Friar Tuck	Lytton Grey
Little John	Signor Guainazzi
Herne, the Hunter	M. Vanara

Scene I. *Ancient Britain. Forest of oaks. Evening.*
Britannia discovered sleeping beneath the sacred oak of the Druids. The Genius of Britain enters. She regards the sleeping Britannia and predicts her future greatness.

Solo (Legnani)

Entrance and March of the Druids, Neophytes, etc.

Rites of the Mistletoe

The High Priest approaches the sacred oak, at the foot of which Britannia lies in sleep. The High Priest, inspired, announces that the sleeping woman is predestined to be the mother of a race which shall be mighty among the Nations of the World. He twines an oak wreath which he places upon Britannia's head.

Britannia awakes and embraces Britain's Genius.

Tableau

SCENE II. *Coming of age in Queen Elizabeth's time.*
Retainers arrive to tender homage and congratulations to the young heir. His old uncle entrusts to his keeping a sword, saying, 'With this I fought for Queen and country'.

Commencement of the Birthday Festivities

SCENE III. *May Day.*
Enter Bag-pipers, Hobby-horses, Robin Hood, Maid Marian, Friar Tuck, Little John, Jack-in-the-Green, Musicians and Revellers. The May Queen enters, enthroned and attended by her Maids of Honour.

Tableau
Historical Quadrille by Britons, Romans, Saxons, and Normans
Morris Dance
Quadrille – Knights of the Sword and Rose Maidens
General Dance
Flirtation Scene and Pas de Deux – Robin Hood and Maid Marian
Comic Scene – Friar Tuck and the Dragon
Dance of Hobby-horses
General Dance
Solo (Legnani)
Maypole Dance and Finale

SCENE IV. *The legend of Herne the Hunter. A wild glade in Windsor Forest. Night.*
Herne the Hunter's weird retainers enter, carrying the spoils of the chase. Herne the Hunter appears. He reproaches them on the insignificance of their offerings, and commands the hunt to be resumed. His retainers urge that they are weary, and refuse to obey. Herne threatens them, upon which they prostrate themselves before him. He orders them to follow him.

Entrance of Wood Nymphs
Dance of Wood Nymphs *Solo* (Nancy Houghton)

SCENE V. *Bringing home the Yule Log.*
Yule Log Procession. Pipers, Drummers, Musicians, Peasants, Masqueraders and Children dancing in front of the Yule Log.

The festivities are abruptly interrupted by the sudden appearance of Herne and his followers. All shrink back terrified at the wild Hunters. But the Snow Fairy appearing, protects the merrymakers and subdues Herne.

Dance Ensemble
Solo (Legnani)
Finale

SCENE VI. *Christmas in the olden time. Hall of an old castle.*
Enter Lord and Lady of the Manor, followed by Nobles, Guests and Jesters.

Procession of the Boar's Head and Roast Beef.

Guests drink the health of their host, who orders the tables to be removed and the doors to be opened, that all may partake of the Christmas cheer.

The Peasants and Vassals enter, and express their good wishes to their liege Lord and Lady.

Jester's Dance (Julia Seale)
Blind Man's Buff
Comic Pas de Quatre
Entrance of Father Christmas, who distributes gifts
Kissing Dance
Finale

Scene VII. *Coronation of Her Majesty Queen Victoria. Tableau vivant.*
Reproducing the celebrated picture by E. T. Parris, illustrating the Coronation of Her Majesty the Queen in Westminster Abbey on June 28, 1838, and dedicated to the British Nation by Thomas Boys.

Scene VIII. *1897. Britain's glory. Entrance of troops.*
Grenadier Guards, Royal Irish, Gordon Highlanders, Artists Volunteer Corps, 22nd Bombay Infantry, Cape Mounted Infantry, Canadian Troopers, Australian Rifles.

Entrance of groups, allegorical of British Colonies
Entrance of British Sailors
Hornpipe
Military Evolutions
'God Save the Queen'

The Four Emblematical Pedestal Groups, representing Europe, Asia, Africa and America, are exact reproductions of the Sculptures on the base of the Albert Memorial, Hyde Park.

The Devil's Forge

Legendary Ballet in two scenes invented and produced by Charles Wilson. Action and Dances by Lucia Cormani. Music by George W. Byng. Scenery by T. E. Ryan and E. H. Ryan junior. Costumes designed by Comelli. First performed at the Alhambra Theatre, January 12, 1903.

Karl	Edith Slack
Heinrich	Miss J. Reeve
The Burgomaster	Mr A. Walcott
Gretchen (the Burgomaster's daughter)	Rosie Dean
Joseph (friends of Karl)	Miss N. Hill
Aans (friends of Karl)	Miss R. Burrows
The Demon of the Forge	Ada Taylor
Melitta (companions of Gretchen)	Miss M. Hart
Rosalie (companions of Gretchen)	Miss J. Arnold
The Fairy of the Mountain	Alma Mari

Scene I. *A German village.*
The action takes place in a German town, and the period may, broadly speaking, be described as sixteenth century.

Karl, a young sword maker, whose skill has made his town famous, is about to be betrothed to Gretchen, the beautiful daughter of the Burgomaster. His friends, who are assembled to witness the ceremony and to participate in the rejoicings, find Karl in his workshop putting the final touches to a sword which is to be presented to his future father-in-law.

Presently the latter enters, accompanied by his daughter, and love tokens having been exchanged, the guests are invited to dance and make merry. While the revelries are proceeding, Heinrich, accompanied by some companions, enters. He is told of the betrothal, and being smitten by the charms of Gretchen, conceives, in a spirit of jealousy, a scheme for the humiliation of her lover. Heinrich draws his sword and, having at a blow partly cleft a helmet, invites Karl to a similar test with the weapon the latter has just completed. Karl, amazed at the wondrous workmanship of Heinrich's sword, attempts the task and fails, his boasted blade falling in pieces. To add to his humiliation, the Burgomaster leads Gretchen away, refusing to sanction her betrothal to a disgraced man.

The guests depart, and Karl, left alone, broods over his misfortunes. From bitter reflections he is aroused by an old woman who, entreating him to listen, tells him of the mystic cavern on the mountain, the fire glow of which can be seen in the distance. She tells him that if he is brave enough to face the eerie dangers of "The Devil's Forge", to place his sword in the fire that bursts from a cleft in the rock, and afterwards to hold it for some moments in the stream that flows through the cavern, such elasticity and power will be imparted to the blade that no armour could possibly withstand it. With the coming of night, Karl, strengthened by his love for Gretchen is seen wending his way to the mountain.

SCENE II. *The Devil's Forge.*
The scene changes to the 'Devil's Forge' with its cauldron of issuing fire, vapour and smoke. Around the seething cauldron, goblins and hideous forms are dancing. Karl is seen standing at the entrance to the cavern. Boldly he advances to carry out the old woman's instructions, but the foul, fiery breath of the place drives him back. Again he tries to reach the flaming rock, from which the demons in vain try to drive him. A step nearer, and the very rocks themselves appear to him to be transformed into dancers, who try to lure him from the fire. Undaunted still, Karl strides forward, and being faint, would drink of the cold stream, but the Spirit warns him of the doom of all who have drunk of these waters.

His love for Gretchen nerves Karl to a mighty effort, and reaching the fire-lapped rock, he holds within it his sword, which instantly becomes red-hot. Then, his task half done, he turns to the stream, which, as the blade is immersed, changes its course and flowing into the furnace, causes an explosion which renders open the mountain.

In the closing tableau Karl's triumph is complete.

APPENDIX E

Ballets produced at the Empire, 1884–1915

Date		Title	Choreographer	Composer	Weeks in Programme
8 Nov.	1884	*Coppélia*	Bertrand	Delibes	6
24 Dec.	1884	*Giselle*	Bertrand	Adam	1
21 Dec.	1885	*Hurly-Burly*			3
22 Dec.	1887	*Dilara*	Lanner	Hervé	45
22 Dec.	1887	*The Sports of England*	Lanner	Hervé	21
19 May	1888	*Rose d'Amour*	Lanner	Hervé	34
31 Oct.	1888	*Diana*	Lanner	Hervé	29
24 Dec.	1888	*Robert Macaire*	Martinetti		5
28 Jan.	1889	*The Duel in the Snow*[1]	Martinetti, Lanner	Hervé	26
20 May	1889	*Cleopatra*	Lanner	Hervé	31
26 Sep.	1889	*The Paris Exhibition*	Lanner	Hervé	33
23 Dec.	1889	*A Dream of Wealth*[2]	Lanner	Wenzel	52
20 May	1890	*Cécile*	Lanner	Wenzel	53
22 Dec.	1890	*Dolly*	Lanner	Wenzel	36
25 May	1891	*Orfeo*	Lanner	Wenzel	30
31 Aug.	1891	*By the Sea*[3]	Lanner	Wenzel	56
24 Dec.	1891	*Nisita*	Lanner	Wenzel	21
23 May	1892	*Versailles*	Lanner	Wenzel	39
26 Sep.	1892	*Round the Town*[4]	Lanner	Wenzel	66
20 Feb.	1893	*Katrina*	Lanner	Wenzel	63
27 Sep.	1893	*The Girl I Left Behind Me*	Lanner	Wenzel	54
21 May	1894	*La Frolique*	Lanner	Ford	50
8 Oct.	1894	*On Brighton Pier*[5]	Lanner	Ford	39
6 May	1895	*Faust*	Lanner	Lutz, Ford	65
25 Jan.	1896	*La Danse*	Lanner	Ford	39
26 Oct.	1896	*Monte Cristo*	Lanner	Wenzel	56
21 Jun.	1897	*Under One Flag*	Lanner	Wenzel	32
14 Feb.	1898	*The Press*	Lanner	Wenzel	34
12 Oct.	1898	*Alaska*	Lanner	Wenzel	30
8 May	1899	*Round the Town Again*[6]	Lanner	Wenzel	70
10 Sep.	1900	*Sea-Side*	Lanner	Wenzel	27
18 Mar.	1901	*Les Papillons*	Lanner	Wenzel	59
6 Nov.	1901	*Old China*	Lanner	Wenzel	29
28 May	1902	*Our Crown*	Lanner	Wenzel	33
14 Jan.	1903	*The Milliner Duchess*[7]	Lanner	Wenzel	46
26 Sep.	1903	*Vineland*	Lanner	Wenzel	24

1 Revived, 23 Mar. 1903
2 Second edition, 13 Oct. 1890.
3 Second edition, 15 Feb. 1892.
4 Second edition, 29 May, 1893. Revived, 28 Jan. 1895.
5 Revived, 12 Aug. 1895.
6 Second edition, 29 Jan. 1900
7 Second edition, 31 Oct. 1904.

Date		Title	Choreographer	Composer	Weeks in Programme
9 Mar.	1904	*High Jinks*[8]	Lanner	Wenzel	34
3 Jan.	1905	*The Dancing Doll*[9]	Lanner	Bayer, Clarke	26
9 Oct.	1905	*The Bugle Call*	Farren, Ad. Genée	Sidney Jones	27
6 Jan.	1906	*Cinderella*	Farren, Ad. Genée	Sidney Jones	18
14 May	1906	*Coppélia*[10]	Al. Genée	Delibes, Glaser	49
6 Aug.	1906	*Fête Galante*	Farren	Glaser	13
15 Nov.	1906	*The Débutante*	Lanner	Clarke, Glaser	24
7 May	1907	*Sir Roger de Coverley*	Lanner	Carr	21
30 Sep.	1907	*The Belle of the Ball*[11]	Farren, Ad. Genée	Clarke	36
7 Sep.	1908	*The Dryad*[12]	Ad. Genée	Bright	2
19 Oct.	1908	*A Day in Paris*	Farren	Clarke	51
5 Jul.	1909	*Roberto il Diavolo*	Al. Genée	Meyerbeer	18
9 Oct.	1909	*Round the World*[13]	Farren	Clarke	41
25 Jul.	1910	*The Dancing Master*[14]	Farren	Clarke	42
10 Oct.	1910	*The Faun*	Farren	Bright	12
15 Nov.	1910	*Ship Ahoy!*	Farren	Clarke	26
18 May	1911	*Sylvia*	Farren	Delibes	21
10 Oct.	1911	*New York*	Farren	Clarke	25
2 Apr.	1912	*The Water Nymph*	Kyasht	Pugni, Kadletz	15
24 Sep.	1912	*First Love*	Kyasht	Glinka, Clarke	5
11 Feb.	1913	*The Reaper's Dream*	Kyasht	Delibes, Tchaikovsky	6
4 Oct.	1913	*Titania*	Kyasht	Mendelssohn, Clarke	13
7 Sep.	1914	*Europe*	E. Espinosa	Guy Jones	25
22 Mar.	1915	*The Vine*	Farren	Schumann, Grieg, Debussy, arr. Pinches	24
6 Sep.	1915	*Pastorale*	Majilton	Pinches	22

8 Second edition, 26 Sep. 1904.

9 Second edition, 3 Apr. 1905.

10 Revived, 10 Jun. 1908.

11 Second edition, 30 Dec. 1907.

12 Originally produced privately, and afterwards danced by Genée at the Playhouse Theatre, 26 Mar. 1907.

13 Second edition, *East and West*, produced 21 Mar. 1910.

14 Revived by E. Espinosa, 27 Feb. 1914.

APPENDIX F

Principal dancers in the Empire ballets, 1884–1915

Mmes

Aenea 1887–88, 1890–91
Ardraghetti, Landamia 1895

Balashova, Alexandra 1914
Bedells, Phyllis 1907–15
Bessone, Emma 1885
Brambilla, Isabella 1894
Brianza, Carlotta 1888, 1893–94

Candida 1894
Carmen 1889
Carozzi, Felicita 1893
Cavallazzi, Malvina 1887–99
Cerale, Luigia 1892–93
Cerri, Cecilia 1899
Clerc, Elise 1891–1908
Collier, Beatrice 1906–10
Coppini, Sofia 1892
Cora 1891–1904
Cornalba, Elena 1888, 1892, 1895
Courtland, Alma 1892–1914
Craske, Dorothy 1896, 1898, 1902–07, 1914

De Sortis, Bettina 1887–92

Farrant, Amy 1915
Ferrero, Antonietta 1902

Gantenberg, Edvige 1896–97
Genée, Adeline 1897–1909
Giuri, Maria 1887–93
Gradella 1896–1900

Hamer, Hetty 1910
Hofschüller, Julie 1884
Holt, Alice 1884–85

Irmler, Martha 1896

June 1915

Kyasht, Lydia 1908–13

Laurent, Marie 1884
Levey, Florence 1893–94
Loveday, L. 1893
Luna [Lauri] 1886

Manneroffer, Amalia 1887–88
Martell, Flo 1906–15
More, Unity 1909–13
Mossetti, Carlotta 1910–11, 1914–15

Nelidova, Lydia 1895

Palladino, Emma 1886–93
Papucci, Quetta 1898–1904
Paston, May 1889–1909
Pavor, Daisy 1910, 1913
Pertoldi, Erminia 1886
Porro, Bice 1894–95

Rossi, Adelina 1887–88, 1891

St Helier, Ivy 1913
Santori, Edea 1887–88
Sarcy, Héva 1893
Savigny, Marie 1892–93
Seymour, Kate 1892–93
Sinden, Topsy 1889–91, 1908
Sismondi 1884–85
Slack, Edith 1891–1900
Sozo, Adelina 1891
Spotti, Angelina 1888

Trevissick, B. 1898–1909

Vaughan, Kate 1886
Vincent, Ada 1888–1905

Walter, Connie 1914–15

Zanfretta, Francesca 1895–1900, 1903–09, 1914–15
Zauli, Delfina 1885

MM.

Albertieri, Luigi 1887–1891

Bishop, Will 1893–1902, 1904
Bolm, Adolph 1908, 1910

Cecchetti, Enrico 1888, 1891–92

De Vincenti, Vittorio 1891–95

Elia, Simone 1892–93
Espinosa, Edouard 1914

Farren, Fred 1904–12
Flexmore, Fred 1893

Gavrilov, Alexander 1913
Genée, Alexander 1908
Guerra, Nicolà 1891

Kurylo, Edward J. 1911–12

Lawton, Frank 1900
Litavkin, Serge 1913

Mordkin, Mikhail 1914

Peshkov 1910

Ridley, John 1887–99
Rosi, Giovanni 1910

Santini, Amadeo 1899–1905
Sundberg, Paul 1903–07

Vincent, George 1892–1901, 1903, 1908
Vladimirov, Piotr 1913

Vokes, William 1904–06
Volinine, Alexandre 1912

Walls, Tom 1907–09
Warde, Willie 1884, 1892–93

Zalewski, Jan 1910–11
Zhukov, Leonide 1913

APPENDIX G

Empire ballets: selected scenarios

NOTE: Five Empire ballets are described in Cyril Beaumont's *Complete Book of Ballets* – *The Press*, *Les Papillons*, *Cinderella*, *The Débutante* and *The Dryad*, all of which date from the years 1898–1908. The scenarios printed in this appendix are representative of an earlier period and have been selected to illustrate the work of Katti Lanner, Leopold Wenzel and C. Wilhelm. *Orfeo, Versailles, Faust* and *Monte Cristo* show the more serious aspect of the Empire ballet; the fifth, *Round the Town*, is an example of the up-to-date ballet.

Orfeo

Mythological Ballet Divertissement in two tableaux. Designed by C. Wilhelm. The Ballet invented and produced by Katti Lanner. Music specially composed by Leopold Wenzel. The scenery by Telbin. First performed at the Empire Theatre, May 25, 1891.

Orfeo	Malvina Cavallazzi
Eurydice	Ada Vincent
Melita	Bettina de Sortis
Malignity	Enrico Cecchetti
Hymen	Cora
Pluto	Mr J. Cazaly
Proserpine	Louise Allen
The Spirit of Fascination	Adelina Rossi

SCENE I. *Arcadia.*

A sacred grove before the temple of Hymen. A golden afternoon. On raising the curtain groups of girls are seen, some picking flowers and weaving garlands, whilst others are dancing to the music of lyres, played by the pupils of Orfeo.

Melita enters with a quantity of flowers, which she distributes amongst her friends. The dance is interrupted by Orfeo, who emerges from the Temple, playing on his lyre a hymn which he has composed to the honour of Hymen. His friends and pupils listen in admiration to the divine melody.

Orfeo enquires after Eurydice. The maidens announce her approach. Eurydice enters, Orfeo meets and embraces her, and then presents her to his friends as his bride. Various wayfarers pass by, amongst them Pluto, disguised as a mortal. He pauses on his way and draws near to the group, casting insolent glances of admiration on Eurydice. Orfeo resents this, and interposes to shield his betrothed from Pluto's advances. Eurydice presents Orfeo with a garland of laurels, with which she decks his lyre, Orfeo takes a garland of myrtle and places it over Eurydice's head; she is then veiled by her attendants, and the bridal procession enters the Temple.

Pluto returning, summons the Spirit of Malignity, and instructs him to secure Eurydice for the Service of Proserpine in Hades. At this moment strains of a marriage hymn are heard from the Temple; the bridal cortege reappears. Hymeneal dance commences. After the dance friends bring presents to the bride. Amongst the others, Malignity appears disguised as an old peasant, carrying a basket of roses, which he offers to Eurydice. She smiles her thanks, and is about to take some, but throws them away, terror-stricken, as a venomous snake concealed in their midst inflicts a mortal wound. Orfeo, with a cry of anguish, catches her in his arms. Movement of horror. Priests and guests advance menacingly on Malignity, who throws off his disguise, and sinks through the ground in flames. Eurydice dies. Orfeo, overcome with grief, snatches a sword from one of his friends, and would stab himself, but is restrained by his companions, who bear away the dead body of the bride.

Orfeo, left alone in a frenzy of despair, his glance falls on the laurel garland with which Eurydice had decked his lyre; he kisses the garland passionately, and throwing the lyre on one side, falls unconscious on the steps of the Temple.

Hymen appears and, looking with sympathy on Orfeo, says, he will protect him. He approaches him and arouses him from his despair.

'Take your lyre,' he says to Orfeo, 'and if you have no fear follow me; you will see Eurydice again, and your lyre will protect you.'

A vision of Eurydice appears, beckoning Orfeo to come to her rescue. Orfeo, overcome with hope and joy, says, 'I fear no danger to see Eurydice again; I devote my life.'

Orfeo and Hymen depart from Hades.

Scene II. *Hades. The realms of Pluto.*

Charon is seen ferrying a barge with Eurydice accompanied by Malignity; he passes the River Styx to conduct her to Pluto. Pluto and Proserpine approach to witness the revels of the demons, which are interrupted by the barking of Cerberus announcing that someone approaches.

Distant strains of Orfeo's lyre are heard, and he appears on the summit of the rocks.

The demons and guards of Pluto oppose his entrance into Hades, but in vain; they have to give way before the melody of the lyre.

Pluto enraged, orders Orfeo to be seized and the lyre taken from him, but as they are about to lay hands on him, a blinding flash of lightning and a peal of thunder proclaim him to be protected by the superior deities. Pluto bids him seek Eurydice for himself; he essays to do so, despite the mocking jeers of the dwellers in Hades.

A beautiful demon attempts to turn Orfeo's thoughts from his pursuit, but in vain, and at length his passionate appeal so melts the heart of Proserpine that she promises to restore Eurydice on the sole condition that Orfeo does not look back on her until he reaches earth. Eurydice appears, trembling, and advances slowly. Orfeo instinctively knows of her approach, and, remembering his promise not to look on her, ascends the rocks slowly, followed by the jeers of Pluto's subjects.

In the far distance above appears a glimpse of sky and a gleam of sunshine. Just as Orfeo reaches the daylight, Malignity, enraged that Orfeo should triumph, runs after them and tries to snatch Eurydice from his arms; this causes Orfeo to forget his promise, and he turns as Eurydice sinks into Malignity's arms fainting from his imploring gaze. A bacchanal ensues, the demons showing their delight. Orfeo breaks his lyre, but Hymen appears, and at a sign from him the demons retire in rage, and love triumphs.

(Reproduced from the synopsis issued with the programme.)

Versailles

Grand Ballet Divertissement in three tableaux, by Katti Lanner. Music specially composed by Leopold Wenzel.[1] Scenery by T. E. Ryan. Costumes designed by C. Wilhelm. First performed at the Empire Theatre, May 23, 1892.

King Louis XIV	Malvina Cavallazzi
The Queen	Miss M. Ford
Louise de la Vallière	Ada Vincent
Athenais de Tournay Charente	Cora
Raoul, Victomte de Bragelonne	Miss R. Johnstone
D'Artagnan, Capitaine des Mousquetaires du Roi	Mr H. J. C. Vernon
Prévôt. Maître de danse du Roi	Vittorio De Vincenti
Lulli, Compositeur de Musique	John Ridley
Répétiteur	Mr F. Artelli
Master of the Ceremonies	Louise Allen
Mlle Sallé	Bettina de Sortis
Mlle Rancourt (2nd Danseuse of the Opera)	Lizzie Vincent
Mlle Camargo	Sofia Coppini

Scene I. *The park at Versailles.*

Gardeners are seen busily preparing for the arrival of King Louis XIV and his Court. Cavaliers and ladies arrive and the latter present their colours to their favourites. Refreshments are served by pages, and a dance follows. The Vicomte Raoul de Bragelonne, it is observed, takes no part in the dance, but stands apart from the gay assembly. His mind is occupied by thoughts of Louise de la Vallière, who was betrothed to him in her childhood. Louise approaches Raoul, and at his request presents him with her colours. Raoul then implores her to fulfil the wish of his own and their parents' hearts by

1 The music used in the second tableau, at Lulli's entrance, for the lesson of the principal dancer, was arranged on themes by Lulli.

naming the nuptial day. Louise is confused and bids him wait. Disappointed, he retires, and the other cavaliers follow. The ladies now freely express their opinion on the merits of their late companions. Louise alone remains silent, and on being questioned answers abruptly that the Sun (meaning the King) absorbs her whole soul, and that she has no thought to bestow on mere planets. She is treated with scorn and deserted. The King, unobserved, has overheard the ladies' conversation; he approaches Louise, who is startled and attempts to escape. The King passionately expresses his affection for her, and learns that his love is reciprocated. Louise, however, declares her intention of leaving the Court for ever. Raoul enters, and is enraged on discovering the situation. He draws his sword and advances, but on recognising the King he breaks his weapon in half and declares himself the prisoner of his royal master. Louise begs and obtains pardon for Raoul, who is commanded to leave the royal presence. He implores Louise to accompany him, but she refuses. He thereupon upbraids her, and accuses her of dishonour. A trumpet call is heard; Louise, bewildered, escapes to the palace, and the King follows.

SCENE II. *An ante-room in the Palace.*
A grand ballet is to take place before the King. Lulli, Prévôt, and the principal danseuses arrive to make the necessary preparations. Before the performance they go through a rehearsal.

SCENE III. *The grand reception room in the Palace.*
The King, Queen and Court enter and take their places to witness the two grand ballet-divertissements, 'The Ages' and 'The Triumph of Flora'. The King invites Louise to take part in a minuet. He is charmed with her graceful movements, and presents her with a bracelet of great value. The act of the King brings upon Louise the envy and reproach of the other ladies, and the jealousy of the Queen, who retires. Louise is overcome with grief. Raoul again implores her to leave the Court. Louise suddenly disappears. Her page hands the King a letter containing the news that she has left the Court, never to return. A vision shows Louise taking the veil. The entertainment is continued in honour of the Roi Soleil.

(Taken from the description in the *Stage* of May 26, 1892.)

Round the Town

Characteristic Ballet in five tableaux, by Katti Lanner and George Edwardes. Music by Leopold Wenzel. Scenery by Telbin and Bruce Smith. Costumes designed by C. Wilhelm. First performed at the Empire Theatre, September 26, 1892.

Frank Mortimer (a carpenter)	Malvina Cavallazzi
Jane (his wife)	May Paston
Nellie (her child)	Miss E. Howard
John Borough (a working man)	George Vincent
Dr Birch (a tutor)	John Ridley

His pupils	MM. Artelli Bertram Griffiths Lewington Perkins G. Vincent F. White
Mr Rapless (the Oofless Swell)	Willie Warde
Polly	Bettina de Sortis
India	Vittorio De Vincenti

SCENE I. *Covent Garden.*
It is summer time in the early morning. Mr Rapless, an 'oofless' swell, in love with some fair lady, comes early to the market in order to get a bouquet. Money, however, is scarce with him, and he has to satisfy himself with purchasing from a flower-girl a penny bunch of violets. Dr Birch, a tutor newly arrived in London with his pupils, wishes to show them the sights, and they begin with Covent Garden market. The pupils, joined by Rapless, surround a coffee stall, a disturbance takes place, and the police interfere, the gentlemen in blue getting much the worst of it. Here is danced a spirited polka, 'La Londonienne'. Jane Mortimer, a poor woman, and her child, deserted by her dissolute husband Frank, and left penniless, take refuge in one of the porches, and fall asleep. The husband appears, and catching sight of his neglected wife immediately demands money of her; he is behaving with violence when the bystanders interfere, and he is hunted from the scene, which closes with more skylarking by Dr Birch's merry pupils.

SCENE II. *The Royal Exchange.*
It is mid-day. Merchants, stockbrokers, smart-looking lady guides with tourists, telegraph and messenger boys, flower girls, and a beadle are all busily engaged. Jane and little Nellie are offering flowers for sale, but find no buyers, when on comes John Borough, a good-hearted workman, who divides with them his dinner. A fight ensues amongst the telegraph and messenger boys, which is quieted by the intervention of the shoeblacks. Dr Birch's pupils also prove troublesome. In this scene takes place one of the best characteristic and most effective dances of the ballet. Eight tall, good-looking girls, attired in becoming outdoor costumes, raise gracefully their skirts and, to the strains of bright music, dance in effective lively fashion, finishing up by coming right down to the footlights, and presenting a dainty shoe to the kneeling shoeblacks to clean.

SCENE III. *The Thames Embankment.*
It is afternoon. A crowd are assembled to witness the return of the Volunteers and Guards. The Salvation Army is passing along, the man with the big drum, the lads with their bright red 'Salvation' vests, and the lassies with their tambourines, presenting a most lively natural picture. A Salvationist

catches sight of Rapless, offers him a *War Cry*, and asks him to join their ranks. Rapless, inspired by the banging of the drums and rattling of the tambourines, joins and marches off to the strains of 'To be there'. This scene also includes a dance *à la* Lottie Collins. Soldiers having come and gone, the crowd gradually disperses, as the shades of evening draw in. Dr Birch is left alone to his reflections, when Jane and Nellie come on, dragging weary feet along. 'Let me die,' whispers Jane, when she suddenly remembers the child. 'No, we will die together.' And she is making her way to the parapet when the Doctor steps forth, and he has hardly convinced her of her folly when Mortimer appears. Hurriedly concealing Jane and Nellie, the Doctor advances and questions him as to the whereabouts of his wife and child. 'Mind your own business,' he replied. 'Your wife and child are dead,' says the Doctor. Incontinently, the penitent ruffian falls fainting to the ground. Nellie ventures forward, and, placing her hand on his shoulder, whispers, 'Father'. Hardly believing his senses, he grasps her, and is thankful that his fears were in vain. The Doctor promises his assistance on Mortimer's assurance that he will change his mode of life; and the latter leaves happily in the company of his wife and child.

SCENE IV. *The front of the Empire.*
It is the first night of a new ballet, and Leicester Square is the centre of excitement. A street piano is playing, and children are dancing to popular tunes. Fashionably-dressed ladies pass to and fro, gentlemen in evening dress are present, and salutations are exchanged. The Doctor and Rapless have arranged to visit the theatre, and, just as they enter, the Doctor has the satisfaction of seeing his *protégé*, Mortimer, returning contentedly from his work.

SCENE V. *'Our Empire'.*
A ballet entitled 'The Daughters of the British Empire' is in progress. England, Scotland, Ireland, Wales, India, Australia, Canada, Cape Colony, British Columbia, the West Indies, Malta, Gibraltar, Ceylon, Hong Kong, New Zealand, Burma, the City of London, Liverpool, Manchester, Coventry, Birmingham, Dover, Portsmouth, Plymouth, Bristol, Newcastle, Cardiff, Newmarket, Nottingham, Burton, Yarmouth, Edinburgh, Glasgow, Dublin, Belfast, Brighton, Cowes, Henley, Oxford, Cambridge, Windsor, and Eton are all represented. 'Commerce' is suggested by four Mercuries in exquisite grey dresses. And finally, when the stage is full, Britannia, mighty and majestic, strides to the front and, clad in a cloak made of a gorgeous Union Jack, waves her commanding and protecting trident over all.

(Based on descriptions in the *Stage* of Sep. 29, 1892, and the *Era* of Oct. 1, 1892.)

Faust

Grand Spectacular Ballet in five tableaux, under the direction of George Edwardes. The Ballet arranged by Katti Lanner from the scenario of C. Wilhelm, and produced under their joint superintendence. The music of the first two tableaux composed by Meyer Lutz, and of last three tableaux by Ernest Ford. The mise-en-scène, costumes and accessories designed and supervised by C. Wilhelm. The scenery painted by Joseph Harker, Glendenning, and Karl Lautenschläger. The organ built expressly for this production. First performed at the Empire Theatre, May 6, 1895.

MORTALS

Faust	Malvina Cavallazzi
Margaret	Ada Vincent
Valentine	May Paston
Siebel	Cora
Martha	Miss F. Banbury
Lisa	Miss E. Tree
Wagner	Will Bishop
Charlatan	George Vincent
Innkeeper	John Ridley
Pedler	Mr C. Perkins
General	Mr Lewington
Soldiers, Drummers, Students, Nobles, Citizens, Pages, Market Folk, Strolling Players, and Villagers	

SPIRITS

Mephistopheles	Francesca Zanfretta
Cleopatra	Constance Collier
Helen of Troy	Miss M. Ford
Phryne	Miss Huxley
Aspasia	Miss Dillon
Lais	Miss Morland
Nymphs of Oblivion, Harpists, Cupids, Angels, etc.	
Fantasy	Elena Cornalba

SCENE I. *A street in Nuremberg.*
The watchmen retire to their rest at the approach of dawn. Then a crowd of students, citizens, and strolling players is gradually formed. In this scene are introduced Faust's infernal compact with Mephistopheles, the business with the fiery wine, and the exorcisation of Mephistopheles with the sword-hilts. After a grotesque *pas seul* by Wagner, suggestive of military life, and a dance of *vivandières*, the troops, among them Margaret's brother Valentine, march away under the city gate. The scene ends with a lively valse and galop.

SCENE II. *Margaret's garden.*
After a dance of animated daisies, Faust and Margaret are seen locked in each other's arms. Valentine returns with the troops, and Siebel informs him of what has befallen Margaret. The duel takes place, and Siebel protects Margaret from the violence of the indignant populace.

Scene III. *Near the summit of the Brochen.*
Faust and Mephistopheles are here, and there is a dance of the will-o'-the-wisps.

Scene IV. *The Palace of Pleasure.*
Mephistopheles has transported Faust to a splendid palace where Cleopatra is holding high revel, attended by Nubians, women, and courtiers. Among the guests are Helen of Troy, Phryne and Aspasia. Here Fantasy tempts Faust from beauty to beauty. At the height of his dissipation a vision of Margaret appears on one of the columns which support the roof of the palace, and for a moment Faust pauses in his wild career. Then, with a sound like thunder, the palace walls are overthrown.

Sene V. *Apotheosis.*
A long golden staircase is revealed, on which angels are grouped, while Margaret stands lower down in white robes with a large lily. Faust bursts from Mephistopheles, who tries to take him 'down below', and kneels at the foot of the staircase.

(Based on the synopsis issued with the programme and the description in the *Stage* of May 9, 1895.)

Monte Cristo

Grand Spectacular Ballet in two acts and seven scenes under the direction of George Edwardes. The scenario by Richard Henry, founded on Dumas' celebrated Romance. Designed and supervised by C. Wilhelm. Arranged by Katti Lanner. The music composed expressly by Leopold Wenzel. The scenery of Act I painted by Joseph Harker, the tableaux curtains and the scene of Act II by J. Telbin. First performed at the Empire Theatre, October 26, 1896.

ACT I

Edmond Dantès	Malvina Cavallazzi
Mercédès (a Catalan girl - betrothed)	Francesca Zanfretta
Fernand (a Catalan - in love with Mercédès)	Alma Courtland
Sergeant of Gendarmes	Will Bishop
Danglars (shipping agent)	John Ridley
Lola (a Catalan girl)	Cora
Caderousse (a tailor)	George Vincent
La Carconte (his wife)	Miss F. Banbury
Babette (Marseillaises)	Edith Slack
Javotte (Marseillaises)	Miss Jenkins
Old Dantès	Mr Perkins
The abbé Faria	Giuseppe Pomé
M. de Villefort (magistrate)	Mr Rockliffe
M. Morrel (a shipowner)	Mr Lewington
Turnkey	Mr Griffiths

Gaoler	Mr Artelli
Haydée (a Greek girl)	Ada Vincent
Guardian Spirit of the Treasure	Mlle Gradella
La Folie des Richesse	Miss E. Tree
The Diamond (première danseuse)	Edvige Gantenberg
Market People, Fisher Folk, Sailors, Gendarmes, Marseillais, Catalans	

SCENE I. *Marseilles – the Catalan village.*
The curtain rises upon the quay at Marseilles, where Fernand is sitting at a tavern. After a Catalan dance led by Lola, Mercédès arrives with old Dantès and is greeted by M. Morrel. Caderousse appears, heralding the arrival of 'The Pharaon', which is seen entering the harbour. Mercédès, escaping from the unwelcome attention of Fernand, runs forward to meet Edmond, who arrives with Danglars and the crew. After a dance by sailors and market girls, Danglars, Fernand and Caderousse arrange the plot against Edmond Dantès, and after Carconte has entered and quarrelled with her husband, the two chief conspirators are left alone, and Fernand finally drops the fatal letter into the box. De Villefort visits the gendarmerie, receives the letter, stops the bridal procession, and orders the arrest of Dantès.

SCENE II. *The cells of the Château d'If, twelve years later.*
Edmond Dantès and the Abbé Faria are planning an escape and discussing the secret of the hidden treasure, when the fatal attack of illness seizes the Abbé, who expires in the arms of his friend. Hearing the approach of the gaoler, Dantès retires to his own cell, and conceives the idea of escaping by taking the place of the Abbé in the sack in which the latter has been shrouded.

SCENE III. *The ramparts of the Prison.*

SCENE IV. *The Mediterranean.*
A series of panoramic effects, showing the exterior of the prison, the sack being thrown into the sea, Edmond struggling with the waves, and the felucca coming from the distance to his rescue.

SCENE V. *The Island of Monte Cristo.*

SCENE VI. *The riches of the cave.*
Dantès arrives on the Island of Monte Cristo and finds the treasure. Smugglers arrive with Haydée and Ali; Dantès comes to their rescue and purchases their liberty. The smugglers leave the island; Haydée relates the story of her life, and then plays to Dantès, who falls asleep and whose dream of the treasure is presented in the form of a grand divertissement.

ACT II

The Count of Monte Cristo (Edmond Dantès)	Malvina Cavallazzi
Mme de Morcerf (the Mercédès of Act I)	Francesca Zanfretta
Vicomte de Morcerf (the Fernand of Act I)	Alma Courtland
Albert de Morcerf (their son)	May Paston
M. Beauchamp (society journalist)	Will Bishop
Baron Danglars	John Ridley
Baroness Danglars	Miss F. Banbury
Mlle Danglars	Miss Esdaile
M. de Villefort	Mr Rockliffe
Mme de Villefort	Miss M. Ford
Valentine	Cora
Maximilian Morrel	Miss L. Hill
Franz d'Epinay	Giuseppe Pomé
Lucien Debray	G. Vincent
Ali (Monte Cristo's Nubian slave)	W. Edwards
Major-Domo	Edith Slack
Guests, Incroyables, Merveilleuses, Pages, Bouquetières, Musicians, Servants	

The gardens of Monte Cristo's mansion, near Paris, six years later.
A floral fête is in progress. Franz d'Epinay shows Albert de Morcerf an attack on their father's character and suggests that their host is responsible for its publication. Albert accuses the Count of Monte Cristo and challenges him to a duel. When the company has dispersed Mercédès, now the Vicomtesse de Morcerf, approaches Monte Cristo and begs for her son's safety; after a severe mental struggle, he promises to sacrifice his own life instead, and Mercédès says she will stop the duel. The guests reappear and there is a Greek dance by Haydée; she recognises the Vicomte de Morcerf (who comes to congratulate her) as her father's betrayer. Morcerf affects indifference, and then in a tableau the old story of his earlier treachery is presented, and Monte Cristo reveals himself as Edmond Dantès. Morcerf, after vainly attempting to attack Dantès, rushes off and commits suicide. The Vicomtesse goes away with Albert, Haydée confesses her love for the Count, and the resumption of the fête brings the ballet to an end.

(Reproduced from the synopsis issued with the programme.)

APPENDIX H

Wilhelm's scenario for 'High Jinks'

The scene represents the entrance Hall of an old English Elizabethan Manor House - solidly built up with heavy fireplace - with armorial bearings - panelled oak walls - lofty mullioned windows - and staircase leading to upper apartments. The Hall is furnished in luxurious modern fashion as a Lounge with settees - carpets - occasional tables, etc., and doors lead in various directions to the Servants' quarters - to the Dining Room - to the Porch - and so forth.

At the rise of the Curtain - a group of ladies is discovered - they are attired in tea gowns - some busy round the grand piano - others reading - a visitor is playing a valse - some few are dancing - servants come in with lighted lamps - bring afternoon tea. Return of the shooting party - who join the ladies. Afternoon tea-and-cake walk (? 'Bedelia') - Arrival of visitors from the station - Fashionable society actress (Mlle Zanfretta) who attracts so much attention from one of the eligible young men of the party that his fiancée (Mlle Genée) a daughter of the house - is jealous. This thread of story will of course be strengthened and developed - a brief rehearsal - with comical diversions - of the play to be presented in the evening is interrupted by the dressing bell. The Company troop off upstairs. The perplexed amateur author busy writing up his dialogue, etc., is dusted 'from pillar to post' - by a bevy of parlour maids and footmen - who, directed by butler and housekeeper, decorate the Hall for the evening festivities. Some fun may be had here by amateur attempts to fit up the scenery, etc., for the stage - (to be prominently seen on a landing of the great staircase) - and the testing of some of the armour suits for stage wear, etc., etc. Then the guests begin to appear for dinner. Firstly some few of the principals to play their little scenes of intrigue and then the bulk of the guests in swell evening gowns - the men possibly in hunt evening dress - red coats and black satin knee breeches. They pair off and dance in to dinner - (air 'Little Mary'). When they are 'off' the preparations for the theatricals are resumed - the stage manager (excused from dinner - the various courses brought to him by a supercilious footman) drills the gardener and the groom and the page boy and some giggling servant girls in their supernumerary business. Then (the guests who are acting having gone off to their rooms to change) the hostess appears to welcome some additional visitors - to form an audience - somewhat eccentric countrified types - the rector and the curate - the local medico, etc., etc., and the play begins. It is proposed that this should be a palpable burlesque of 'Faust' as being a well-known story, not requiring actual dialogue to make the action clear, and lending itself admirably to parody and to mixing up the well-known airs of the opera with popular tunes of the day. This will be worked up with comic incident and interspersed with characteristic dances to employ the rest of the Ballet. The daughter (Mlle Genée) of course scoring largely over the actress from Town and getting plenty of opportunity for dance and pantomime. In the opera she of course will be Marguerite - and a skirt dance of daisy dresses - contrasted with a revel of gipsies and of Mephistopheles ladies in red skirts will be a bright and striking mass of colour. The scene ends after some absurd denouement of the play - with the reconciliation of the lovers and a general dance of the actors and their audience - perhaps 'Sir Roger de Coverley' to bring the curtain down.

Santini will be a fashionable singer or violinist amongst the guests - the pet of the ladies. Miss Vincent, the hostess. Papucci, a French maid. Craske, the young lover. Jenkins the chief footman. Cora, a mischievous girl of the sporting type. Paston, a society journalist lady of the Connie Ediss type, and various eccentric characters will be worked in.

Bibliography

ANON., 'Stage morality, and the ballet' *Blackwood's Edinburgh Magazine*, 105 (March 1869), 354–60
BEAUMONT, CYRIL W. *Bookseller at the Ballet* (London, 1975)
BEAUMONT, CYRIL W. *Complete Book of Ballets* (London, 1937)
BEDELLS, PHYLLIS *My Dancing Days* (London, 1954)
BESANT, SIR WALTER *London in the Nineteenth Century* (London, 1909)
BOOTH, CHARLES *Life and Labour in London* 2nd series, vol. 4 (London, 1902)
BOOTH, J.B. *London Town* (London, 1929)
[BYRNE, MRS WILLIAM PITT] *Gossip of the Century: personal and traditional memories – social, literary, artistic, etc.* (London, 1892)
CHESHIRE, DAVID *Music Hall* (Newton Abbott, 1974)
DISHER, M. WILLSON *Winkles and Champagne* (London, 1938)
EDWARDS, HENRY SUTHERLAND *The Lyrical Drama: essays on subjects, composers and executants of modern opera* (London, 1881)
ESPINOSA, EDOUARD *And Then He Danced* (London, n.d.)
FLEETWOOD, FRANCES *Conquest* (London, 1953)
FLITCH, J. CRAWFORD *Modern Dancing and Dancers* (London, 1912)
GUEST, IVOR *Adeline Genée* (London, 1958)
GUEST, IVOR *Adeline Genée: a pictorial record* (London, 1978)
HADDON, ARCHIBALD *The Story of the Music Hall* (London, 1935)
HÁJEK, LADISLAV *Pvameti Augustina Bergra* (Prague, 1942)
HOLLINGSHEAD, JOHN *My Lifetime* (London, 1895)
HOLROYD, MICHAEL *Bernard Shaw, vol. I:* 1856–1898 (London, 1988)
JACOBS, ARTHUR *Arthur Sullivan: a Victorian Musician* (Oxford, 1984)
KIRWAN, D.J. *Palace and Hovel* (Hartford, CN, 1871)
KYASHT, LYDIA *Romantic Recollections* (London, 1952)
LUMLEY, BENJAMIN *Reminiscences of the Opera* (London, 1847)
LYNHAM, DERYCK *Ballet Then and Now* (London, 1947)
MACKENZIE, COMPTON *Figure of Eight* (London, 1936)
MACQUEEN-POPE, W. *The Melodies Linger On: the Story of Music Hall* (London, 1950)
MANDER, RAYMOND AND MITCHENSON, JOE *The Lost Theatres of London* (London, 1968)
MAYHEW, ATHOLL 'The building of the ballet' *The Idler*, 2 (August 1892), 61–9
MORTON, W.H. AND NEWTON, H.C. *Sixty Years' Stage Experience* (London, 1905)
PATERSON, PETER *Glimpses of Real Life as Seen in the Theatrical World and in Bohemia* (Edinburgh, 1864)
PERUGINI, MARK E. *The Art of Ballet* (London, 1915)
PERUGINI, MARK E. *A Pageant of the Dance and Ballet* (London, 1935)
PULLING, CHRISTOPHER *They Were Singing* (London, 1952)

Ralph, Richard 'Stewart Headlam – the dancing priest' *About the House*, 7, 1 (Christmas 1984), 56–61
Rendle, T. McDonald *Swings and Roundabouts* (London, 1919)
Ritchie, J. Ewing *The Night Side of London* (London, 1869)
Rivière, Jules *My Musical Life and Recollections* (London, 1893)
Schneider, Louis *Les Maîtres de l'opérette française: Hervé, Charles Lecocq* (Paris, 1924)
Scott, Harold *Early Doors* (London, 1946)
Shaw, George Bernard *The Diaries, 1885–1897* Edited by Stanley Weintraub (Penn. State University, 1986)
Shaw, George Bernard *Immaturity* (London, 1930)
Shaw, George Bernard *London Music in* 1888–89 as heard by Corno di Bassetto (later known as Bernard Shaw) (London, 1937)
Shaw, George Bernard *Music in London, 1890–94* (London, 1932)
Sherson, Erroll *London's Lost Theatres of the Nineteenth Century* (London, 1925)
Sims, George R. *Glances Back* (London, 1917)
Sims, George R. *My Life* (London, 1917)
Sitwell, Osbert *Laughter in the Next Room* (London, 1949)
Smith, Albert *The Natural History of the Ballet-Girl* (London, 1847)
Soldene, Emily *My Theatrical and Musical Recollections* (London, 1897)
Stuart, Charles Douglas and Park, A.J. *The Variety Stage* (London, 1895)
Sullivan, Herbert and Flower, Norman *Sir Arthur Sullivan, His Life, Letters and Diaries* (London, 1927)
Survey of London, vol. XXXIV
Symons, Arthur 'At the Alhambra' *Savoy*, 5 (September 1896), 75–83.
Tillett, Selwyn *Victoria and Merrie England* (Saffron Walden, 1980)
Walford, Edward *Old and New London* (London, n.d.)
Wiley, Roland John *Tchaikovsky's Ballets* (Oxford, 1985)
Williamson, Audrey 'Sullivan's ballets' *Dancing Times*, 486 (April 1951), 394-6, 400

Newspapers and Periodicals

All the Year Round
Daily Graphic
Daily Telegraph
Dancing
Dancing Times
Day's Doings
Era
Evening Standard
Globe
Illustrated London News
Illustrated Sporting and Dramatic News
Morning Chronicle
Morning Post
Observer
Pall Mall Gazette
Punch
Saturday Review
Sketch
Stage
Tatler
Theatre World
The Times
Times Literary Supplement
Weekly Dispatch

Collections of Programmes etc.

Bibliothèque de l'Opéra, Paris (Wenzel scores, Justament notebooks)
Bodleian Library, Oxford (Johnson collection of ephemera; programmes)
Royal Academy of Dancing, London (Adeline Genée collection)
Theatre Museum, London (London Archives of the Dance; Jacobi scores. General collection: programmes, documents, cuttings)
Westminster Reference Library, London (Broadley collection)

Index

I. PERSONS

II. BALLETS, MUSICAL COMEDIES, OPERAS, PLAYS, &c.